HOLOCAUST AND THE STARS

This book is a groundbreaking study of one of the greatest science fiction writers, the Polish master Stanisław Lem. It offers a new direction in research on his oeuvre and corrects several errors commonly appearing in his biographies. The author painstakingly recreates the context of Lem's early life and his traumatic experiences during the Second World War due to his Jewish background, and then traces these through original and brilliant readings of his fiction and non-fiction. She considers language, worldbuilding, themes, motifs and characterization as well as many buried allusions to the Holocaust in Lem's published and archival work, and uses these fragments to capture a different side of Lem than previously known. The book discusses various issues concerning the writer's life, such as his upbringing in a Jewish, Zionist-minded family, the extensive relations between the Lem family and the elite of Lviv at that time, details of the Lem family killed during the German occupation and attempts to reconstruct what happened to Lem's parents and to the writer himself after escaping the ghetto.

Part of the *Studies in Global Genre Fiction* series, this English translation of the Polish original, which has already been considered a milestone in Lem studies, offers a fresh perspective on the writer and his work. It will be an important intervention for scholars and researchers of Jewish studies, Holocaust literature, science fiction studies, English literature, world war studies, minority studies, popular culture, history and cultural studies.

Agnieszka Gajewska is professor at the Faculty of Polish and Classical Philology at Adam Mickiewicz University in Poznań, Poland.

Katarzyna Gucio is an experienced and highly accomplished translator of Polish and English.

Studies in Global Genre Fiction

Series Editors: **Bodhisattva Chattopadhyay**, University of Oslo, Norway and **Taryne Jade Taylor**, Embry-Riddle Aeronautical University, USA

Studies in Global Genre Fiction offers original insights into the history of genre literature while contesting two hierarchies that constrain global genre fiction studies: (1) Anglophone literature and other global language literatures and (2) literary fiction and genre fiction. The series explores the exchanges between different literary cultures that form aesthetic concerns and the specific literary, sociopolitical, geographical, economic, and historical forces that shape genre fiction globally. A key focus is understudied genre fictions from the 'global South' — where geographical location or language often confines works to the margins of the global publishing industry, international circulation, and academic scrutiny, even if they may be widely read in their own specific contexts.

Contributions to this series investigate the points of disruption, intersection and flows between literary and genre fiction. The series analyses cross-cultural influences in literary classifications, translation, transcreation, localization, production, and distribution while capturing the rich history of world and global literatures.

Books in this series

Indian Genre Fiction
Pasts and Future Histories
Edited by Bodhisattva Chattopadhyay, Aakriti Mandhwani and Anwesha Maity

For more information about this series, please visit: https://www.routledge.com/Studies-in-Global-Genre-Fiction/book-series/SGGF

HOLOCAUST AND THE STARS

The Past in the Prose of Stanisław Lem

Agnieszka Gajewska

TRANSLATED BY KATARZYNA GUCIO

LONDON AND NEW YORK

Cover image credit: Katarzyna Swinarska, Deserted Lviv (Lwów wyludniony) , 2016, charcoal, watercolor on paper and collage, 21 × 28 cm, Gdańsk, Poland. Used with permission.

First published in English 2022
by Routledge
2 Park Square, Milton Park, Abingdon, Oxon OX14 4RN

and by Routledge
605 Third Avenue, New York, NY 10158

Routledge is an imprint of the Taylor & Francis Group, an informa business

Translated by Katarzyna Gucio

Published in Polish by Adam Mickiewicz University Press 2016

British Library Cataloguing-in-Publication Data
A catalogue record for this book is available from the British Library

Library of Congress Cataloging-in-Publication Data
Names: Gajewska, Agnieszka, author. | Gucio, Katarzyna, translator.
Title: Holocaust and the stars: the past in the prose of Stanisław Lem/ Agnieszka Gajewska; translated by Katarzyna Gucio.
Other titles: Zagłada i gwiazdy. English
Description: Abingdon, Oxon; New York, NY: Routledge, 2022. | Series: Studies in global genre fiction | Includes bibliographical references and index. |
Identifiers: LCCN 2021032597 | ISBN 9780367428723 (hardback) | ISBN 9780367428730 (paperback) | ISBN 9780367855642 (ebook)
Subjects: LCSH: Lem, Stanisław–Criticism and interpretation. | Holocaust, Jewish (1939-1945), in literature. | History in literature.
Classification: LCC PG7158.L392 G3513 2022 | DDC 891.8/5373–dc23
LC record available at https://lccn.loc.gov/2021032597

ISBN: 978-0-367-42872-3 (hbk)
ISBN: 978-0-367-42873-0 (pbk)
ISBN: 978-0-367-85564-2 (ebk)

DOI: 10.4324/9780367855642

Typeset in Bembo
by Deanta Global Publishing Services, Chennai, India

CONTENTS

Biographical Notes *vi*
Author's Note *vii*
Series Editors' Preface *viii*

Introduction 1

1 Lem(berg) Land 36

2 The split 72

3 Holocaust in space 118

Conclusion *157*
Index *161*

BIOGRAPHICAL NOTES

Agnieszka Gajewska is Professor at the Faculty of Polish and Classical Philology at Adam Mickiewicz University in Poznań, Poland. She is the author of *Zagłada i gwiazdy. Przeszłość w prozie Stanisława Lema* [The Holocaust and the Stars: The Past in the Prose of Stanisław Lem], Poznań, Wydawnictwo Naukowe UAM 2016, for which she received the postdoctoral title of *doktor habilitowany*. In her earlier research work, she focused on feminist criticism (the monograph *Hasło: feminizm*, 2008), minority discourses (she edited an anthology of Polish translations: *Teorie wywrotowe*, 2013) and political prisoners (various articles). She is currently working on a biography of Stanisław Lem. She is the director of the Interdisciplinary Centre for Gender and Identity Studies at Adam Mickiewicz University.

Katarzyna Gucio is an experienced and highly accomplished translator of Polish and English. Her credits include literature (for her Polish translation of *The Tattooist of Auschwitz* by H. Morris, she received the Best Foreign Book of the Year Award), monographs and other scholarly works (including English editions of books by award-winning scholars, such as *Wire-Bound State. The Lodz Ghetto* by A. Sitarek, *British Diplomacy and the Concept of the Eastern Pact* by D. Jeziorny or *Kantor. A Monograph* by Dominika Łarionow, to be released in 2020). She has completed numerous translation projects in collaboration with most major art institutions and museums in Poland and continues to work with them on a regular basis. Since 2013, she has been part of a team (and as of this year—the chief translator) tasked with translating the enormous collection of documents saved from the Warsaw Ghetto (the so-called Ringelblum Archive) into English. She also translates poetry—a collection of her translations of poems by W. B. Yeats will come out in April 2020.

AUTHOR'S NOTE

This book, *Holocaust and the Stars: The Past in the Prose of Stanisław Lem*, was published in English thanks to the financial support of the Faculty of Polish and Classical Philology AMU in Poznań. Additional funding for this translation and editing have been provided by the University of Oslo under the "Frie Midler til Forskning" scheme as well as by CoFUTURES (European Research Council grant agreement no. 852190).

The monograph was created as part of a project financed by the National Science Center, granted on the basis of decision no.DEC-2011/03 / B / HS2 / 0348.

SERIES EDITORS' PREFACE

In *Holocaust and the Stars*, Agnieszka Gajewska offers a groundbreaking study of one of the greatest science fiction writers, the Polish master Stanisław Lem. Lem is an industry by himself; his works have been filmed (most famously Andrei Tarkovsky's *Solaris* from 1971 and Ari Folman's *The Congress* from 2013) and have been the inspiration for scientific and technological theories such as the cutting-edge constructor theory, and he has been both highly controversial and highly influential. While there are a number of critical studies on Lem, including several in the last few years alone since his death in 2006, such as works by Peter Swirski and the translation of his 1964 non-fiction masterpiece *Summa Technologiae* (U Minnesota Press, 2014) among others, little light has been shed on the impact of the Holocaust on his oeuvre.

In this book, Gajewska painstakingly recreates the context of Lem's early life and his traumatic experiences during World War Two due to his Jewish background, and then traces these through original and brilliant readings of Lem's fiction and non-fiction. Gajewska considers language, worldbuilding, themes, motifs and characterization, as well as many buried allusions to the Holocaust in Lem's published and archival work. She uses these fragments to capture a different side of Lem than previously known, since Lem himself rarely discussed his early life and his wartime experiences. The book was published in 2016 in Polish as *Zagłada i gwiazdy. Przeszłość w prozie Stanisława Lema*. This edition has been specially translated and revised for English language publication. The book has already been considered a milestone in Lem studies, receiving a stellar reception in academic and popular reviews.

We are elated to present *Holocaust and the Stars* in our Studies in Global Genre Fiction series. One of our main goals for this series is to raise critical awareness of non-Anglophone genre literatures, and Gajewska's brilliant insights on Lem's oeuvre certainly accomplish this and more.

– **Bodhisattva Chattopadhyay and Taryne Jade Taylor**
Series Editors, Studies in Global Genre Fiction

INTRODUCTION

At the end of the hall in Stanisław Lem's Lviv apartment, its current owner, displaced from Lemkivshchyna, has hung a painting depicting Cossack Mamai. Like a curator of a literary museum, she kindly offers a tour to visitors who knock on her door and, citing *Highcastle*, reconstructs the pre-war layout of the rooms and furnishings. Underpinning her story is the belief that the contemporary Lemkos who now live in Lviv and the Poles who left for Wrocław and Kraków after World War Two share a common fate. Cossack Mamai, placed in the very center of the apartment, symbolizes the time and space paradox of the displaced: the Cossack rides through a vast steppe, but when a song transports him back to Zaporozhye, he reminisces about long lost places, more important than the new landscapes he is passing. Mamai is riding a horse, though at the same time he is standing still, because his mind is occupied by the views he left behind. One of Mamai's main attributes is his *bandura*, a music instrument similar to a *kobza*, which lends him a resemblance to blind troubadours—for this reason the Cossack is sometimes referred to as the "Homer of Ukraine."[1] Mamai's song is a *dumka*, filled with dramatic scenes, often devoted to the themes of death, pain and injustice, reminiscent of a lament.[2] It has been suggested that the depictions of this Cossack might have been inspired by Buddhism, especially since the way he is seated is reminiscent of the position of the body during meditation. Many nineteenth-century representations of the Cossack include inscriptions that leave no doubt as to the social divisions that existed at that time, as well as a desire for a reckoning with Poles and Jews that had inhabited the territory of present-day Ukraine since the sixteenth century. The caricatures of Poles, as well as the blatant anti-Polish and anti-Semitic lyrics of Mamai's song,[3] reflect the centuries-old belief in the exploitation of the Ukrainians by Polish colonizers. However, for contemporary Ukrainians displaced from Lemkivshchyna, the Cossack has turned into a universal metaphor of the situation of refugees.

DOI: 10.4324/9780367855642-1

In my book, I propose to read Stanisław Lem's prose through the prism of the writer's continuous return to the past, to the time before the war, before the occupation, as well as to his exile from Lviv. In his works, Lem returned time and time again to the catastrophe of the war, which turned the world of his childhood and youth into ashes, forced him to leave his hometown and wiped out the majority of Lviv's population. Other researchers have made similar observations regarding the significance that Lem's youth had for his entire oeuvre. This was most clearly articulated by N. Katherine Hayles in her article "Chaos as Dialectic: Stanisław Lem and the Space of Writing." The scholar interpreted the writer's self-referential statements, citing Lem's autobiographical essay "Chance and Order," published in 1984 in *The New Yorker*. It was in that text that Lem shared some of his wartime experiences with the public, in a way providing his readers with a supplement to *Highcastle*, dating back to 1939. Hayles links his carefree childhood and youth, interrupted by the outbreak of war and occupation, with the philosophy of chance that he often employed in his prose and critical writings, thus seeing this biographical fracture as a multilayered dialectic reflected in Lem's literary and philosophical works. From this perspective, critical writing about his own books becomes for him an attempt to negotiate between chaos and order, offering him a chance to reclaim, at least partially, control over his own destiny.[4] Jerzy Jarzębski also associated Lem's philosophical stance with his early experiences during the German and Soviet occupation.[5] In my research I extend these insights into all of Lem's work, while also seeking interpretative links between individual texts and historical events. For this reason, in the Introduction I explain the key concepts that are fundamental for my reflections, situating them in the context of the reception to Lem's prose to date. In the following three chapters I focus on the interpretation of this prose through the prism of Lviv's history, autobiographical themes and the status of the witness and the survivor. In the first part of the book I analyze the traces of the history of Lviv Jews in the *Time Not Lost* trilogy and in *Highcastle*. In the second part, I discuss autobiographical themes interwoven into the lives of several of Lem's protagonists, and in the third I uncover the scars of the twentieth-century history that marked his science fiction works. In the late 1940s, Lem depicted wartime violence realistically, but in the early 1950s, censors blocked the publication of a volume of short stories previously printed in magazines.[6] When censors approved *The Astronauts* for printing, the writer won popular acclaim as a science fiction author and is now usually associated with this genre. In all his science fiction works, he undoubtedly obscured any traces of his own Lviv past, although he never entirely abandoned the theme of the Holocaust and war, choosing instead to portray his experiences from the occupation through allusions, associations and similes, additionally masked by the setting of space travel and alternative time. The complex, narrative song about the death of the world persists in these works, and themes of wartime violence emerge unexpectedly from narrative cracks, seemingly pointless anecdotes, unpredictable twists and grotesque visions.[7] The experience of a man subjected to Nazi persecution, pseudonymized in science fiction and shining through in protagonists' biographies, reveals Lem's artistic strategy, both in terms of games he played with censors and the mechanism he developed to express the profound anxiety and fear of the victim of such persecution, who also happens to be one of the few surviving witnesses to the crimes.

Moreover, the figure of Cossack Mamai brings to mind a protracted, brutal civil war, intermingled with bloody pogroms. The memory of the Great War and its consequences casts a persistent shadow also on Lem's post-Holocaust works,[8] especially where it led to the disruption of the social fabric. The hole in the glass pane in Lem's Lviv apartment left by a bullet from World War One, which he mentions in *Highcastle*, refers to historical events and at the same time portends another ethnic conflict, one which would cost hundreds of thousands of Lviv residents and refugees their lives, and which would also become immensely useful for the Soviet and German armies. In spite of the widespread contemporary nostalgia over *Kresy*—the Borderlands, Lviv is not an easy element in Polish collective memory: there, instead of peace and independent statehood, November 1918 brought fratricidal fights and pogroms;[9] in Lviv, the chronology of occupation and military operations was different, the underground state was also less successful in terms of organization and, instead of the advent of peace, 1945 marked the beginning of displacement and expatriation.

As Jan M. Piskorski notes, asylum-seeking, expulsions and resettlement during World War Two destroyed the ethnic structure of East-Central and Eastern Europe.[10] While the arrival of forced resettlers in the so-called Recovered Territories was conducive to the cultural unification of the population, as Tomasz Zarycki points out, staying in Małopolska—as was the case with Lem, who in July 1945 settled in Kraków with his family—meant living on the outskirts of the state established by the communists after the war. The Treaty of Yalta and the USSR's patronage over Poland, as Zarycki emphasizes, facilitated the return of the modernist national state, enthusiastically advocated by the Polish National Democracy before the war.[11] Although the communists rejected the notion of the Catholic Church as the foundation of the community, as Dmowski had imagined it, they followed the nationalist program in other regards and symbolically enhanced the significance of Wielkopolska, whereas the Borderlands were Orientalized in their plans. Therefore, while in the interbellum era of the Second Polish Republic (1918–1939) the center of the country's symbolic space was located in the east, with the capitals in Vilnius and Lviv, after the war—as Zarycki points out—individual groups from those areas were marginalized in an attempt to blend them together and form a single homogenous population.[12] The communist-era People's Republic of Poland (PRL) was characterized by centralization of power and homogenization of society, which, according to the cited scholar, means that many regions did not have separate symbolic representation. Quoting Bohdan Jałowiecki, Zarycki states that the symbolic space of the PRL was dominated by members of former gentry and intelligentsia hailing from the Russian partition, who cultivated national myths and the memory of uprisings and thus imposed such representation on other regions.[13] Viewed in such a sociological-historical context, Stanisław Lem's oeuvre—including his science fiction works—can be interpreted as an attempt to offer an alternative version of the symbolic imagination of those regions whose history was consigned to oblivion or overlooked.[14] The central role of Lviv (not just for Lem, but for many other writers, too) as well as the story of a city resident watching the world from the point of view of the so-called "intelligentsia"—these elements go against the vision of the symbolic representation that the post-gentry preached in the PRL era. An important element of this marginalization is also the phenomenon that Zofia Wóycicka described as the "interrupted mourning" of the Holocaust. As a consequence of the Stalinization of historical memory, the tragedy of the Jews was sidelined in public life and gradually pushed out of the official narratives. This process affected particularly severely the victims of atrocities committed by the Nazis in the areas occupied by the USSR after 1945.[15] Lem's writings remind us of events suppressed in the collective memory, of victims of the German occupation and of the wartime exile of survivors.

Such an approach to reading alternative history and the search for historical traces are highly reminiscent of Andrzej Zieniewicz's idea of autobiographical studies, as he points out that the experience of artists in the twentieth century had a significant impact on how they wrote fiction:

> it is not about historical prose as literature, but about literature as historical prose, a prose of discovery that some of the most important issues of Polish historicity cannot be presented as fiction, and one has to move away from it towards autobiography, concluding a peculiar pact with the reader, a pact of statement that is both assertive and unassertive, fictional and, at the same time, non-fictional in various dimensions.[16]

Alternative histories require distortions, genre shifts and chronological instability, and the autobiographical theme is usually broken down and distributed among several protagonists. Building a story that does not yield to the mainstream of collective memory, blurring the traces of personal experiences, combined with an ethical appeal to bear witness to those who died—all that in times of ubiquitous political scrutiny—required a strategy based on allusions, Aesopian language and a transformation of existing narrative models. Particularly helpful in that regard was science fiction, especially books featuring the theme of catastrophe, the philosophy of chance inspired by Darwin and the history of philosophy of science, including the history of medicine.

Science fiction?

> "So what does literature mean to you, then?" Stefan dared to ask after a while.
>
> "For readers, it is an attempt to forget. And for the author, an attempt to find redemption … like everything else."
>
> (Stanisław Lem, *Hospital of the Transfiguration*)

Historical literary syntheses devoted to contemporary literature hardly ever mention Lem's name or the titles of his novels.[17] This absence may, of course, be explained by the fact that he was assigned a separate place as the author of works classified as science fiction[18] (SF), a genre that researchers of post-war literature have rarely found interesting. Another problem may also be the fact that the subject matter of the novels is essentially incompatible with mainstream Polish prose. Nonetheless, the above reasons for such scarcity of references to his prose seem somewhat questionable. Popular literature has never ceased to be of interest to literary scholars, and Lem's oeuvre includes both an autobiographical book and realistic novels, in which he addressed fundamental ethical issues and tackled totalitarian systems. What, therefore, are the reasons for Lem's absence from the mainstream of the contemporary history of Polish literature? And let us bear in mind that this question covers books that have been frequently translated and reprinted. Dominika Oramus notes that the division into mainstream literature and science fiction is arbitrary and not based on any convincing arguments. According to the researcher, the best proof is the fact that George Orwell's *Nineteen Eighty-Four*, *We* by Yevgeny Zamyatin and Aldous Huxley's prose are excluded from the SF category, while Stanisław Lem's books are classified as science fiction.[19] "Lem 'does not fit,'" Oramus says, "into the standard history of recent literature and there is no school or trend to which he belongs."[20] In the mid-1970s, the writer himself pondered the lack of references to his work even in footnotes in books on Polish contemporary literature and came to the conclusion that this was mainly due to the attitude of researchers interested in works that meted out justice on an *ad hoc* basis, constructing temporary national myths and provisionally depicting Polishness against the background of the West.[21] He noted ironically:

> First, Polish critics pushed me, as a writer, DOWN from literature in the strict sense to entertainment for young readers, and now I am pushed out UP (namely, to philosophy). First, it seems, it was not literature YET, and now it is not ANYMORE.[22]

It is the philosophical and scientific aspect of the writer's works that has been appreciated by the German-speaking readership and critical circles (Austria, East Germany, Germany and Switzerland), where critics and readers alike appreciate Lem's prose for its rationalism, bold visions of technological development and references to natural sciences. One must notice—as Jacek Rzeszotnik stresses—that all these qualities go far beyond the generic framework of science fiction. Despite the admiration for the intellectual significance of this prose, German-speaking researchers point out that Lem's writing as such is hardly avant-garde in terms of technique, but rather conservative and firmly rooted in the eighteenth-century tradition.[23] In the USSR, however, Lem's prose replaced—as Konstantin Dushenko notes—not only banned philosophers, but also theologians, although the Soviet editions of his novels were heavily censored:

> The Russian translation of *His Master's Voice* (1970) reduced the original text by exactly one-third; in addition, the title was changed to *Heaven's Voice*. Nearly until the end of the 1970s, each edition of *Solaris* was drastically abridged and the penultimate chapter was cut out almost in its entirety. … Censors and editors were terribly afraid of all that "metaphysics" and "mysticism." And they were almost equally afraid of the pessimistic worldview. In order to ensure a proper reception to Lem's texts, each edition was supplemented with ideologically appropriate prefaces and afterwords. *Summa Technologiae* had as many as two prefaces, one afterword, and a commentary on top of that.[24]

The translator reminds us that party activists in the USSR blamed Lem for the pessimism of Soviet science fiction and were critical of his futurological visions. In their view, politically engaged science fiction should envisage the future of the communist revolution in the brightest possible terms.[25]

From the perspective of his American reception, Lem's work does not fit into the mainstream of science fiction literature due to the excessive philosophical potential of his books, unusual characters and unexpected failures during space expeditions. In the mid-1970s, Ursula Le Guin wrote that Lem's space was too modest for the sci-fi prose to which American readers were accustomed. They did not want to hear that there were things people could not comprehend and could not "even make plastics out of."[26] In May 1981, in an interview with writer Raymond Federman, when asked whether he saw himself as a science fiction writer, Lem demurred. At the same time, he stressed that he employed various literary genres in his work and that although his prose could be seen as an example of thought experiments, this was mainly due to the fact that realistic prose usually narrows the field of vision to small groups of people, whereas he was interested in the fate of humanity as a whole.[27] Federman was inclined to categorize Lem's writings as experimental prose, which was akin to his own approach, as his protagonists were usually doubled, tripled, sometimes with multiple personalities, populating an absurd world governed by chance. Lem agreed with that diagnosis insofar as, as he emphasized, prose enabled him to express problems that were difficult to present discursively.[28]

Regardless of which side of the Iron Curtain Lem was read, the reception focused mainly on the philosophical aspects of his works, pointing out that the thematic scope and manner of constructing fantastic stories went far beyond the genre boundaries of science fiction, although no new genre definitions were proposed. Differences in the response to his works concern formal issues unresolved by researchers, related to attempts to classify Lem's oeuvre as traditional and fossilized, or, on the contrary, as experimental and avant-garde. Critic Peter Haffner noted that this prose was far less likely to become outdated than most science fiction texts because it concerned ethical dilemmas that continued to be all too important. The researcher suggested that Lem was positioned outside the tradition of Polish literature because the latter had been focused on the national cause for decades. Meanwhile, Lem's writings were more in line with the best and most interesting satirical books, such as *Don Quixote* by Cervantes, *Jacques the Fatalist and His Master* by Diderot or Flaubert's novel *Bouvard et Pécuchet.*[29] Viewed from this perspective, Lem would be the author of non-heroic stories, disillusioning and presenting confusing philosophical problems through jokes and the grotesque.

In my opinion, the works of Stanisław Lem can also be regarded as part of Polish mainstream contemporary literature. It is interesting to consider his prose in the context of the so-called generation of Columbuses[30] with whom he shares references to catastrophic themes. Jerzy Jarzębski noted the author's generational experience mainly in *Hospital of the Transfiguration*, although he did not extend that observation into his science fiction works.[31] In my proposed approach, the biographical experience associated with the Nazi occupation can actually be applied to the writer's entire oeuvre. The only difference is that Lem drew on catastrophism from the science fiction tradition, including catastrophic satires, and was more likely to seek inspiration in world literature than in the works of Polish inter-war poets. I realize that the writer's generational affiliation is elusive and difficult to pinpoint. Sławomir Buryła, for example, voiced his doubts as to whether Lem, as an author operating on the sidelines of political life and underground resistance, could be included in the generation of Columbuses, and pointed out that few researchers would agree to such a qualification.[32] It is my belief that there are more than enough grounds to include Lem's writings in that category, although the writer should probably be associated with the generation described by Buryła as "Jewish Columbuses." During the occupation, Lem's peer group, young Jewish men and women, were, as the researcher puts it, "destined to die in gas chambers and mass graves."[33] In such a context, it is worth noting both the writer's involvement with the underground resistance and the heroism associated with life on the so-called Aryan side.[34] Perhaps, however, as Lawrence L. Langer suggested, we should stop clinging to "a grammar of heroism and martyrdom"[35] in our Holocaust research, because it makes it impossible to understand the choices the survivors had to make. More precisely, they could not make any decisions, and every act of heroic opposition to the occupant was usually tantamount to committing suicide and involuntarily contributing to the death of other prisoners or random strangers.[36]

In the history of twentieth-century literature, Lem's oeuvre occupies a separate (that is to say marginalized) place, for similar reasons as the works by Jan Józef Szczepański, Jerzy Zawieyski or Leo Lipski. His prose eludes classification into particular trends and historical turns because of its ideological incompatibility, references to ambiguous literary traditions and skepticism about every attempt to build a community. In his writings, he often returned to the past, ignored the literary heritage of the nineteenth century[37] and drew on the tradition of the Enlightenment,[38] which, in a way, eliminated the "national"—meaning "recognizable"—character of his work, imposed by literary syntheses. Even his works from the Stalinist era are considered unrepresentative of the literary trends of the time.[39] Through the Enlightenment ideals, Lem becomes a "citizen of the planet" and endeavors to avoid unequivocal national labels, aware of the dangers they entail. Lem's artistic creations feature references to the seminal works by Jonathan Swift and H. G. Wells. Also not without significance are the scientific interests of the writer—after all, he evokes an entire gallery of the nineteenth-century pioneers of space research that inspired thinking about interplanetary expeditions—and his medical education, because technology and its ethical consequences are hardly consistent with the notions of important literary subjects in Poland.[40]

The reasons for such a "separate place" in the literary canon can also be explained by referring to Hayden White's ordered, structuralist categories. White lists three strategies for styles of historical explanation: emplotment, ideologies and argumentation. Each of these consists of specific patterns. In the case of emplotment, these are, respectively: tragic, comedic, romantic and satirical; as for ideologies: anarchic, conservative, radical and liberal; and in argumentation: formist, mechanicist, organicist and contextualist. If such a structured system were to be applied to Lem's prose, the narrative he proposes would be based on a satirical, conservative and formist model. It is, in my opinion, this unusual combination of thinking style that is most problematic and often makes it impossible to include Lem's oeuvre in a particular literary trend, school or patriotic canon. The satirical pattern presupposes the impossibility of freeing oneself from the rule of evil and the weakness of people aware of the inadequacy of their efforts in a hostile world. According to the formist mode, the world becomes comprehensible when a proper form is indicated, which serves to identify all its elements.[41] Lem's protagonist is usually doomed to failure, because the rule that describes the world presented is chance and the calculus of probability.[42] All this is usually set in an extremely conservative social model, in which defending the status quo guarantees the stability of a world that is subject to constant shocks and disasters. As the writer himself puts it: "I am, in fact, a conservative and a visionary, so to speak, somewhat exaggeratingly. Some things I foresee, but I don't want them."[43] In Lem's work, special emphasis is placed on presenting the unpredictability of human behavior, as well as on sudden changes in decisions due to accidental events. Balanced scientists—physicists, biologists, philosophers and anthropologists—are keen to get to know a foreign civilization and, as a result of numerous failures, decide either to use atomic weapons or to deprive aliens of their lives in some more sophisticated manner. The science fiction setting blurs the traces of allusions to historical events and contemporary realities of life in communist Poland, yet seems no less readable than the parables of Jerzy Andrzejewski, Jerzy Zawieyski or Andrzej Szczypiorski.

It must not be forgotten that Stanisław Lem never gave a full testimony about his own experiences from the times of the occupation; we have only interviews in several languages, often with contradictory information, in which the writer talked about the past, usually replacing his life story with an anecdote. This may change with the publication of his correspondence, as so far only a small fraction of his home archive has been released, and the significance of the information in

Lem's letters—also for this book—cannot be overestimated. In my opinion, the ethical and philosophical consequences of the experience of being a victim and a witness of the Holocaust were articulated primarily in the disputes conducted by the protagonists of Lem's prose and at other levels of the narrative. In her analysis of autobiographism through the categories of testimony, confession and challenge, Małgorzata Czermińska points out that in internal tensions on the side of personal document, "The authorial stance makes itself felt above all in the shaping of the narrative perspective and may be modelled to a certain extent independently of genre convention."[44] The researcher is mainly interested in non-fiction prose, although she does not lose sight of parallel transformations of novels, literature of fact and essays, particularly intensive in the second half of the twentieth century. In my opinion, reflections on autobiographical themes can be extended particularly to Stanisław Lem's fiction, because the writer constantly employed genres reminiscent of personal documents. In several novels—such as *Star Diaries*, through *Memoirs Found in a Bathtub*, the quasi-autobiography in *His Master's Voice*, or *Tales of Pirx the Pilot* and *Solaris*—alternative ways of telling stories about the past have been established using formal mimesis. In his autobiographical *Highcastle*, the writer addresses the problem resulting from the multitude of autobiographies of characters he had already written:

> With several science fiction books and one contemporary novel behind me, I have put together biographies of fictitious persons so many times that the addressing now of my own person, and my own person of years ago, should be done only with the utmost self-control.[45]

At the same time, *Highcastle*, when read alongside *Tales of Pirx the Pilot*, begins to reveal the autobiographical background of the adventures of Lem's most famous character. This applies especially to the first stories, featuring anecdotes from the writer's schoolboy years, and the descriptions of group dynamics and the protagonist's appearance bring to mind the depreciating tone of the autobiographical essay. This gives rise to the hypothesis that, on planet Earth, Pirx—"the nicest character in Polish classical science fiction"[46]—must reside in Lviv, and it is there that the library the pilot abandoned is located.

Lem's protagonists and his narrators constantly justify writing memoirs by the need to explain their position on projects of cosmic importance, address widespread views about the past and devote separate chapters to their reading testimonies—impressions on books read in libraries on ships and space stations.[47] The tension between testimony and confession, triggered by parallels in the events in the story and one's own experiences, leads to the forming of cracks in the principal narrative, from which the writer's personal account unexpectedly emerges, mediated by fictional characters and unrelated to the central storylines of novels and stories.

Such a phenomenon of sudden interference of the past world in everyday and creative life is akin to the process of releasing traumatic memories. It is also confirmed by the main characteristics of Lem's writing, such as illogical descriptions of nightmares, breakdown of the cause-and-effect order, chronological inconsistencies, analyses of numbness, panic anxiety, melancholy and depression and the ubiquitous sense of the futility of any attempts to convey one's own experiences. The narrative solutions entail repetition; it is usually only the recently experienced, dangerous adventures of the protagonists that make it possible to understand the cataclysm from the past. This happens in the Pirx stories, but also in *His Master's Voice*—an attempt to understand the horror of the Hiroshima and Nagasaki bombings. In *Ananke*, one of the most melancholic and dark tales from the Pirx series, the protagonist describes the inner state of a witness to a transporter accident, in which many of his colleagues died:

> It was odd, but, being among strangers, he had been viewing the accident as an outsider, as one of the many witnesses not really involved, even when he had detected the hostility, the irritation in their questions … True, he'd been shaken, but he'd kept his head, always the observer, never entirely overwhelmed by events because of the way they lent themselves to systematic analysis: for all their inexplicability, they could be sifted, categorized, posited according to the method dictated by the solemnity of the investigation. Now all that was giving way. His mind was a blank, he evoked nothing, the images reasserted themselves on their own, from the beginning … He might have been the struggling ship itself, and, though painfully aware of the hopeless inaccessibility, the finality of what had happened, he returned to those fragmentary seconds with a silent, unremitting question in search of the cause.[48]

There is an emotional chasm that opens between the publicly made account-testimony and experiencing the catastrophe in solitude. The chronologically recounted events, supplemented by hypotheses as to their cause, are conducive to cognitive and emotional distance. In solitude, the distance crumbles, and as a result of complete identification with the victims, every second of the catastrophe is relived over and over. These two modes of storytelling permeate all of Lem's oeuvre and contribute to repeated cognitive dissonance in readers, because the rhythm of the protagonists' emotions does not harmonize with the rhythm of the narrative. Affected by tragic events and the death of their companions, Lem's protagonists succumb to melancholy, while at the same time striving to bear the imperative of memory, realizing that they are one of the few witnesses of those deaths. Such an approach to the narrative is reminiscent of the post-war discussions on the challenges of attempting to write about the Holocaust. Addressed in those scholarly disputes were issues such as ethical duties towards other people's suffering, the obligation to testify about the scale of the crimes and the description of the internal ruin of witnesses. In Lem's prose, the cosmic catastrophe,[49] combined with the fear of the consequences of nuclear explosions and the Cold War conflict, became a prism that made it possible to break the genre's limitations and ambiguously point to genocide.

Hannah Arendt and science fiction

In the context of the Holocaust, Lem's most frequently cited text is *Prowokacja* [Provocation], a review of a non-existent book whose equally non-existent author (a German scholar) explains the main principles of Nazi politics. Although it seems that in this review Lem simply expressed his own views on the "anthropology of evil" and Nazism,[50] one cannot forget that he articulated them through a whole range of intermediaries, and some of the views in *Provocation* contradict the analyses in his early books, written immediately after the war (for example on the mercantile purpose of the Holocaust). Even the name of the fake author is ironic, as Lem associates Aspernicus with Copernicus, and Horst with "another Horst," most likely Horst Wagner, a Third Reich diplomat responsible for the deportation and extermination of European Jews. Although captured after the war, Wagner nevertheless managed to escape from prison and flee to South America.[51] It may also be an allusion to the author of the National Socialist German Workers' Party (NSDAP) anthem, Horst Ludwig Wessel. The avalanche of associations prevents us from fully grasping the speaker's position and from considering the argument presented in the review to be the same as Lem's views. Moreover, in columns published in *Tygodnik Powszechny* in the 1990s, the writer once again commented on *Provocation*:

> I tried to elevate the narrative onto a kind of black buskin in order to create and substantiate the impression—which was actually false—that the Germans had a diabolic and devilish goal, but one that could be placed in some negative transcendence.[52]

Reviews of non-existent books can therefore be treated as subsequent versions of thought experiments, presenting consistent arguments in order to face seemingly correct views. At the same time Lem emphasized that attempts to understand the mechanisms of the Holocaust are too abstract because the scale of the crime exceeds the capacity of human imagination.[53]

It is possible that *Provocation* was inspired by Hannah Arendt's book *The Origins of Totalitarianism*, the French translation of which—*Sur l'antisémitisme*—the writer read in 1973 (a Polish translation was not published until 1989). In a letter to Michael Kandel, he reported:

> Such a strange impression from reading! Both totalitarianisms are undoubtedly made diabolical .... This is a (somewhat) fantastic sociological essay—that is, in a word, sci-fi ... And yet it was through exaggeration, simplifications and abuse of factual material, adapted to the concept *a priori*, that she managed to materialize a certain "aura," a certain "genius temporis acta"—of that time with which I am very much familiar personally. It is interesting that it is through hyperbolization, emphasis, macabrization, "black sublimation," in a word—ersatz of an infernal transcendence, in the

> guise of a strictly quasi-scholarly lecture—that social states can be evoked, states of things that the laborious objectivity of ordinary sociological analyses has failed to tackle.[54]

The interpretation of *The Origins of Totalitarianism* resonates with the main themes that later featured in *Provocation*, and it can even be assumed that it is an attempt to reiterate some of Arendt's assertions in a form that imitates a sociological-historical essay. In an autobiographical essay written for American readers, Lem discussed *Provocation* as an example of his own commitment to developing science fiction that tackles serious historical and philosophical problems, posing important questions about mass crimes.[55] In this context, Arendt's and Lem's respective books are proof that science fiction can put forward cognitively interesting theses on social and political issues. In his letter to Kandel, Lem emphasized the double nature of his experience of the Soviet and German occupation, and from the very beginning of his career he reflected on the overlapping features of both totalitarianisms, although he usually pointed out Nazism as the crueler of the two and often disagreed with the notion that extermination camps could be compared to gulags.

At the same time, the writer argued that in order to demonstrate the scale of German crimes, it is necessary to transgress the limits of what is appropriate, even at the expense of historiographical attention to detail. By liberating the story from the "laborious objectivity" of sociological research, Lem points to the need to have impact on the level of sensory perception, that is, to evoke a feeling of horror through "black sublimation" and hyperbolization, which help to imagine the "aura" accompanying the victims and witnesses of the genocide. Thus, based on Arendt's philosophical rationale, the writer contributes to the debate on how to write about the Holocaust and asserts that provocation is necessary. Holocaust literature researcher David Roskies applied the category he dubbed "scandalous memory" to such type of writing and focused on texts that go beyond the boundaries of appropriateness and break with previous writing practices, which means playing a game with readers' expectations. At the same time, he noted that moving and provocative works keep the theme of the Holocaust alive, while attempts to sacralize it in fact render it dead.[56] The title of Lem's review itself is a self-referential commentary, but apart from the aspect of transgressing the decorum principle, the term "provocation" may refer to the legal category. *Provocatio* also means summons and appeals. Considered from this perspective, the essay *Provocation* is a court trial of the perpetrators of genocide.

The fundamental ethical challenge for victims is the memory of the crime committed. In a letter to Professor Władysław Kapuściński dated May 30, 1976, Lem shared his reflections on his scholarships in Germany:

> Although Germans (both factions) lavish me with attention and gifts, in the depths of my soul I still harbor some fundamental reservations against

> them. There are things one has no RIGHT to forgive ... all the more so because the Germans haven't done these things just to me personally.[57]

He also dryly recounted the achievements of German science, built on the looting of ghettos and concentration camps: about the anthropological museum in Dahlem, he wrote:

> Simply wonderful, it cost millions, half of Polynesia and, naturally, they have catamarans there, a whole village, it's unbelievable, it was from the time when the Bonn government had no idea what to do with money, but that "Kanada"[58] [prosperity] is over now.[59]

Underlying the letter are both mockery and ironic detachment: here are Germans building an ethnographic museum with money pulled from the linings of torn Jewish coats, in which they put on display the peoples of Polynesia and their culture in an attempt to demonstrate the ethnic diversity of the world. Five years later, in a conversation with Raymond Federman, Lem recapitulated *Provocation* in answer to a question about the experiences of the occupation, stressing that he wrote this review of a non-existent book as a response to the increasingly prevalent German trend of thinking about overcoming the past (*Bewaltigung der Vergangenheit*). The writer asserted that nobody could forgive the Germans for what they had done because nobody had the right to do so. That could only be done by their victims, which, as we know, is not possible. *Provocation* is, therefore, a warning against attempts to overcome the Nazi past, but also against texts published in the United States, France and Germany that deny the existence of extermination camps. Federman agreed with Lem, noting that as survivors, they were both obsessed with history and mass death, and that their experience did not only affect the way they perceived the past, because for them both, as artists, the central question was how to live in the post-Holocaust era. Lem agreed with the fellow author, emphasizing:

> I believe that this Holocaust has not yet ended. That is to say, yes, in a sense it ended with World War Two; but it keeps re-appearing in various forms and versions here and there. What about Cambodia? Strange efforts to make people happier by exterminating half of the nation. All this is an extension of the Holocaust.[60]

In response to this statement, Federman asked Lem directly whether his work as a science fiction writer could be considered a part of the post-Holocaust era. The Polish author confirmed and added:

> I would even go further and say that the boom in sci-fi since World War II may have something to do with this post Holocaust era in which we live ... in which we survive.[61]

Science fiction of the Cold War era reflected the fears of survivors and showed the scale of destruction, referring to the models of catastrophic novels, adding to them the knowledge of mechanized mass death and using war rhetoric associated with nuclear weapons for its own purposes—on both sides of the Iron Curtain.

The prose of nuclear pacifism

> "Sci-fi? Sure, I like it, but only the trashy stuff."
>
> Stanisław Lem, *Pirx's Tale*

There is no denying the researchers' suggestion that an important point of reference in Lem's grotesque visions is the philosophical parable, the thematic and narrative limitations of which the writer exceeds in his subsequent works.[62] Those who explore inspirations and influences of specific literary traditions in Lem's prose often forget that he is a contemporary writer, and that his fiction falls entirely within the timeframe of the People's Republic of Poland. An attempt to set Lem within the context of Polish literary history may prove to be as interesting and inspiring as a search for borrowings from forgotten and peripheral genres. Let us start from the beginning, though Lem's first three books were blocked by censors, and until *The Astronauts* he was banned from publishing.[63] In 1954, *Sezam i inne opowiadania* [Sesame and other stories] was released—a collection of texts in which Lem openly criticized the politics and science of the United States; no wonder, then, that censors had no objections. It seems that it was that volume that marked the moment when Lem developed a strategy of playing a game with the censors,[64] without giving up the development of his own artistic concept. For the unpublished author, the solution to the stalemate was to focus on the socialist-realist anti-imperialist novel. While the so-called *produkcyjniak* ("factory literature," socialist-realist novel or short story, usually set in the workplace and concerning the socialist reconstruction of the country) provoked the reader into adopting a distanced approach right from the outset, it cannot be denied that anti-imperialist novels and short stories from the Cold War era did offer some accurate diagnoses of capitalism and its inherent exploitation, as well as correct assessments of the US policy on racial segregation or the practice of employing Nazi scientists in senior positions in American research centers. The anti-imperialist story has another advantage, namely that it criticizes the imperial, total, terrorizing power, unconcerned with any ethical boundaries. Thus, the talented writer manages to exploit it as a double-edged weapon against both the imperialist power of the United States and Soviet policy.[65] Therefore, Stanisław Lem could be listed alongside writers who made use of the possibilities offered by anti-imperialist narratives, such as Mirosław Żuławski, the author of *Rzeka czerwona* (1953) or Julian Stryjkowski, who published *Bieg do Fragala* in 1951.[66]

Lem's anti-imperialist story employs pre-war genres, especially the pacifist novel in its science fiction variant, represented in particular by the prose of H. G. Wells and Karel Čapek. Censors considered the pacifist novel to be a "bourgeois genre."[67] Therefore, they required that such prose focus on criticizing the policies of Western countries. For reasons clear from the point of view of the interests of the socialist state, praising pacifism was not desirable at a time when peace rhetoric was harnessed to fuel the arms race and legitimize the position of the Eastern Bloc on the Korean War. In his volume of short stories, as well as in his later texts, Lem developed an anti-imperialist novel and transformed it into a new form of thematic prose, which I would call the prose of nuclear pacifism. In the post-war era, the direct use of naturalistic and expressionist poetics (characteristic of the pacifist novel written after World War One) made it difficult to present the events of World War Two. The pacifist novel of the science fiction variety, particularly that invented by Čapek, was a prose genre, easily adaptable to the nuclear age and the Cold War arms race. This is evidenced by the Czechoslovakian film adaptation of the novel *Krakatit (*1947) directed by Otakar Vávra, where the detonation of highly explosive material invented by the protagonist was presented in the same way as the explosion of the atomic bomb in Hiroshima. In his analysis of the screen adaptation of Čapek's 1924 novel, Tomáš Pospíšil points out that Vávra's film, produced not long after the hostilities ended, had a profoundly anti-war message and aimed to bring attention to the ethical challenges associated with the production of weapons of mass destruction. At the same time, communists came to power in Czechoslovakia, and the film, made in response to the destruction caused by nuclear bombs in Japan, unintentionally began to resonate with Soviet propaganda, which accused the United States of using the nuclear weapons in their possession to put pressure on international organizations.[68] Similar relations between the artistic project and political slogans can be seen in the case of Lem's prose, as the author's observations are in no way parallel with the principles of socialist indoctrination. In Lem's writings, historical references to war and colonial expansion play a significant role, which, despite the apparent convergence with the media policy of the communist Poland, lends his books a universal appeal, revealing both the violence in the vision of a total war and the political abuse on this side of the Iron Curtain.

The subject of nuclear extermination captured the collective imagination of science fiction authors throughout the Cold War era, although it remained entangled in current political conflicts.[69] Both American writers and Stanisław Lem referred in their work to one of the most influential reports of the atomic age, namely John Hersey's *Hiroshima*, published in the United States in 1947 and consisting of testimonies of survivors of the bombing.[70] A year later, the book was released in Poland in Józef Wittlin's translation, although its traces are evident in Lem's texts written back in 1947. The short story *Człowiek z Hiroszimy* [The man from Hiroshima] accuses the United States of both the destruction of the city and racism against the Asian population. Terrifying descriptions of people who survived, only to realize that nothing can stop the radiation-induced decay of their bodies, are intersected with the story of the double agent Sato, sentenced to a slow death after the nuclear explosion as a result of radiation poisoning. Sato shares his experiences with a friend:

> And those who lived, without hands and feet, and without children, old men and little girls, sat in front of houses or in large squares, surrounded by a rim of fire and smoke, and dust, in silence. I didn't hear a single scream, a single moan. Not a moan.[71]

It is the silence of the victims that seems to be the most shocking in Hersey's reportage. Lem's story concludes with a detailed description of the catastrophe, and the focus on mothers killing their newborn children lest they become subjects for American experiments, pointing to the cynicism of politicians, the intelligence network and scientists. In the face of inevitable death, Sato can evaluate their actions:

> American and English newspapers have proclaimed a new era—so its first day was in Hiroshima? Who found this city on the map? Who put the red cross on paper, who dared to say: here? Your pilots used to come here and say: "That's some scrambled eggs we made!" It was not all right to kill Germans like that because they were human beings. And we're what? Japs.[72]

For the Allied forces, the Japanese became a group unworthy of mourning and respect, and the laughter mocking the victims proves that the sense of community with the suffering was destroyed. Their disintegrating bodies, the fact that they have become living corpses, is set within the narrative about victory, heroic struggle and the new era of war technology. Through the perfect annihilation of thousands of bodies of reified people, technological progress is being made in the arms race. The echoes of John Hersey's report haunted Lem for decades, and in the 1970s the writer wrote to his translator that he had used the text for his "private spiritual retreats" in times of profound self-doubt and depression.[73]

As a writer, Lem responded passionately to changes in social life and tried to anticipate the consequences of the decisions made by world leaders, who would not hesitate to destroy half the planet. Daniel Muzyczuk stresses that cybernetics, the subject that fascinated Lem, played an important political role in the 1960s:

> Rudolf Carnap's research into the objectivity that the natural language of science makes possible to achieve reached a new dimension in the 1960s. It also reflected a desire to find some agreement across the Iron Curtain. In this context, shouldn't we read Lem's novels featuring the theme of contact with a foreign civilization as a commentary on the Cold War?[74]

Muzyczuk maintains that already in Lem's debut novel, namely *The Astronauts*, we can attempt to read metaphorically encoded information from space, sent by extraterrestrial beings. Extraterrestrialism, the scholar argues, could have come from people "who at that time, depending on the nationality of the author of the sci-fi text, were metaphorical representatives of NATO or the Warsaw Pact, or simply Americans or Soviets."[75] These findings seem to be confirmed by a 1959 column by Lem, where the author analyzed American science fiction:

> The conflict between two parts of the world is reflected in this literature virtually from its inception. The image of the "red hemisphere of the Earth" found its most skillful pamphletist, most adept "negative utopist" in Orwell. Everything that has been written after him on this subject is at best a simplification, and at worst nonsense.[76]

In *Return from the Stars*, however, many references to the contemporary political and social situation can be traced, albeit not obviously. Stanisław Welbel points out that the ideas employed in this novel to describe the protagonist's entertainment "are close to the utopian art projects of the 1960s, based on enhancing the senses and experiencing reality through technology."[77] Welbel sets Lem's work within the context of the experiments and discoveries in art and science after the Polish October. Analyzing science fiction in the broad context of the changes that took place in Poland after 1956, the researcher notes that "in science fiction from the Cold War era, apart from the fascination with cybernetics and the competition between humankind and machines, film games are a transference and a depiction of the worldwide conflict."[78] Nuclear threats, space expeditions and arms races infuse science fiction with relentless specters of war.[79] The annihilation of bodies through burning must also evoke associations with the extermination of millions of people, after which nothing remains, not even graves or documents. The overlapping of the images of Hiroshima and the Holocaust paves the way for new ways of talking about the past and breaks the silence in confrontation with the burning pits. As it turned out, one of the ways to express the scale of violence in Lem's prose is the focus on carnality, a thorough analysis of the physiological fragility of human animals and descriptions of objects made of human bodies.

Protein

> We are, after all, my dear Jurek, ordinary protein animals, bred by evolution, and I don't think we can "know everything ourselves."
>
> Stanisław Lem in a letter to Jerzy Wróblewski[80]

It is not only history and politics that make Lem's writing so important to world literature. Equally significant and corresponding to the vision of the constant threat of war are the philosophy of chance and the approach to the human condition. The writer focuses his philosophical problems on the category of chance, drawing on the history of medicine—full of mistakes and cruel experiments.

One must not forget about his careful reading of the writings of Charles Darwin. It is to this philosopher that we owe Lem's descriptions of human bodies as "protein [that] pops up," "greasy jelly" (*Hospital of the Transfiguration*), "malleable substance" (*The Astronauts*) or "sticky matter on limestone scaffolding" (*Fables for Robots*). A venomous caricature of humankind can be found in the first novel *The Man from Mars*, published in installments in the press in 1946. One of the protagonists, Professor Widdletton, tries to imagine how a visitor from another planet could perceive the scientists gathered in the secret laboratory:

> I think that if the Martian were familiar with the notion of the ridiculous, then it would seem ridiculous to him if he saw a man smoking or devouring some carcass covered in dead sauce and boiled in dirty water ... or with those leg casings made of donkey and cow skin.[81]

Lem's protagonists ridicule people who, when confronted with aliens, pale in comparison—just like palefaces—mainly because of the organic protein structure of their bodies and the specific way they produce life energy.

The way the body is conceptualized in many of Lem's works is one of the most characteristic features of his writing. The body subjected to experiments, dead, dismembered, reduced to a medical preparation, and the metal bodies of robots, become an argument in a game of metaphysics and binary opposites. By this I mean that Lem is not so much close in his views to Jacques Derrida, for example, although—contrary to appearances[82]—he certainly shares many cognitive doubts with the philosopher, but rather owes much to the philosophical legacy of Darwin,[83] whose writings clearly impacted the notions of the body in his prose, and also—as he himself admitted in his letters—to his entire philosophical concept of humankind.[84] This makes it evident that the author of *His Master's Voice* is not so much a pessimistic writer[85] as his attitude is firmly rooted in the knowledge of the philosophical implications of Darwinian thought. And although researchers have often pointed to evolution as an important subject in Lem's oeuvre,[86] I would like to consider it differently, bearing in mind the interpretation of Darwinism proposed by Elizabeth Grosz. The philosopher stresses that Darwin's writings offer a comprehensive critique of essentialism and teleological thinking, taking into account the power of differences and introducing an anti-humanistic, algorithmic and mechanistic analysis of biological dynamics that rejects the identification of change with development and progress.[87]

It seems that Lem himself suggests interpretations that embed his work both in historical context and in Darwinian thought, when in *One Human Minute*, in a review of a non-existent book entitled *Das kreative Vernichtungsprinzip. The World as Holocaust*, he prophesizes that books with such titles would be published at the end of the twentieth century, but they would not be understood until the following century. There is an interesting ironic game present already in the title: in German, "the world as the Holocaust" is translated as "the principle of creative destruction," evoking associations with the language of the Nazi propaganda, critically analyzed, for example, in *Provocation*. Contrary to appearances, the essay "The World as Holocaust" does not concern wartime memories; rather, Lem plays an ironic game with readers, because instead of telling stories about Nazi crimes, he includes statistical and probability calculations, by means of which he proves that there is no life in the universe, and even if there is, then our ideas about it are naive because they are the product of an anthropocentric image of the world. In order to prove his point of view, he shifts smoothly from the birth of stars to the evolution of life on Earth, indicating its randomness. Lem constantly mocks the belief in the teleological aspect of human life, its uniqueness, pointing to the fortuitousness of existence.

A grotesque vision of evolution and a mockery of the sense of uniqueness of the human species can be seen in Trurl's journey and in the tale of the third machine constructed for King Genius, one that tells stories that are "profound and compelling."[88] In this tale, Trurl, the Great Constructor, is blinded by a comet and driven away from its path. He then throws whatever lies in his reach out of the spaceship window: gunpowder barrels, chess pieces, kitchen utensils. Finally, he tosses a jug:

> This jug, accelerating in accordance with the laws of gravity and boosted by the comet's tail, crashed into a mountainside above the dump, fell, clattered down a slope of junk toward a puddle, skittered across some mud, and finally smacked into an old tin can; this impact bent the metal around a copper wire, also knocked some pieces of mica between the edges, and that made a condenser, while the wire, twisted by the can, formed the beginnings of a solenoid, and a stone, set in motion by the jug, moved in turn a hunk of rusty iron, which happened to be a magnet, and this gave rise to a current, and that current passed through sixteen other cans and snips of wire, releasing a number of sulfides and chlorides, whose atoms linked with other atoms, and the ensuing molecules latched onto other molecules, until, in the very center of the dump, there came into being a Logic Circuit[89], and five more, and another eighteen in the spot where the jug finally shattered into bits. ... That evening, something emerged at the edge of the dump, not far from the puddle which had by now dried up, and this something, a creature of pure accident, was Mymosh the Selfbegotten, who had neither mother nor father, but was son unto himself, for his father was Coincidence, and his Mother—Entropy.[90]

The story continues with a grotesque description of Mymosh gazing at himself in a puddle and admiring the incidental arrangement of garbage on his body. And here comes the ridicule of anthropocentrism and metaphysical usurpations: "Truly, I am beautiful, nay, perfect, which clearly implies the Perfection of All Created Things!! Ah, and how good must be the One Who fashioned me!"[91]

The tale of how the Great Constructor Trurl "created a local fluctuation, and what came of it"[92] is a reworking of the story of the creation of man from the Book of Genesis. The bluntness of this fragment points to the philosophical inspirations with Darwin's theory and puts an end to all discussions about the purposefulness of existence.

Such an approach was undoubtedly influenced by the books by Norbert Wiener, whom Lem held in great esteem. In *The Human Use of Human Beings*, the founder of cybernetics hypothesizes that living organisms and some machines "are precisely parallel in their analogous attempts to control entropy through feedback."[93] Wiener points out that the words "life," "vitalism," "purpose," "soul" do not meet the requirements of strict scientific thinking and as such are better avoided.[94] For the mathematician struggling with machines capable of communication, Darwin was an extremely important philosopher, as he gave up thinking about the theory of evolution as a gradual transition to ever higher and better forms, instead pointing out that, on the one hand, living beings demonstrate a spontaneous tendency for multidirectional development, while on the other, they tend to follow the pattern set by their ancestors, which in consequence leads to adaptation to the environment.[95] According to Darwin, "this residual pattern," Wiener emphasizes, "assumes the appearance of universal purposiveness."[96] A commentary to the story of the machine about Mymosh could be a fragment of Wiener's reflections on the relationship between energy and information:

> Thus the question of whether to interpret the second law of thermodynamics pessimistically or not depends on the importance we give to the universe at large, on the one hand, and to the islands of locally decreasing entropy which we find in it, on the other. Remember that we ourselves constitute such an island of decreasing entropy, and that we live among other such islands.[97]

Wiener's worldview runs parallel to Lem's storytelling solutions, which ridicule the belief in progress, and the inevitability of extermination—as individuals, species or civilization—is one of the few certainties. For example, in *His Master's Voice*, the narrator Peter E. Hogarth asserts that

> For the disinterestedness of evil is the only support, in man, for the theological argument; theology answers the question where does a quality come from that has its origin neither in nature nor in culture. A mind immersed totally in the human experience, and therefore anthropocentric, might finally agree with the image of Creation as a somewhat sick joke.[98]

Challenging theodicy—not just by this protagonist—is deeply immersed in Darwin's legacy. It is what makes it possible to point out the anthropocentric cognitive limitations of humankind. The randomness of existence reveals the grotesqueness and futility of searching for an answer to the question *unde malum?* treating evil as a result of various environmental factors.[99]

Evolutionary biology

The theme of medicine and doctors marks one of the principal directions of my research. It is closely associated with the writer's own education, started at the Medical Institute in Lviv (which had been separated from the University of Lviv by the Soviet authorities) and continued at the Jagiellonian University in Kraków after the war. Hospital internship and knowledge of anatomy and physiology, as well as some scholarly papers written at the time (such as an article by the future writer, then a student, titled "Etiology of cancer"[100]), provide the background for many novels and short stories, in particular at the beginning of the 1950s.[101] Studying medicine must have been particularly difficult during the occupation and after the war, when the extent of doctors' involvement in Nazi politics was gradually being discovered. Also frequently recurring in Lem's prose is the theme of disinclination to perform autopsies. Additional factors included the awareness of pseudo-medical experiments and the sources of some preparations, as well as the state of science in post-war Poland. At the same time, it was the knowledge of biology that had a significant impact on shaping the writer's worldview. In a letter to Michael Kandel in 1977, Lem emphasized:

> I begin to agree with the idea that the rightness of my "intuition" stems from the fact that thinking is based on generalizations straight out of evolutionary biology, "chance," "stochastics," "randomness," all this from there, in a biological interpretation, and not in the present—physical.[102]

Already in *Hospital of the Transfiguration*, Sekułowski, one of the most cynical characters of Lem's prose, tells the protagonist: "It seems to me that we have no more knowledge of our bodies than of the most distant star."[103] Combined in this self-referential statement are the principal themes of the writer's work: the philosophy of science, the history of medicine, interplanetary travel and doubts about the cognitive capabilities of humankind.[104]

In the contemporary humanities, ethical issues related to life, evolution and the transformation of social relations, taking place as a result of the impact of technological changes, occupy a central place. Some researchers analyze extreme situations and, through categories such as "vile bodies" (Grégoire Chamayou) or a life "undeserving of grief" (Judith Butler), demonstrate complex political and legal issues that make wars possible and deprive individuals and populations of citizenship and human rights, thereby developing earlier biopolitical concepts. These projects are firmly anchored in the anti-humanism of the second half of the twentieth century and an attempt to undermine the anthropological definitions of "human" and "humanity." In her collection of essays *Frames of War: When Is Life Grievable?* Judith Butler analyzes how contemporary media paved the way for certain groups of people to be perceived as meaningless:

> We might think of war as dividing populations into those who are grievable and those who are not. An ungrievable life is one that cannot be mourned because it has never lived, that is, it has never counted as a life at all.[105]

Although her findings relate to the wars that took place after September 11, 2001, Butler taps into the broader context of racism and all armed conflicts, citing a number of historical examples.

Out of the philosophical spectrum Butler presents, the most important for my examination are her observations about the precariousness of human life and the potential for mourning. Awareness of the precariousness of life, constant threats and susceptibility to injury and annihilation help people to cross-cultural boundaries and identify with others: "Precariousness implies living socially, that is, the fact that one's life is always in some sense in the hands of the other."[106] These observations, just like the critique of anthropocentrism, resonate with the ethical implications of Lem's prose and essays, as the author was fascinated by discursive demarcation lines intended to justify violence against others. For we cannot be misled by the fact that the nuclear weapons in his novels are aimed by the protagonists at foreign, potentially dangerous civilizations, because—and this is not just my opinion—Lem touches upon the ethical obligations of Earthlings and their relationship to other populations of the Earth during the Cold War era. Lem's decisions to annihilate the incomprehensible aliens are preceded by hours of debates focusing on the difference between human life and one that is non-human and thus less worth protecting. The aliens in Lem's prose are usually annihilated, but instead of sadness, envoys from the Earth feel a mixture of shame, disgust and relief. As Butler put it,

> Forms of racism instituted and active at the level of perception tend to produce iconic versions of populations who are eminently grievable, and others whose loss is no loss, and who remain ungrievable.[107]

Butler's work focuses on the identification of gaps in the mechanisms of creating boundaries between life worth mourning and life that is not worth mourning. For this reason, her attention is focused on the ontology of the body and its social dimension. The fragility of the body allows us to see the external conditions necessary to preserve life:

> It is outside itself, in the world of others, in a space and time it does not control, and it not only exists in the vector of these relations, but as this very vector. In this sense, the body does not belong to itself.[108]

The interdependence of the bodies of human animals and their mutual recognition of each other in the precariousness of life are the basis for actions that make it possible to escape from the omnipotent military political machines and their media representations.

I also draw on the category of "vile bodies" proposed by Foucault's disciple, Grégoire Chamayou, who studied the history of this concept (Latin *corpore vili*; French *corps abject*) in medicine. In his dissertation, Chamayou tentatively posits that the nineteenth-century imperial, technopolitical idea of a camp as a ground for experiments on the inhabitants of the colonies was reused and imported to Europe, where concentration camps were set up in a different historical context.[109] In my opinion, it is this notion that best conveys the issues underpinning Lem's prose, because in his alternative worlds, the writer presents a broad spectrum of violence: colonialism and physical exploitation, as well as medical experiments done in the name of progress. Thus, the history of medicine paves the way for philosophical reflection on the ontological status of the body and reveals how certain subjects are deprived of legal and ethical protection in the name of development and usefulness.

Fragments

The purpose of my reading of Lem's prose is not just to reconstruct historical and biographical events, nor do I seek a coherent interpretation frame that would bind together this vast collection of prose. On the contrary, I strive to present narrative loops, point out seemingly non-functional anecdotes, broken threads and abandoned concepts, which is why I rarely interpret all aspects of the novel, focusing instead on particular themes, motifs and biographies of the protagonists. Such a mode of reading was inspired by Grzegorz Niziołek's book *The Polish Theatre of the Holocaust*, in which the author emphasizes, for example, the need to reread works written during the era of socialist realism and argues that a special place in them is occupied by Jewish characters, who "usually have an episodic status, their storylines are loosely related to the entire composition, some even give the impression of unnecessary amplification, may seem unclear to readers, broken, poorly integrated into the course of events."[110] I do not restrict such an approach only to the period of socialist realism, but extend it to cover the whole of Lem's genre prose, including texts from later periods. I am interested in masks, mediation, narrative shadows—hiding behind ostensibly indirect speech, but also behind an omniscient narrator, suspending fictional worlds in space and alternative worlds, apocryphalism and false clues. In reading Lem's prose, I focus mainly on jagged, broken, scattered stories without a conclusion, set aside from the principal storyline, seeing in them traces of testimony.

In her book *Unclaimed Experience: Trauma, Narrative and History*, Cathy Caruth emphasized that the important aspect of Sigmund Freud's essay "Beyond the Pleasure Principle" is the notion that trauma disrupts the experience of time, whereas she interprets it as events experienced too suddenly, too unexpectedly, to be fully comprehended and assimilated by the subject in such a way that they reach consciousness, until they return, multiplied by nightmares and repetitive actions of the survivor.[111] Like Caruth, I read a literary text, searching for recurring numbers, words and images in Lem's prose; I focus on their rhetorical potential (such as the word "selection"), which cannot be reduced to the thematic meaning of a literary work, because it stubbornly bears testimony to a number of unhealed wounds.[112]

In this, I follow Niziołek, who interprets post-war Polish theater and often does not respect the fictionality of the story,[113] because such a reading strategy makes it possible to recreate a testimony encoded in subsequent works. I approach Lem's prose as a form of personal document and in its interpretation I apply the postulates of Michał Głowiński, who points out that

> literary works about the Holocaust can (and even should) be asked questions of the kind posed by historians who deal with such or such documents. It must be immediately added that questions that can be interpreted as typical for history have never, in fact, been applied to works of literature (or akin thereto).[114]

Caruth, on the other hand, stresses that the screams and crying of a traumatic wound does not need to relate to the past events experienced by the subject, but may be associated with the trauma of the other person, thus making it possible to meet the Other and listen to his/her story.[115] Langer puts it in a similar way: "Former victims are thus pursued not only by their own earlier traumatic moments but by the traumas of others too."[116] For this reason, I endeavor not to relate events described in the prose to the writer's personal experience, pointing to the role of intermediaries, and thus writing about protagonists, narrators and characters. The only exception to this principle is when the writer (especially in his correspondence) refers his own experiences to the worlds he created.

Too much history

> How to read Holocaust literature?
> In all languages. From the beginning:
> before time, in time, and against time.[117]
>
> David G. Roskies, *What Is Holocaust Literature?*

When it comes to interpreting texts written just after the war, Michał Głowiński believes that it might be worthwhile to take biographical categories into account:

> in the decades following the Holocaust, almost all Holocaust narratives, in particular early ones, are highly evocative of the life-writing genre, including those that employ fiction and are, from a certain point of view,

> fully-fledged literary works, meaning that they exhibit characteristics usually attributed to literature.[118]

Lem's story, thousands of pages long, is the testimony of a former victim who assembles horror-filled images from a broken kaleidoscope of events. In his earliest novels and stories, the writer employs the medium of realistic convention to recreate the reality of life under the Nazi occupation. He also took an active part in public debates on the representation of the Shoah and its meaning, from the dispute on the "penchant for martyrdom" held just after the war up until the analyses of terrorism published after the political transformation, for which the point of reference was the annihilation of the Jewish nation. In the 1950s, his story had no chance of breaking through the wall of censorship, and once it finally did, it turned out to be of little interest to readers. In his *Polski teatr Zagłady* [The Polish theatre of the Holocaust], Grzegorz Niziołek addresses, among other things, the reception to theater in the post-war era, arguing that:

> Forms of representation of past events with too historical a structure often contributed to the marginalization of theatrical productions: if we know all about it, why are we being told about it time and time again? … On the other hand, all forms of deformation, displacement and condensation, provoked—through a déjà vu mechanism—a profound shock and intense emotional response from the audience.[119]

At this juncture, it is difficult to extend these insights onto the entire contemporary history of Polish literature, although perhaps such a perspective would make it possible to remake the twentieth-century canon. Niziołek maintains that the audience's indifference to the historical representations of the extermination of Jews stemmed from insufficient empathy, as well as the separation of Polish and Jewish suffering in the immediate aftermath of the war and later. If we were to apply these remarks to the interpretation of Stanisław Lem's prose, we could point out that the writer's unsuccessful debut inspired him to search for a niche that would enable him to express his experiences as a victim and witness in the form of, as Niziołek put it, "deformation, displacement and condensation." The realistic convention did not so much prove inadequate to convey the extermination of the Jews of Lviv as it was constantly at odds with the historical politics of the People's Republic of Poland, which, incidentally, was subject to continuous alterations during the Cold War era. By choosing the genre of science fiction,[120] in the eyes of censors Lem became a writer of fiction for young readers, and the atomic fables he wrote had the added advantage of promoting scientific discoveries among the young.[121] Nevertheless, the writer never lost sight of the crisis caused by World War Two, nor of the threats posed by nuclear weapons, the Cold War and other ethical challenges of modern times. In an interview published in 1986 in *Science Fiction Studies*, Lem explained how he understood literary realism, albeit with the caveat that his definition was not universal. Literary realism is literature's response to real problems of at least two types: one concerns the phenomena that people are having to face now or that they have just started to notice, and the other is a quandary that they will need to solve in the future. At the same time, the writer cautioned that any attempt to distinguish "possible problems" from those "fictitious" or probable, even though they might seem outrageous or "highly unlikely" now, would ultimately prove unsuccessful. Thus defined, Lem was still a realist writer, especially since—following his own examples—his literary output, categorized as science fiction, is no different from the method of forming research hypotheses, e.g. in physics. [122]

In the context of science fiction, it is also symptomatic that in their testimonies, victims and survivors compare their experience of the Shoah to "otherworldly"' situations, likely a reference to pre-war catastrophic science fiction novels, which served as a sounding board for social fears.[123] When asked how the so-called Aryan side looked from the perspective of the ghetto, Israel Gutman said: "Quite a different world: people dressed in regular, clean clothes, laughing, a family walking together, people carrying flowers … It was as if I was looking at something that was happening on the moon."[124] Krystyna Żywulska and Dina Gottliebova compared their arrival in Birkenau to landing on another planet.[125] In her account of her time in Auschwitz, Edith P. recalled that she believed that there was a black sun over the camp, as if she found herself in a different solar system.[126] The comparison between the Shoah and space travel reflects various complex relationships generated by the traumatic experience of forced isolation and expulsion. In Dawid Kahane's testimony, it is the area outside the Lviv ghetto that is likened to an alien planet:

> Inside the Yura [cathedral], the walls upstairs made a peculiar impression on me. … There was such gentle silence amidst those walls that we could hear our hearts beating. After the frantic noise of the ghetto I really thought I was on another planet.[127]

Langer, on the other hand, cites the survivors' imagery of "another planet" as a metaphor depicting the meanders of the memory of former victims. Bessie K., for example, says in her testimony:

> it seems to me that Hitler chopped off part of the universe and created annihilation zones and torture and slaughter areas. You know, it's like the planet was chopped up into a normal [part]—so-called normal: our lives are not really normal and this other planet, and we were herded onto that planet from this one, and herded back again, [while] having nothing, virtually nothing in common with the inhabitants of this planet.[128]

There are parallels between the latter testimony and the storyline of Lem's *Return from the Stars*, explaining how alienated the protagonist feels when faced with the ordinary lives of people on Earth after returning from his time-loop journey.

Hal Bregg confronts the memories of his friends' deaths, while at the same time trying to forget the paralyzing fear that gripped him in space.

According to Maciej Dajnowski, the fears of Lem's protagonists stem from the fact that they constantly get lost in labyrinth-like, alien spaces inhabited by monsters.[129] Some of the most frequently evoked *loci horridi* in his prose are cemeteries and ruins; the eerie quality of the landscape is enhanced by a feeling of being torn apart, helpless and restless, and the main dramatic axis of many of his works is death, accompanied by various shades of red, often reminiscent of blood (e.g. the ocean in Solaris).[130] In my opinion, these themes are linked to the experiences of the victim of the German and Soviet occupation, and the horror-story setting[131] provides an opportunity to give testimony. Therefore closed, claustrophobic rooms play a significant role in this prose, bringing depression and anxiety to the characters. In one of his interviews, the writer even shared an anecdote about *Memoirs Found in a Bathtub*, saying that upon finishing reading the novel, Hanna Malewska asked Jan Józef Szczepański if Lem was suffering from paranoia. For the writer himself this was proof that, even though he was free from claustrophobia or agoraphobia, he was still capable of conveying the atmosphere of the fear of closed spaces convincingly.[132] We should bear in mind that all those spatial elements in Lem's prose are depicted with a certain degree of detachment, distorted by gallows humor and irony. Chaya Ostrower points out that in the accounts of survivors, humor alleviated the subjective feeling of horror and offered a chance to distance oneself from it. The researcher concludes her analysis by pointing out that humor has been an effective means of coping with atrocities experienced, and that stories about that period of life are woven, as she puts it, out of horror stories stitched together by threads of macabre humor.[133] A grotesque horror story seems to be an important point of reference in reflections on Lem's writing and the traces of his own experiences found in his works.

Just as playing with time, irony and distortion in Lem's prose contribute to the confusion of interpretative traces related to the historical context and lend a "universal" character to his prose. In the opening story in *The Cyberiad*, entitled *How the World Was Saved*, designer Trurl boasts to Klapaucius, telling him about a machine that could create anything starting with "n." Jealous and angry, Klapaucius commands the machine to produce Universal Nothingness, and as it systematically executes his command, annihilating things and concepts alike, one by one, he begs it to stop and admits that it has been well designed. The machine cautions Klapaucius:

> Take a good look at this world, how riddled it is with huge, gaping holes, how full of Nothingness, the Nothingness that fills the bottomless void between the stars, how everything about us has become lined with it, how it darkly lurks behind each shred of matter.[134]

Having wreaked such havoc, the machine is unable to reproduce all the destroyed phenomena and objects. As a result, the world has lost many of them irretrievably, since the machine was programmed only to create things that begin with "n." The answer to the title question—how the world was saved—is, therefore, that it was only by chance and, in addition, by no means whole, and that it is now inhabited by mutilated, imperfect and grotesque characters.

Bestiaries

In Lem's *Bestiariusz Lema według Mroza* [The bestiary according to Mróz], an illustrated album published in 2012 after the death of both authors, the inhabitants of the Universe are presented with an ironic detachment. In the afterword, Piotr Sitkiewicz provides a detailed account of the subsequent stages of cooperation between the artist and the writer, supplementing it with reproductions from *Monstrorum Historia* by Ulisse Aldrovandi and from the treatise on monsters and miracles by Ambroise Para, as well as paintings by Hieronymus Bosch, Albrecht Dürer, Pieter Breughel and William Hogarth, which served as a source of inspiration for the illustrator of Lem's stories about expeditions to unknown planets.[135] The publisher does not explain why illustrations featured at the exhibition entitled simply *Mróz and Lem*[136] have been published as a bestiary, although the reference to the medieval genre[137] in the case of Lem's prose seems justified. After all, bestiaries are semi-scientific, semi-fantastic works, and as such should perhaps be perceived as predecessors of the science fiction genre. In bestiaries, drawings depicting mythical and fairy-tale creatures are mixed with illustrations of reptiles or mammals encountered by travelers in distant parts of the world, and the allegorical and symbolic potential of animal images is combined with the medical knowledge of the era. The narrative potential of this genre was discovered by such writers as Lewis Carroll, T. H. White and Jorge Luis Borges.

It is evident that authors of bestiaries must have had a sense of humor. They also documented groundbreaking moments in natural history and exploited the philosophical potential of reflection on monsters. They become problematic only when they are harnessed for purposes such as racial superiority, violence, expansion and conquest, while at the same time justifying mass killings. Ewa Kuryluk emphasizes:

> Artists of the Nazi propaganda were inspired by exhibits in anatomy cabinets and collections of curiosities, by fantastic treatises on savages and freaks, by the grotesque, the fantastic, and church art. The mentally ill at times resemble beasts, at other times—dwarfs, Siamese twins, black people or monkeys, or bring to mind a bunch of sinners—repulsive cripples and gimps, burned and quartered in the visions of Catholic hell.[138]

At the other pole of Nazi propaganda is the New Man, who has revolutionized the way we perceive the body. The image of the New Man was seductive because it referred to the need to build a strong community bond, exploiting the dream of physical and political unity, especially attractive in times of social, political and cultural crisis. Such an idealistic and impossible-to-achieve image of body was intended to contribute to the creation of a new soul: resistant to compassion and empathy, determined to fight in the name of progress, regardless of how cruel the methods.[139] In Lem's prose, characters often have physical deformities, scars and nervous tics, so that the readers do not have too high expectations of the protagonists whose story they intend to follow. The writer attempted to predict the consequences of both the concept of the New Man and the Nazi science that supported it, focused on improving the operation of the state and individuals. In 1948, for example, he wrote in "Życie Nauki":

> The question of subordinating medicine and biology to National Socialism was only one of the links in the process of the Nazification of German science, whose representatives, with astonishing obedience, broke basic scientific principles and tried to adorn political theories of entirely ad hoc nature.[140]

Nazi science was meant to tear apart the social fabric, segregate, break ties and introduce determinants that often broke the identity of individuals. As a result, it discursively created a population of people whose lives—as Butler put it—were not worthy of grieving, and their annihilation was not met with any significant opposition from their fellow residents.

Notes

1 *Cossack Mamai. A Phenomenon of an Image and an Attempt at Deciphering Its Cultural 'Identification' Code*, S. Bushak (research), V. and I. Sakharuk (catalog), Radovid Press 2008, p. 92. I would like to thank Nadiya Polishchuk for pointing out the painterly theme during our visit to Stanisław Lem's former home and for explaining the link between Cossack Mamai and the theme of Jew the Eternal Wanderer.
2 Ibid., p. 94–95.
3 Ibid., p. 84–90, 110–117.
4 K. N. Hayles, "Chaos and Dialectic: Stanisław Lem and the Space of Writing," *Chaos Bound: Orderly Disorder in Contemporary Literature and Science*, Ithaca NY, 1990, p. 115–140.
5 J. Jarzębski, "*Kosmogonia i konsolacja*" [in:] idem, *Wszechświat Lema*, Kraków 2003, p. 90. Biographical themes also intrigued the younger generation of researchers, but the lack of information about the writer's life before 1945 prevented them from drawing interpretative conclusions. Cf. K. Bałżewska, *Czarny wariant "Bildung." O relacjach między "Czarodziejską górą" Thomasa Manna a "Szpitalem Przemienienia" Stanisława Lema*, "Pamiętnik Literacki" 2012, no. 1, p. 111–128; P. Majewski, *Lem fantastyczny czy makabryczny? O możliwym źródle pisarstwa nierealistycznego*, "Przegląd Filozoficzno-Literacki" 2009, no. 1, p. 127–153.
6 The volume was to be published under the title *Wywiad i atomy*. Cf: K. Budrowska, *Literatura i pisarze wobec cenzury PRL 1948–1958*, Białystok 2009, p. 149–156.
7 On the subject of narrative gaps in texts on the Holocaust see A. Ubertowska, *Aporie, skandale, wyrwy w tekście. Etyka opowieści o Zagładzie*, "Teksty Drugie" 2002, no. 1–2, p. 135–139.

8 Cf. *"Nie spieszy mi się domykać kanon." Rozmowa z Profesorem Davidem Roskiesem, współautorem książki "Holocaust Literature. A History and Guide,"* interview by Paweł Wolski, "Narracje o Zagładzie" 2015, no. 1, p. 18.
9 "From Lviv's point of view, World War One turned out to be just a prelude to the ultimate catastrophe." K. Kotyńska, *Lwów. O odczytywaniu miasta na nowo*, Kraków 2015, p. 49. Cf. K.S. Jobst, *Układy i konfrontacje. Kwestia narodowa w Galicji*, Polish translation from the German by B. Andrunik [in:] *Mit Galicji*, eds. J. Purchla, W. Kos, Ż. Komar, M. Rygier, W.M. Schwarz, Kraków 2014, p. 161–164.
10 J.M. Piskorski, *Wygnańcy. Przesiedlenia i uchodźcy w dwudziestowiecznej Europie*, Warszawa 2010, p. 128.
11 T. Zarycki, *Peryferie. Nowe ujęcia zależności centro-peryferyjnych*, Warszawa 2009, p. 197–199 (the researcher uses Marcin Zaremba's ideas).
12 Ibid., p. 199.
13 Ibid., p. 201.
14 This does not apply, of course, to the works of émigré authors. Cf. B. Hadaczek, *Historia literatury kresowej*, Szczecin 2008, p. 308–327. In his book, Hadaczek compares Lem's *Highcastle* to works by such writers as Józef Wittlin, Stanisław Vincenz, Kazimierz Wierzyński and Marian Hemar, treating Lem as "a writer in exile," albeit the comparison is made solely in a footnote (cf. idem, p. 317, footnote 15). The scholar lists Julian Stryjkowski, Andrzej Kuśniewicz and Leopold Buczkowski in the same category.
15 Z. Wóycicka, *Przerwana żałoba. Polskie spory wokół pamięci nazistowskich obozów koncentracyjnych i zagłady 1944–1950*, Warszawa 2009.
16 A. Zieniewicz, *Pakty i fikcje. Autobiografizm po końcu wielkich narracji (szkice)*, Warszawa 2011, p. 12.
17 In one column published in the early 1990s, Lem wrote: "I have the impression that I live on the terrible margin of literary life in Poland—and I am actually happy about it." S. Lem, *Powrót do prajęzyka* [in:] idem, *Lube czasy*, ed. T. Fiałkowski, Kraków 1995, p. 72. In a letter to Jerzy Wróblewski dated September 24, 1964, Lem complained, "this literary life of mine is like Robinson's on a desert island." Letter courtesy of Barbara and Tomasz Lem.
18 "I never believed in any *homo sovieticus*, which was supposed to be so wonderful, I escaped into the Universe from the realities of local existence." Lem, *Goście z Petersburga* [in:] *Lube czasy*, p. 132. In the 1970s, Leszek Szaruga was convinced that Lem's work should be seen as an attempt to interpret the present day, disregarding props such as space travel and technical inventions. The researcher emphasized that "the convention adopted by Lem has the same character as that of Aesop, Swift or Moore, for whom the props serve simply as a protective garment." L. Szarga, *Lema przypadki konieczne*, "Nurt" 1972, no. 8, p. 17.
19 D. Oramus, *O pomieszaniu gatunkow. Science fiction a postmodernizm*, Warszawa 2010, p. 95.
20 Ibid., p. 104.
21 S. Lem, *List z 3 listopada* [in:] idem, *Sława i fortuna. Listy do Michaela Kandla 1972–1987*, Kraków 2013, p. 301–302 (original spelling).
22 S. Lem, *List z 15 listopada 1974* [in:] ibid., p. 311.
23 J. Rzeszotnik, *Rekonstrukcja portretu "dialektycznego mędrca z Krakowa." Stanisław Lem w zwierciadle niemieckojęzycznych źrodeł* [in:] *Lem i tłumacze*, eds. E. Skibińska i J. Rzeszotnik, Kraków 2010, p. 137–149.
24 K. Duszenko, *Teolog „częściowo dozwolony,"* "Tygodnik Powszechny" 2000 [online], <http://www.tygodnik.com.pl/apokryf/17/duszenko.html> [access: October 10, 2015].
25 Ibid.
26 U.K. Le Guin, European SF: "Rottensteiner's Anthology, the Strugatskys, and Lem," *Science Fiction Studies* 1975, vol. 1, no. 3, p. 184.
27 R. Federman, "An Interview with Stanisław Lem," *Science Fiction Studies* 1983, vol. 10, p. 3; Antoni Smuszkiewicz noted that already in the early 1950s in an article

entitled *Imperializm na Marsie* [Imperialism on Mars], Lem stressed the relationship between contemporary criticism, realism and science fiction. A. Smuszkiewicz, *Stanisław Lem*, Poznań 1996, p. 33.
28 R. Federman, An Interview with Stanisław Lem, p. 5.
29 P. Haffner, "Stanisław Lem: A Moralist Who Doesn't Moralize," *Science Fiction Studies* 2001, vol. 28, no. 129, p. 53. Federman also pointed out that humor and irony make Lem's writing significantly different from science fiction prose, which takes itself very seriously and tends to be moralizing. R. Federman, An Interview with Stanisław Lem, p. 4.
30 Generation of Polish writers born circa 1920, who entered adulthood during World War Two. It was the war that was the primary factor that shaped their literary output.
31 J. Jarzębski, *Przypadek i wartości. (O aksjologii Stanisława Lema)* [in:] idem, *Wszechświat Lema*, p. 193.
32 S. Buryła, *Tematy (nie)opisane*, Kraków 2013, p. 19–20.
33 Ibid., p. 27.
34 Discussing the notions of heroism in the post-war debates about the Holocaust, Zofia Wóycicka cites the views of Betti Ajzensztajn, who believed that it was heroic "to escape from the ghetto and the camp, get some 'Aryan papers' and live on the 'Aryan' side, teach clandestine classes, participate in religious, scientific and cultural life, be involved in self-help, document German crimes and save treasures of culture; it was also an expression of heroism to die out of solidarity." Z. Wóycicka, *Przerwana żałoba*, p. 167.
35 L. L. Langer, *Holocaust Testimonies: The Ruins of Memory*, New Haven and London 1991, p. 162.
36 Ibid., p. 182–183.
37 Maciej Dajnowski disagrees, although in his *Pejzażysta Lem*, the researcher cites nineteenth-century concepts mainly from the Western culture (in the broad sense), and so does not include Lem in the paradigms of Polish Romanticism.
38 "Of course, I belong to the Enlightenment tradition and I am a rationalist, albeit somewhat desperate. A desperate rationalist is sometimes quite akin to a madman." S. Lem, *List z 1 sierpnia, 1972* [in:] idem, *Sława i fortuna. Listy do Michaela Kandla 1972–1987*, p. 79.
39 I wrote about it in the article *Parodie, pastisze i recykling w prozie Stanisława Lema*, *Zagadnienia Rodzajów Literackich* 2014, no. 2, p. 65–75.
40 See M. Szpakowska, *Dyskusje z Stanisławem Lem*, Warszawa 1996, p. 9.
41 E. Domańska, *Wokół „Metahistorii"* [w:] *H. White, Poetyka pisarstwa historycznego*, eds. E. Domańska, M. Wilczyński, Kraków 2010, p. 7–30. Cf. *Teorie literatury XX wieku. Antologia*, eds. A. Burzyńska, M.P. Markowski, Kraków 2006, p. 504–508.
42 J. Jarzębski, who in his article *Chaos jako wyzwanie* stressed that Lem was a modernist thinker that believes in reason and progress, and that randomness never played a significant role in his work, would probably disagree with such a statement. J. Jarzębski, *Chaos jako wyzwanie: późna eseistyka Lema* [in:] idem, *Wszechświat Lema*, p. 243.
43 S. Lem, *Zmienna niezależna* [in:] idem, *Lube czasy*, p. 91.
44 M. Czermińska, *The Autobiographical Triangle. Witness, Confession, Challenge*, Peter Lang, Berlin 2019, transl. by Jean Ward, p. 24.
45 S. Lem, *Highcastle*, transl. Michael Kandel, 2017, p. 54.
46 A. Smuszkiewicz, *Stanisław Lem*, p. 73.
47 See M. Czermińska, *Autobiograficzny trójkąt*, p. 71–96 for the meaning of libraries and testimonies of reading in personal documents.
48 S. Lem, *Ananke* [in:] idem, *More Tales of Pirx the Pilot*, transl. Louis Iribarne with the assistance of Magdalena Majcherczyk, and by Michael Kandle, New York 1982, p. 185.
49 Such an approach to the relationship between catastrophism and stories about the Holocaust is reminiscent of the concept of post-catastrophic narratives. Cf. *Po*

Zagładzie. Narracje post-katastroficzne, eds. A. Artwińska, P. Czapliński, A. Molisak, A. Tippner, "Poznańskie Studia Polonistyczne. Seria Literaturoznawcza" no. 25, 2015.

50 One of those who interpreted *Provocation* that way was Małgorzata Szpakowska, who stated that "The quasi-essay ... is simply a way of attracting attention, an advertising trick employed in a just cause. Lem's reasoning could have been as follows: a provocative thesis (the Holocaust as an epiphenomenon of the state of European culture) would not be harmed in any way by provocative form; on the contrary, by breaking the convention of a funerary lament, it would facilitate cold reflection on the phenomenon itself." M. Szpakowska, *Dyskusje ze Stanisławem Lemem*, p. 152.

51 Hiding Nazis is one of the most important themes in Lem's early works, and can be traced back to the collection *Sezam i inne opowiadania* (1954).

52 S. Lem, *Zagłada i jej uwertura* [in:] idem, *Lube czasy*, p. 13.

53 Ibid., p. 14.

54 S. Lem, *List z 30 sierpnia* 1973 [in:] idem, *Sława i fortuna. Listy do Michaela Kandla 1972–1987*, p. 161, 162 (all emphasis in the quotations from the writer's correspondence follows the original).

55 S. Lem, *Chance and Order*, translated from the German by F. Rottensteiner, *The New Yorker* 1984, No. 59 [online], p. 88–98, <http://csc.ucdavis.edu/~chaos/ courses/ncaso/Readings/Lem_CAO_NYi984.html> [access: May 7, 2015].

56 "*Nie spieszy mi się domykać kanon.*" Interview with Professor David Roskies, p. 28–29.

57 Stanisław Lem's letter to Professor Władysław Kapuściński dated May 30, 1976, Muzeum Literatury w Warszawie, ref. no. 3740.

58 Section of Auschwitz-Birkenau, located several hundred yards from gas chambers and crematoria, with warehouses where possessions of people brought to the camp were taken upon their arrival to be sorted; any valuables were later sent to the Reich. The colloquial name "Kanada" was the outcome of a widespread belief that Canada was a particularly wealthy country.

59 Stanisław Lem's letter to Professor Władysław Kapuściński dated December 27, 1977, Muzeum Literatury w Warszawie, ref. no. 3740.

60 R. Federman, An Interview with Stanisław Lem, p. 13–14.

61 Ibid., p. 14.

62 "Although it would be overly simplistic to frame Lem's grotesque series within the category of a philosophical parable—for this paradigm is likely of the most significance here—to some extent they do indeed continue this tradition, with their satirical fervor, intellectual and background, and normative or better: persuasive, instructions of reception." M. Płaza, *Umysł i nauka wobec chaosu historii w "Czasie nieutraconym" Stanisława Lema*, "Pamiętnik Literacki" 2006, no. 2, p. 108.

63 K. Budrowska, *Literatura i pisarze wobec cenzury PRL 1948–1958*, p. 148–168.

64 It is worth remembering that, as Kajetan Mojsak emphasizes, "the Aesopian language was, to a degree, fiction—in the sense that it was comprehensible to officials and it was they who controlled its social functioning (demonstrating considerable tolerance)...as it was practically harmless. ... It was a complex system of understatements, winking at the reader and deliberate omissions; a combination of actual, rigorous censorship and a kind of mimicry—in which each side was involved. K. Mojsak, *Cenzura wobec prozy groteskowej w latach 1956–1965* [in:] *„Lancetem, a nie maczugą." Cenzura wobec literatury i jej twórców w latach 1945–1965*, ed. K. Budrowska, M. Woźniak-Łabieniec, Warszawa 2012, p. 247–248.

65 I will not expound further on this subject since I have discussed these issues in my article *Parodie, pastisze i recykling w prozie Stanisława Lema*, p. 65–75.

66 In his book *Słowo o socrealizmie*, Wojciech Tomasik mentions these two artists as authors of anti-imperialist prose. Cf. W. Tomasik, *Słowo o socrealizmie: szkice*, Bydgoszcz 1991.

67 See K. Budrowska, *Literatura i pisarze wobec cenzury PRL 1948–1958*.

68 T. Pospíšil, "The Bomb, the Cold War and the Czech Film," *Journal of Transatlantic Studies* August 2008, vol. 6, no. 2, p. 142–147.
69 Cf. A. Jelewska, *Ekotopie. Ekspansja technokultury*, Poznań 2013, p. 55–75.
70 Por. M. K. Booker, *Monsters, Mushroom Clouds, and the Cold War. American Science Fiction and the Roots of Postmodernism, 1946–1964*, Greenwood Press 2001, p. 65–66.
71 S. Lem, *Człowiek z Hiroszimy*, [in:] idem *Człowiek z Marsa. Opowiadania młodzieńcze. Wiersze*, Warszawa 2009, p. 291.
72 Ibid., p. 293.
73 S. Lem, *List z 3 marca 1975* [in:] idem, *Sława i fortuna. Listy do Michaela Kandla 1972–1987*, p. 346.
74 D. Muzyczuk, *Czy sztuka może być obiektywna? O próbach projektowania wzorów dla języka uniwersalnego*, [in:] *Kosmos wzywa! Sztuka i nauka w długich latach sześćdziesiątych*, ed. J. Kordjak-Piotrowska, S. Welbel, graphic design by M. Frankowska, A. Frankowski, Warszawa 2014, p. 72.
75 Ibid.
76 S. Lem, "Science Fiction," [in:] idem, *Wejście na orbitę*, p. 36.
77 S. Welbel, *Nauka—bezkresna granica* [in:] *Kosmos wzywa!* p. 92.
78 Ibid., p. 93.
79 In a study on the Cold War nuclear arms race, Piotr Osęka points out that the US and USSR authorities realized quite late that the nuclear war could not be won due to the scale of destruction it would entail. However, even when they were aware of this and estimated the number of victims at 30–50 million, numerous crises arose that could have potentially triggered a Third World War, the last one in 1983. P. Osęka, *W cieniu atomowych grzybów*, "Ale Historia!" supplement to "Gazeta Wyborcza" February 23, 2015, p. 8–10.
80 S. Lem, a letter to Jerzy Wróblewski, undated, 1960s, courtesy of Barbara and Tomasz Lem.
81 S. Lem, *Człowiek z Marsa*, p. 94.
82 Cf. S. Lem, *Dwa pantofle i drabina* [in:] idem, *Lube czasy*, p. 97–99. Jerzy Jarzębski discussed the parallels between Lem's views and those of the philosophers he officially criticized, such as Nietzsche and Derrida. J. Jarzębski, *Lektura świata. Stanisław Lem jako czytelnik* [in:] idem, *Wszechświat Lema*, p. 254.
83 Cf. B. Korzeniewski, *Hybryda światów* [in:] *Stanisław Lem: pisarz, myśliciel, człowiek*, eds. J. Jarzębski, A. Sulikowski, Kraków 2003, p. 243–255.
84 Discussing the history of the reception to his works, Lem stressed that critics had failed to note that "the concept of humans as beings created through a stochastic process; the search for God as a rescue maneuver—not so much in the area of the existential future of the soul as in the sphere of senses that should save such an evolutionary product from being discredited on the execution plane—all that (it is not a list, just an example) comes straight from Darwin, interpreted in the spirit of the 20th century technological revolution." S. Lem, *List z 5 kwietnia 1974* [in:] the same, *Sława i fortuna. Listy do Michaela Kandla 1972–1987*, p. 222.
85 Anti-utopian visions, cognitive skepticism and disbelief in humankind in Lem's prose also provoked objections from censors, who refused to accept them unless they were formulated in the science fiction genre or set in grotesque realities. K. Mojsak, *Cenzura wobec prozy groteskowej w latach 1956–1965* [in:] *"Lancetem, a nie maczugą,"* p. 243.
86 See, for example, M. Szpakowska, *Dyskusje ze Stanisławem Lem*, p. 54–89.
87 E. Grosz, "Darwin and Feminism: Preliminary Investigations for a Possible Alliance," *Australian Feminist Studies* 1999, vol. 14, no. 29, p. 34–35. Lem's interest in the mechanisms of the origin of life, evolution and heredity is also evidenced by his articles published as part of his work at the Science Conservatory. See e.g. S. Lem, *Omówienie książek Jeana Rostanda*, "Życie Nauki" 1948, no. 33–34, p. 298–299.
88 S. Lem, *The Cyberiad*, p. 174.
89 Most likely an allusion to Bertrand Russel's "logical type." Cf. N. Wiener, *The Human Use of Human Beings*, London 1989, p. 59.

90 S. Lem, *The Cyberiad*, p. 233.
91 Ibid., p. 234.
92 Ibid., p. 231.
93 N. Wiener, *The Human Use of Human Beings*, p. 26.
94 Ibid., p. 32.
95 Ibid., p. 37.
96 Ibid.
97 Ibid., p. 39.
98 S. Lem, *His Master's Voice*, transl. Michael Kandel, Evanston 1999, p. 11.
99 Cf. B. Zielińska, *Oskarżenie bez oskarżonego. Pytania teodycei w twórczości Stanisława Lema* [in:] *Stanisław Lem: pisarz, myśliciel, człowiek*, p. 171–188.
100 I would like to thank Marek Bukowski from the Gdańsk Medical University Museum for his advice on the bibliography of Lem's works related to medicine and conversations on the situation of doctors in Poland after 1945.
101 I discuss Lem's allusions to his own diploma work entitled *Etiologia nowotworów* (Warszawa 1947) found in the title story in *Sezam* in my article *Parodie, pastisze i recykling w prozie Stanisława Lema*, p. 72.
102 S. Lem, List z 7 maja 1977 [in:] idem, Sława i fortuna. Listy do Michaela Kandla 1972–1987, p. 570.
103 Idem, *Hospital of the Transfiguration*, transl. William Brand, San Diego–New York–London 1988, p. 54.
104 In 1976, Bogusława Latawiec interpreted the new edition of *Hospital of the Transfiguration* through the prism of themes, tropes and plot structures in Lem's later science fiction works, pointing to the thematic coherence between a realistic novel and the adventures of protagonists in space. B. Latawiec, *Kosmos i medycyna*, "Odra" 1976, no. 7–8, p. 43–45.
105 J. Butler, *Frames of War: When Is Life Grievable*? 2009, p. 58.
106 Ibid., p. 14.
107 Ibid., p. 24.
108 Ibid., p. 52.
109 G. Chamayou, *Les Corps vils. Expérimenter sur les êtres humains aux XVIIIe siècle et XIXe siècle*, Éditions la Découverte, 2008; for the purpose of this book, I have consulted the Polish edition, *Podłe ciała. Eksperymenty na ludziach w XVIII i XIX wieku*, transl. J. Bodzińska, K. Thiel-Jańczuk, Gdańsk 2012, p. 276–311.
110 G. Niziołek, *Polski teatr Zagłady*, Warszawa 2013, p. 191–192.
111 C. Caruth, *Unclaimed Experience: Trauma, Narrative and History*, The Johns Hopkins University Press 1996, p. 8.
112 On Caruth's interpretative method see ibid., p. 8–9.
113 G. Niziołek, *The Polish Theatre of the Holocaust*, p. 32–33.
114 M. Głowiński, *Oczy donosiciela*, "Zagłada Żydów. Studia i Materiały" 2014, no. 10, p. 857.
115 Ibid., p. 11.
116 L.L. Langer, *Holocaust Testimonies. The Ruins of Memory*, p. 13.
117 D.G. Roskies, "What is Holocaust Literature?" [in:] D. Roskies, N. Diamant *Holocaust Literature: A History and Guide*, p. 19.
118 M. Głowiński, *Oczy donosiciela*, p. 856.
119 G. Niziołek, *Polski teatr Zagłady*, p. 58–59.
120 In the first published letter to Stanisław Lem, dated January 20, 1956, Sławomir Mrożek states, "You have said once, if I remember and understand correctly, that for you the science fiction setting serves also as a kind of ruse, intended not just for literature, but also for the literary market." S. Mrożek, *List z 20 stycznia 1956* [in:] S. Lem, S. Mrożek, *Listy 1956–1978*, Kraków 2011, p. 17–18. In 1975, Lem wrote Michael Kandel that he wanted to publish *Imaginary Magnitude* or *A Perfect Vacuum* in the United States because this "would at least radically put an end to the slander

about 'Science Fiction,' which to me is more or less the same as slander about syphilis in polite company." S. Lem, *List z 6 września 1975* [in:] idem, *Sława i fortuna. Listy do Michaela Kandla 1972–1987*, p. 398.

121 K. Budrowska, *Literatura i pisarze wobec cenzury PRL 1948–1958*, p. 170–171.

122 I. Csicsery-Ronay, Jr., "Twenty-Two Answers and Two Postscripts: An Interview with Stanisław Lem," translated by M. Lugowski, *Science Fiction Studies* 1986, vol. 13, p. 244.

123 On the subject of Auschwitz as another planet, see "*Nie spieszy mi się domykać kanon.*" Interview with Professor David Roskies, p. 21.

124 *O tym, jak z wewnątrz getta patrzono na stronę aryjską*. Barbara Engelking's interview with Israel Gutman, "Zagłada Żydów. Studia i Materiały" 2005, no. 1, p. 233.

125 L. Ostałowska, *Farby wodne*, Wołowiec 2011, p. 18. Krystyna Żywulska wrote, "I knew that the house, Warsaw, were somewhere very, very far away, probably on another planet. K. Żywulska, *Przeżyłam Oświęcim*, Warsaw 2004, p. 34 (I owe the last example to Agnieszka Kłos).

126 Edith P., *Holocaust Testimony* (HVT-107). Fortunoff Video Archive for Holocaust Testimonies, Yale University Library [online], <http://web.library.yale.edu/testimonies/excerpts/edithp> I owe this example to Agnieszka Kłos. A series of Andrzej Wróblewski's paintings depicting stars, sun and planets in previously unknown configurations and colors was presented in a similar context, as a response to the annihilation of millions of people, at the exhibition entitled *Zaraz po wojnie. Zaraz po wojnie*, Zachęta—Narodowa Galeria Sztuki (October 3, 2015–January 10, 2016), curators: J. Kordjak, A. Szewczyk, cooperation: M. Komornicka.

127 Dawid Kahane, report from Lviv, translated from the Yiddish by A. Bielecki [in:] *Życie i zagłada Żydów polskich 1939–1945. Relacje świadkow*, ed. M. Grynberg, M. Kotowska, Warsaw 2003, p. 267.

128 Testimony of Bessie and Jacob K., cited in: L. L. Langer, *Holocaust Testimonies. The Ruins of Memory*, p. 53.

129 M. Dajnowski, *Pejzażysta Lem. Szkice z motywiki*, Gdańsk 2010, p. 59–62.

130 Ibid., p. 105–113.

131 Istvan Csicsery-Ronay noted that Lem uses "tropes from a ghost story" in his prose. I. Csicsery-Ronay, Jr., *Obcy u Lema*, transl. into Polish E, Nowakowska, [in:] *Stanisław Lem: pisarz, myśliciel, człowiek*, p. 222.

132 Idem, "Twenty-Two Answers and Two Postscripts: An Interview with Stanisław Lem," p. 248.

133 Ch. Ostrower, Humor as a Defense Mechanism during the Holocaust, *Interpretation: A Journal of Bible and Theology* 2015, vol. 69, no. 2, p. 194–195.

134 S. Lem, *The Cyberiad*, p. 7.

135 P. Sitkiewicz, *Bestiariusz Lema według Mroza* [in:] *Bestiariusz Lema according to Mroza*, ed. P. Sitkiewicz, graphic design by J. Górski, Gdynia 2012, p. 61-86.

136 *Mroz i Lem*, exhibition at the Centrum Designu Gdynia, August 23–October 11, 2012, curated by Janusz Górski.

137 On bestiary as a genre see, for example, I. Dines, "The Problem of the 'Transitional Family of Bestiaries,'" *Reinardus. Yearbook of the International Reynard Society* no. 24, 2011–2012, p. 29–52.

138 E. Kuryluk, *Norma—zabobon—getto—"eutanazja." Pożegnajmy raz na zawsze drzwi bez klamek* [in:] *Zagłada chorych psychicznie. Pamięć i historia*, eds. T. Nasierowski, G. Herczyńska, D.M. Myszka, Warszawa 2012, p. 446.

139 E. Gomel, "From Dr. Moreau to Dr. Mengele: The Biological Sublime," *Poetics Today* 2000, no. 21:2, p. 395. In this article, aside from an insightful analysis of the figure of the Nazi New Man, Elana Gomel discusses the links between the *fin de siècle* bioideology and Nazism.

140 S. Lem, *Omówienie artykułu Edwarda Howarka „Światopogląd lekarza III Rzeszy,"* "Życie Nauki" 1948, no. 35–36, p. 474.

1
LEM(BERG) LAND

Resentments and the history of Lviv Jews

In each of his many passport applications,[1] Stanisław Lem consistently gave his date and place of birth as September 12, 1921, in "Lwów" [Lviv]. The document issued by the authorities of the People's Republic of Poland was, however, annotated: "place of birth: USSR." The official anachronism supported the policy of casting Lviv's Polish past into oblivion, ignored historical knowledge and disciplined the bearer of such a passport.[2] Expatriates were also the cause of many other, much more serious, problems for the communist authorities, mainly due to the documents lost during the war and the Galician past of the city, which, in the case of people older than Lem, involved military service in the Austro-Hungarian army. However, even in communist Poland, Lviv was not entirely and automatically erased from official documents. In the internal report constituting the Questionnaire of the Individual under Surveillance, Security Service officers refrained from using the anachronistic form in Lem's file (the writer was under surveillance from the end of the 1960s[3]) and entered "Lwów" as his place of birth, apparently realizing the political significance of whether someone was born in the USSR or in the territory of the pre-war Second Polish Republic.

Just as with many other cities in that particular corner of Europe, such a creationist and anachronistic narrative about the past is part of Lviv's history, and not just during the Cold War era. Nevertheless, Lviv's case seems to be particularly illustrative in this regard, mainly because it used to be the third-largest city in the Second Republic of Poland, and international historical policy concerning its significance for individual ethnic groups remains a diplomatically incendiary issue to this day.[4] It is difficult to disregard the political entanglement of Lviv that manifests in the representations, especially since the history of the city is depicted mainly from the Ukrainian and Polish perspective, and—as George

DOI: 10.4324/9780367855642-2

G. Grabowicz notes—the points of view of the Austrian, Jewish and Armenian minorities have yet to find representation.[5] Moreover, the entire region of Galicia is associated with the myth of the harmonious coexistence of ethnic minorities, even though, as historian Krzysztof Zamorski comments:

> In Galicia, the cacophony of traditions, intentions and aspirations must be heard. We must see the ocean of mutual accusations, more or less warranted. It is a land where Poles and Ukrainians despised one another. Poles detested Russians, Ukrainians detested Poles, both hated Jews, and the latter responded in kind. Besides, intensifying nationalisms and growing anti-Semitism pushed them effectively out of Galicia.[6]

While the researcher appreciates the role of such mythical imagery in assimilating knowledge about the past, he also realizes the threats it poses, as it is usually exploited for current purposes, based mainly on stereotypes.[7]

After 1989, the Polish publishing market saw a sudden plethora of memoirs about Lviv, a city that Poles had to leave between 1945 and 1946 lest they become Soviet citizens. The nostalgic and sentimental tone of those tales situates Lviv once again in the Galician myth,[8] rendering it a lost Arcadia, with no mention, however, of its poorest districts or the wartime fate of Jewish residents.[9] A broad spectrum of resentments associated with the post-Yalta order is particularly evident in Jerzy Janicki's Lviv cycle, first published in the early 1990s. The author, 7 years Lem's junior, devoted his memoirs to the "Polish city," whose center is the Roman Catholic Church of St. Anthony in Lychakiv, and while he does, in fact, mention both Ukrainian and Jewish residents, his ironic tone blurs social inequalities, making it impossible to evaluate political decisions detachedly: "So the Poles are a minority in Lviv? That sounds like saying that the blacks are a white race today."[10] Janicki's books are rife with such racist and misogynistic similes. For example, he described a Ukrainian woman who worked for his grandparents as a model servant, calling her a "real workhorse."[11] At the same time, he complained that contemporary domestic workers have social expectations that are too high. While Janicki makes decidedly more references to the extermination of Lviv Jews than most authors of memoirs about the city, he nevertheless reduces the survivors' accounts to an anecdote with a catchy punchline. In *Podróż Edmunda Zajdla do miasteczka Bełżec* [Edmund Zajdel's journey to the town of Bełżec], for example, he tells the story of the title character, who witnessed the death of his parents and five brothers and managed to escape from the transport to Bełżec and take refuge in the countryside. After the war, he graduated from university and started a family, and Janicki concludes as follows: "So our good Lord recompensed Edmund Zajdel for all the wrongs he had suffered in the war."[12] Other witnesses' accounts and tales about the fate of the Jews are conveyed in a similar tone, not to mention that they are mainly intended to give readers a better idea of the city's topography. The author of the memoirs uses chiefly pre-war street names.[13]

The mechanisms of such simplifications in such memoirs, so many of which have been published over the past 25 years, are thoroughly examined by Katarzyna Kotyńska in her books *Lwów. O odczytywaniu miasta na nowo* [Lviv. Rereading the city] and *Eseiści o Lwowie. Pamięć, sąsiedztwo, mity* [Essayists on Lviv. Memory, neighbors, myths], and many insightful observations can be found in the volume she has edited, namely *Lwów: lustro. Obraz wzajemny mieszkańców Lwowa w narracjach XX i XXI wieku* [Lviv: a mirror. The mutual image of Lviv residents in the narratives of the twentieth and twenty-first centuries]. In one of the papers from that volume, Magdalena Semczyszyn presented the results of her research on historical information about Lviv contained in Polish, Ukrainian and Russian tourist guides published in the twentieth century, noting that although tour routes take tourists to the same historical sites, each language group hears a decidedly different story. For example, in the contemporary Polish narrative, the city flourished in the Second Polish Republic, while Ukrainian guides describe the same timeframe as a dark age of suffering, with political prisoners, atrocities committed by the Polish police and pacification intended to suppress the national liberation movement.[14]

The history of Lviv's Jews remains on the fringes of those national narratives, even though before World War Two they constituted one third of the city's population, and in the 1920s and 1930s Lviv was one of the most important centers of Jewish life in Europe.[15] After the war, the life of Jews in Lviv concentrated around one of the synagogues that survived the German occupation,[16] albeit seriously damaged.[17] The last rabbi of Lviv died in 1962 and the Jewish community was not revived until 1991, when they reclaimed the synagogue. The early 1990s was also when sites associated with the extermination of Jews were commemorated for the first time—in 1992, a monument devoted to the murdered in Lviv was erected, and a multilingual (Ukrainian, English and Hebrew) plaque was placed at the Kleparów station, dedicated to the victims of transports to Bełżec.[18] Jewish victims have also been commemorated by the museum located in the former prison on Łąckiego Street. In 2003, a monument dedicated to the prisoners of the Janowska camp executed in the forest was erected at the Piaski ravine, although, sadly, the execution site where thousands of people lost their lives is neither fenced off nor regularly cleaned up. In the case of Lviv, the Yalta peace agreements made it possible for the Soviet authorities to break with the past of the city: survivors were expelled and people from distant parts of the Soviet Union or displaced villagers were resettled there. Jewish inhabitants of post-war Lviv deported from the east could not identify with the history of the murdered inhabitants of the city or commemorate their fate,[19] especially since, according to the 1959 statistical survey, they made up only 4 per cent of the population.[20] Many of the material traces were irretrievably erased, and the individual stories of survivors can be reconstructed mainly based on testimonies and accounts given after the war, during the trials of war criminals.[21] It remains unknown who should be the custodian of the memory of the Lviv Jews who were murdered and starved during the German and Soviet occupation. What can be done to include Lviv Jews in the Polish,[22] Ukrainian[23] and Russian[24] memory? How to address and process the participation of Poles and Ukrainians in the crimes for this inclusion to be possible?[25] We should bear in mind that any such process would also require a critical analysis of studies written in German and American circles, which focus on mythicizing the life of Galician Jews, referring mainly to its exotic, mystical ritual, and this very version of the past is nowadays happily accepted by both Poles and Ukrainians.[26] As David G. Roskies argues,

> Out of several Jewish cultures that received a deadly blow from the Germans – German-Jewish, Polish-Jewish, secular Yiddish and Hasidic – only the latter, which after the war merged into one pious ultra-orthodox bloc, regained its strength and vitality.[27]

Survivors from assimilated Polish–Jewish families had no chance to form any community, and remembrance became a challenge for their descendants, because—as the researcher emphasizes—they have only just begun to discover the past of their ancestors and realize their diminished kinship with Jewish culture.[28]

Stanisław Lem decided not to return to his hometown because the murder of the inhabitants of Lviv and the expatriation of survivors stripped it of any sentiment: "Stones are not enough – it is people that matter, and those people are no longer in Lviv."[29] In his memoirs written after the political transformation, the images of carefree childhood are constantly overshadowed by the tragic, and sometimes tragicomic, specter of occupation. Although the writer was highly critical of the politics of the Second Republic, including the detention camp in Bereza Kartuska and the Brest trials, he also pointed out that for him, that era was associated with solid and durable foundations, which he felt he had lost forever:

> After all, there is a foundation, some core principles and rules, a base for everything, which bears the burden of human fate. All of a sudden it turned out that it was fragile, that it could change so easily. To see how easy it is for such changes to occur, for the migration of peoples – such a thing deforms or distorts many a person.[30]

In Lem's prose, the shock of resettlement is reflected in the fate of the protagonists travelling through time and space, from one place to another. Deprived of a home base and a permanent residence, they seem to have nowhere to return.[31] And even when they do go back to Earth—as in *Return from the Stars*—they can hardly cope in changed circumstances and among people whose behavior they do not understand.

Time travel

In 1921–1945, that is, within the timeframe of the writer's residence in Lviv, the city was under Polish, Soviet, German and then again Soviet administration, and while a new set of maps came with each change of power, Lviv residents continued to use the names they remembered from the times of the Austro-Hungarian monarchy. Regardless of the changing names, the topography of the district where the writer and his parents lived has several fixed elements. From one side, the house is close to the university, a park on a hill and the polytechnic. From the front balcony, on the right, there is a view of the old town and Lviv's most important landmarks. Here begins the district with beautiful tenement houses, the famous school of philosophy and mathematics, the zoological collection of Benedykt Dybowski and Włodzimierz Dzieduszycki, libraries and archives. On the other side, Lem's house was adjacent to one of Lviv's two main streets, leading from the station to High Castle (Polish: *Wysoki Zamek*). Along this street there are prison buildings (*Małe Brygidki* –"Little Bridgettines" and *Brygidki*—"Bridgettines"), and behind them stretches (or rather used to stretch) the poorer section of the Jewish quarter, with numerous synagogues, mikvahs and a historic Jewish cemetery located at the back of the Israelite Hospital. Buildings are denser, lower, covered with inscriptions in several languages, and life concentrates on market squares, such as the so-called Krakidały, that is, Krakowski Square behind the Jewish Colosseum Theater—the flea market mentioned by Lem in *Highcastle.* The tenement is surrounded by buildings—the church of St. Yura on the hill, at the foot of which there is a circus, and, not far from the house, the church of St. Anne. The main rabbi of Lviv used to live on a parallel street. I find this location at the intersection of two worlds fascinating—urban poverty alongside universities visited by world-famous scientists, wealthy bourgeoisie and intelligentsia of Jewish, German and Polish origin. Living in such a place, one must have been aware of the misery of human life in prisons, hospitals, shelters and orphanages. And all that was intertwined with Lviv's metropolitan aspirations and scientific discoveries, which had a major impact on modern science.

Another issue is that of time configurations. The rhythm of Catholic (also in the Armenian rite), Evangelical, Greek Catholic and Orthodox holidays, evoking a sense of *déjà vu* (when we realize that Easter or Christmas would be celebrated again several weeks later), overlapped with Jewish holidays and different calendars.[32] In addition, at the turn of 1939–1940, the Soviet calendar was introduced in Lviv, canceling the existing holidays and introducing 6-day work weeks. It was not until June 26, 1940 that the old calendar was restored in the USSR.[33] The new authorities introduced Moscow time, setting clocks back 2 hours. Investigating the everyday life of Poles in Lviv between 1939 and 1944, Grzegorz Hryciuk pointed out that the residents often measured the rhythm of family and social life according to Central European time, while Soviet time was reserved for the opening hours of offices and work.[34] Grotesque visions of synchronizing clocks and defining the time of day are the subject of several of Lem's stories, most notably *The Conditioned Reflex*:

> It was eleven by his watch, seven by the room's electric clock, and ten past midnight by Langner's. They switched their watches to Lunar Time,

knowing they would have to change again soon. The Mendeleev station was in a different time zone. The whole Far Side was in another time zone.[35]

Pirx is somewhat tired after eating several lunches in one day, since it was lunchtime everywhere he went.

Thus, between 1921 and 1944, there was a spatial and temporal paradox in Lviv, unlike the one associated with Cossack Mamai. Without ever leaving the city, one traveled in time and space, living in alternative times and crossing seemingly invisible demarcation lines. Without ever setting foot elsewhere, people the crossed spaces of political systems, and familiar places were suddenly given unknown names. These transformations manifested through multiplied nomenclature, written in at least three alphabets, although usually plaques with former names were not removed, but only crossed out in red so as not to lose orientation in space completely.[36]

Coexisting within the same timeframe was the time of events in the ghetto, the rhythm of Nazi operations, usually set to coincide with most important Jewish holidays, and deportations to the death camp. This confusion of temporal orders had a significant impact on the way of reporting on the past. Lawrence L. Langer described in detail the space–time folds associated with the long duration of the occupation time in the memory of those who were victims of Nazism and managed to survive. In his research on testimonies, he drew attention to the transformation of identity affected by the experience of the Holocaust:

> For example, one of the curses willed by the Nazis to their victims is how deep memory continues to infect their experience of time. … Life goes on, but in two temporal directions at once, the future unable to escape the grip of a memory laden with grief.[37]

Langer points to time discontinuities in the narratives of witnesses who are also former victims, consisting in the use of two time constructs in their accounts: *in medias res*, "which views the Holocaust as an event sandwiched between prewar and postwar periods"; and *in principio*, in which "the Holocaust has a different beginning for each witness and provides closure for none."[38] The inability to come to terms with the loss of the murdered affects survivors' present and the way they think about the future. As a result, they live their lives in two time modes, which breaks down the identity attempts at integration, hence Langer's references to "hidden," "split," "besieged," "improvised" and "reduced" subjectivity. The difference between the analyzed testimonies and the literary representations of nightmarish memories is that in fiction, the echoes of deep memory are transformed and altered, engaging the existing conventions and genres as well as historical knowledge in a dialogue. These findings are of great significance for Lem's oeuvre, as in his realistic prose the author misleads the reader, providing dates inconsistent with historical events, thus avoiding the interference of censorship. His science fiction books, however, are set simultaneously on several time planes, becoming a palimpsest of different chronological orders. Any attempt to establish what timeframe it is requires many modes of expression to be taken into account, making historical, social and political allusions more comprehensible.

The lost city

> Autobiography and history are two key categories of literature studies.
>
> Jerzy Madejski, *Deformacje biografii*[39]

The belief that writing about Lviv was banned in communist Poland has been mostly refuted by now, despite the fact that such suppositions often appear in the memoirs of refugees published after the political transformation. Katarzyna Kotyńska's research was an important turning point in such an interpretation of the censor's ban. The author analyzed fiction devoted to the city in a broad comparative spectrum, juxtaposing Polish, Ukrainian and Russian literary works and essays written in the twentieth century, demonstrating that it was not so much writing about Lviv as such that was banned by the censorship, but just depicting Lviv as a center of Polish culture.[40] In the chapter *Białe plamy a rebours. Lwów w literaturze PRL i USRR* [White spots *a rebours.* Lviv in the literature of the People's Republic of Poland and the USSR], Kotyńska mentions a number of post-war works set in the former capital of Galicia. All those publications were approved by the censors, including *Zegar słoneczny* by Jan Parandowski (published as early as 1953) and new editions of Kornel Makuszyński's books, as well as genre prose: adventure and crime novels[41] published in the 1960s and 1970s, set in the interwar and wartime realities, with numerous references to the Lviv of the Austro-Hungarian era.[42] Stanisław Lem's 1966 autobiographical essay *Highcastle* also proves that references to Lviv were not entirely banned, although admittedly in this case, all events described in this particular book are set before the war. The images of Lem's idyllic childhood correspond to the pre-existing model of writing about Lviv as a unique city, with exceptional atmosphere, delightful sweetshop displays and a perfect background for schoolboy adventures. In a way, in *Highcastle*, Lem follows the themes and chapters of Parandowski's book, although *Zegar słoneczny* is set mainly in the Lviv of the Austro-Hungarian era.[43] Such a reference was all the easier since, as Kotyńska emphasizes, in Parandowski's work Austria is only a secondary setting.[44] The use of an already familiar pattern may explain why Lem's book did not provoke any objections from the censor. Another source of inspiration was undoubtedly Józef Wittlin's essay *My Lwów*, a significant portion of which is devoted to a reflection on memory and forgetting.

In his reflections on the meanders of memory, the narrator of *Highcastle* confesses the temptation to supplement the "anarchic dictate"[45] of memories with knowledge he gained later. Destroyed or lost private archives make it impossible to tell a personal story, and the perspective of collective memory and its rituals recorded in—as he puts it—"old books and albums" turns out to be useless when one attempts to reconstruct memories. When writing about the past, what is useful is a city map. Seen from above, Lviv is reminiscent of a labyrinth, which, as Michał Głowiński argues in his analysis of the Minotaur myth, is a space of alienation.[46] The feelings associated with the city oscillate between the safety of the house and its surroundings and the monstrous and dangerous space that can become hell, prison or execution site. In his examination of myths, Głowiński compares the entire history of the twentieth century to the structure of a labyrinth:

> The image of labyrinth is associated primarily with alienation, fear, loss, the feeling of being surrounded and not in control of one's own fate, dependent on the powers whose knowledge and understanding exceed human capabilities.[47]

In the labyrinth-like Lviv, told from the perspective of the second half of the twentieth century, there lives a monster of national, ethnic and class conflicts. As Jan Sowa points out in *Fantomowe ciało króla*:

> The belief that the culture of the Borderlands was particularly hybrid is an ideological illusion, just as the notion that they were harmoniously multicultural – it serves to obscure the nightmare of the social relations there.[48]

The nearly complete absence of Ukrainians in *Highcastle* (with the exception of one teacher), the lack of direct references to the Jewish minority or the poverty of the Hutsul population, mentioned only in passing, seem to underscore the impenetrability of the demarcation lines of social divisions in Lviv and anticipate future events.

In the 1960s, Lem created a fantasy about Lviv, which was disassembled, reshuffled not only in terms of the resettlement of the population, but also the evacuation of its landmarks (such as the transfer of the Jan III Sobieski monument to Gdańsk or the *Racławice Panorama* and the Aleksander Fredro statue to Wrocław). Like former inhabitants of Lviv, principal landmarks in the city's space were scattered around the world, and a "kinesthetic melody"[49] is all that Lem had left from the city—an embodied kinship with the landscape, a sensual memory of the way home. Richard Sennett points out that in the imagination of engineers, the urban space is based on the need to liberate the body from resistance and is associated with the fear of touch.[50] In this context, the narrator's "kinesthetic melody," which reproduces childhood experiences, focuses precisely on recreating the resistance of stone space that a young child feels, and for this reason touch is the most frequently evoked sense.

For decades, the space of Lviv had a multiplied nomenclature, generated by several temporal and political orders. There is a digression between the descriptions of balloon games in *Highcastle*: "the University then was still called

Parliament [Sejm], perhaps out of inertia, from the Austrian time, when the building housed the Galician parliament."[51] City residents do not keep up with the political changes, the memory of the place lasts longer than prescribed by the new maps, Soviet names—from Lem's time—fail to evoke the memory of familiar sites, just as German names fail to do. However, the world of childhood is also marked by amusement parks, sweetshops and mobile trade, which brings back the memory of the problems faced by Lviv's residents during the economic depression—a fixed feature of the writer's adolescence in the 1930s.

The eponymous *Highcastle* is a place suspended in time, described by blasphemous comparisons: "It was not a Christian heaven full of modest prayer, but a nirvana—no temptations or desires, but blessedness that existed independently."[52] Descriptions of school breaks, extended by the illness of teachers, offering a moment of respite from school, annihilate historical knowledge. The narrator learns the meaning of the name of that place 30 years later, at the same time presenting childhood as freedom from historical memory, which imposes the narrative about Polish settlement, Cossack invasions and the Swedish deluge on a space associated with pleasure.

Highcastle, however, is not Lem's first book about Lviv, the city where he grew up and survived two Soviet occupations and one German. Written in 1965, the autobiographical essay is a prequel to a novel published 10 years earlier, titled *Time Not Lost*.[53] The trilogy consists of the well-known and often reissued *Hospital of the Transfiguration*, as well as two novels hastily written in accordance with the censor's recommendations: *Wśród umarłych* [Among the Dead] (1949) and *Powrót* [Return] (1950). The series devoted to the life of Stefan Trzyniecki was blocked by the censors during the Stalinist era; *Hospital of the Transfiguration* was shelved the longest, namely for 7 years.[54] In 1965, the trilogy was released for the third and—by the author's decision—last time;[55] at the same time, Lem was writing *Highcastle*.

Although in *Time Not Lost* the writer used a similar trope as Parandowski in his *Zegar słoneczny* (not once did he refer to the city by name),[56] researchers of Lem's oeuvre have no doubt that the trilogy is set in Lviv or its vicinity, although they do not inspect this issue in greater detail. The topography of the city can be reconstructed through references to architectural landmarks and addresses where the protagonists meet.[57] As in Jerzy Janicki's essays on Lviv published in the 1990s,[58] Lem's story seems to be addressed to people who remember what the city looked like before the war and during the occupation. However, who is it that remembers Lviv, and what narrative about the city made its way into the collective memory? Who is the heir to the city's occupation-era history? While it is extremely difficult to establish basic statistical data in "bloodlands,"[59] Grzegorz Hryciuk estimates that only 20,000–26,000 Jews survived the Holocaust in the entire District of Galicia.[60] Some data indicate that a little more than 800 Lviv Jews lived to see the end of the war, and it was very rare for whole families to survive,[61] such as Lem's parents and himself. In the second half of 1945 and the first half of 1946, about 30,000 Jews, Polish citizens, were resettled from that area to Poland, but many of them survived the occupation outside the District of Galicia.[62]

In post-war Poland, Jews were not included in the unofficial Borderland communities, which reflected the pre-war and occupation-era relations between Poles and Jews. Anna Wylegała, researcher of the biographical narratives of Lviv Poles at Ośrodek Karta, emphasizes that:

> In the narratives about the Holocaust – forced, usually evoked by interviewers – there is no sense of solidarity and loss, but there is a separation of suffering; our own suffering effectively obscures the suffering of the Other.[63]

In this context, Lem's *Highcastle*, written in the 1960s, is more in tune with the expectations of Polish expatriates. In fact, traces of Jewish presence in the city are removed from the autobiographical essay, and even if they are mentioned, it is in such a way so as to be understood only by those who knew the Jewish district well, or who were friends with the writer. Lem also omitted the history of the occupation:

> I wanted something impossible to attain – to extract the essence of my childhood, in its pure form, from my whole life: to peel away, as it were, the overlying strata of war, of mass murder and extermination, of the nights in the shelters during air raids, of an existence under a false identity, of hide-and-seek, of all the dangers, as if they had never existed.[64]

Nevertheless, the specter of the Holocaust haunts the story of childhood, although it is decipherable mainly for those who are aware of how the historical events unfolded.

Jan Błoński, a close friend of Stanisław Lem's, considered the meaning of *Highcastle* in his essay on Jewish literature, included in the volume *Biedni Polacy patrzą na getto* [The poor Poles look at the ghetto]:

> There are such novels in Polish literature where only a reader familiar with the era can recognize the background or social mentality of the characters. These include, for example, Adam Ważyk's *Mity rodzinne* [Family myths] or Stanisław Lem's *Highcastle*. However, it is difficult to consider such stories together with [Stryjkowski's] *Głosy w ciemności* [Voices in the dark], whose exoticism is not only shown but also named.[65]

One cannot but agree with Błoński that Julian Stryjkowski's story is not exactly parallel to Lem's autobiographical essay, because—despite the fact that they both grew up in Lviv—their generational and communal experiences and their writing choices are significantly different.[66] *Highcastle*, as the researcher emphasizes, features a recognizable family background, associated with the life of the assimilated Jewish intelligentsia. Lem did not become the eulogist of the "exotic" shtetl community, because there is little evidence that he knew that tradition and—we might venture to assert—he most likely did not identify with it.[67]

Discussing the writer's relationship with Jewish culture, many researchers cite Lem's confession in his autobiographical essay titled "Chance and Order":

> But this high I.Q. certainly was of no help in surviving the Occupation of the General Gouvernement (to which administrative unit Poland had been reduced by the Germans). During that period, I learned in a very personal, practical way that I was no "Aryan." I knew that my ancestors were Jews, but I knew nothing of the Mosaic faith and, regrettably, nothing at all of Jewish culture. So it was, strictly speaking, only the Nazi legislation that brought home to me the realization that I had Jewish blood in my veins. We succeeded in evading imprisonment in the ghetto, however. With false papers, my parents and I survived that ordeal.[68]

Both in online sources and in academic papers, this quotation replaces the reflection on the writer's pre-war life and the reasons for hiding during the occupation. Even critics who were friends with Lem cite this excerpt without any comment, as a sign of respect, I suppose, for the writer's right to tell his own story himself. He made similar statements about Jews and the inter-war era in two lengthy interviews, with Stanisław Bereś and Tomasz Fiałkowski, respectively,[69] both of which include numerous anecdotes and reflections on the situation of Jews in Poland, although the writer seems to be speaking from the perspective of someone who is not directly affected by anti-Semitism.[70] Lem undoubtedly protected his privacy, and only a handful of people knew his family history. He did not make it public, and the post-war history of Poland proved time and time again that he was right to employ such a strategy. Nevertheless, as a student of secondary school, Lem attended Judaism classes taught by Dr. Kahane, who was also on his school-leaving examination board.[71] This does not mean, of course, that he came from a religious family, but only indicates how the Polish education system of that era perceived the relationship between one's origin and religion.[72] It might be worthwhile returning to Lem's earlier works and inspecting whether Błoński's postulate that Jewish literature should not be defined by the author's ethnicity, but by references to the "Jewish experience" in their writings,[73] is executed in his novels. At the same time, Błoński pointed out the difficulties that such explorations may engender: "The Jewish experience was therefore sometimes obscured or concealed. It was simultaneously a testimony to the kinship with Polishness … and the fear of Polish readers."[74] In one short sentence, Błoński conveys the tension that writers associated with pre-war Jewish culture had to face in their work after World War Two.[75]

In his tribute to Stanisław Lem, Władysław Bartoszewski noted that "if Staszek had written directly about the Lviv ghetto, about the Holocaust, about his war experiences, he would have received the Nobel Prize, but he almost never talked about it, never wrote about it."[76] Contrary to that assertion, Lem had actually focused his writing interests on the occupation in Lviv from the beginning of his literary career, but at that time, his point of view was confronted with the historical politics of the communist authorities. One can hardly imagine a worse moment for a literary debut than the beginning of the 1950s in the Eastern Bloc. Nevertheless, Lem's first novels and short stories from the 1940s directly addressed the war and the extermination of Lviv Jews,[77] and required a narrative model that would meet the ethical challenges of testimony.

Sanatorium

In a 1957 review of Albert Camus's *The Plague*, titled *Mówi głos ciemności* [The voice of darkness speaks], Stanisław Lem noted that this literary parable would fail to move those who had witnessed much more violent events. They are unable to identify with the mourning processions gathered over pits full of human flesh, because in Camus's world, funeral participants have time for despair and mourning. The reviewer criticizes his own attitude as barbaric, as he realizes that his artistic output cannot consist of the constant repetition of one phrase, "They made soap out of people."[78] At the same time, Lem stressed the importance of experiencing a complete doubt in humankind, which permeated the present times and electrified the air not just in "bloodlands," and seems to have eluded the author of *The Plague*. "There is an excess of knowledge about humanity," Lem said, "that forces the artist to keep silent, at least within the existing poetics, old conventions."[79] Such an inadequacy of poetics is closely linked to the experience of treating the human body as a resource, which, like the bodies of slaughtered animals, can be used to produce insulation, gloves or lampshades.[80] Erstwhile images of despair over open graves are overshadowed by efficient devices used to transform corpses into useful objects. Traditional representations of mass death cannot cope with such changes of perspective: "For there is a difference between dead bodies and dead bodies that have been dismembered and cooked," says Bożena Shallcross,[81] and that was one of the stages in the production of soap. According to Lem, a parable that presents the greatest existential dilemmas of modern times on the example of historical parallels with the Holocaust cannot withstand the test of time. In this context, Lem's experiments with literary genres and poetics, altering familiar plots and conveying philosophical reflections in grotesque forms, enable him to break the impasse of silence about the crisis of ethics and the end of humankind. In his case it is not always science fiction, but sometimes realistic prose as well.[82]

In *Hospital of the Transfiguration*, the writer aimed to reconstruct the image of a world in which there is no time to process grief, empathy and remorse. Jerzy Jarzębski calls this novel a philosophical and moral treatise[83] because it is filled with discussions about the responsibility of individuals for events beyond their control. It is set between February and October 1940, when a young doctor, Stefan Trzyniecki, takes up a job in a sanatorium for the mentally ill, and it concludes with German soldiers taking over the hospital and shooting more than 180 patients in the sanatorium garden. The problem is to find a point of reference in terms of time and place of the events described in the novel, which, in my opinion, could be crucial for its interpretation. There is a temporal anachronism here, namely the fact that the liquidation of patients takes place in the autumn of 1940, and that, in addition to the German soldiers, Ukrainian auxiliary units are involved, which is inconsistent with historical facts. This could have been a means to avoid the interference of censors when writing about former territory of the Second Polish Republic occupied by the USSR in September 1939. The liquidation of psychiatric hospitals continued until 1941; therefore the novel could actually be set a year later, but even then the involvement of Ukrainian battalions in the murdering of psychiatric patients is dubious. Another problem concerns the location. It is said to be near Nieczawa, from where the Carpathians can be seen, and the sanatorium is surrounded by Bierzyniec hills and located near Bierzyniec. It comes as no surprise that no such places can be found on the map. Some interpretations of the novel based on comparisons with historical facts suggest localities such as Owińska, Gostynin,[84] Chełm Lubelski or Kobierzyn, near Kraków.[85] It is evident that the layout of buildings described in the novel do not resemble any of these hospitals. Moreover, patients were shot on site only in Chełm Lubelski; in the other three sanatoriums listed above, they were murdered by gassing.[86] The history of psychiatric hospitals during the occupation is usually reconstructed based on testimonies given after the war by doctors and medical personnel, including interrogation protocols compiled by commissions to establish the exact course of events in cases where medical records were destroyed and it was difficult to verify the number of victims. Such documents are scattered in various archives, such as the Institute of National Remembrance or the Jewish Historical Institute, and many are probably kept locally or abroad. The situation of hospitals is also featured in the recollections of the Holocaust witnesses, the few survivors of the Lviv ghetto. In her testimony, Janina Masłowska mentions that the Germans chased mentally ill Jewish patients from the Kulparków hospital to the newly established Jewish district and placed them under the supervision of the Judenrat, who put them in one of the synagogue buildings.[87] This incident is significant for my explorations, although it is not verified in any other documents or historical studies I have found. From my point of view, it is important that the Jewish residents of Lviv remember the event.

In an unpublished letter to an unknown addressee dated April 17, 1967, Lem stressed that *Hospital of the Transfiguration*

> is not based on any data that I have derived from any biography or observations, in the sense that I have never worked in a psychiatric hospital, although I have medical education, and I have never known people such as those I described in this book. In a word, apart from the background in the double sense (Poland, and during the occupation) – everything was "made up" there.[88]

The word "made up" is in quotation marks, since the author, painstakingly and in great detail, reconstructed the mechanism of operation of German troops and doctors in psychiatric hospitals. As for the novel's location, it is worth noting the description of the space in the sanatorium and the architectural detail, which is the Moorish (Turkish[89]) tower, of unexplained purpose, located in the center of the Bierzeniec sanatorium for the mentally ill.[90] Stanisław Lem did not leave Lviv until 1945,[91] so it is quite easy to identify the building described by the protagonist. It is one of Lviv's most important landmarks, erected in the last years of the nineteenth century close to the street where the writer lived before the war—the Israelite Hospital.[92] The building was designed in Moorish style and is richly decorated with Eastern and Jewish symbols. Architecturally, the hospital resembles the Budapest temple, the largest synagogue in Europe. The hospital, which could house 100 patients, was designed by the famous Lviv architect and architectural theoretician Kazimierz Mokłowski.[93] During the German occupation and the forced resettlement of Jews, the hospital (including the old Jewish cemetery[94]) was not within the borders of the ghetto,[95] but before the war it dominated over the Jewish district. If it is indeed the same tower as in *Hospital of the Transfiguration*, it is not just the fate of mentally ill patients that the novel describes, but also that of the Jewish residents of Lviv (a city surrounded by hills). Thus, the tale about the liquidation of a psychiatric hospital becomes not so much a parable or a philosophical treatise as a way to tell the story of inhabitants of a city seized by the Soviet Union that could not be mentioned in writing and about whose suffering no-one wanted to hear in post-war Poland. Analyzing the history of psychiatric hospitals, Ewa Kuryluk points out that they are a relic of the nineteenth-century approach to psychiatric treatment, which entailed isolating the ill from the rest of society; and that the architectural principles of the sanatorium resemble a ghetto-town.[96] This is another argument in favor of reading the story of the psychiatric hospital as a tale about the fate of the inhabitants of the Lviv ghetto, over which the hospital tower loomed. Marcin Zaremba brought attention to the social and psychological consequences of creating separate Jewish districts, emphasizing that "the resettlement of Jews into ghettos meant their symbolic objectification, their expulsion from the human world."[97] No wonder, then, that the progressive isolation and exclusion from social structures—"for safety reasons," as the German authorities cynically argued—inspired ghetto inhabitants to compare their situation to the pre-war treatment of mentally ill people, including the ban on leaving the Jewish quarter.

In his study, Timothy Snyder demonstrates that the largest number of victims of two totalitarian regimes died as a result of starvation, with shooting and gassing being the second-most common cause of death. Most of the Jews murdered during World War Two died in their place of residence.[98] Everyday murders on the streets and the great pogrom that accompanied the entry of German troops into Lviv provide the context that might explain the presence of Ukrainian auxiliary units in *Hospital of the Transfiguration*. Tatiana Berenstein pointed out that the extermination of the Jewish population in Galicia was extremely brutal, because the administrative board of the district was established at a time when the plan for the mass liquidation of the Jews was in its final stage of development. From the beginning of the German rule, Jews from that area—unlike in other districts of the General Government—were being killed *en masse* already in the second half of 1941, and mass executions became a routine, daily experience for the local population.[99]

Figuren

Lem's prose tackles the Nazi anthropological experiment—the 1935 Nuremberg Laws—in a number of ways. In his monograph *A History of Habsburg Jews 1670–1918*, William O. McCagg analyzes the complex and ambiguous processes entailed in the assimilation of national, ethnic and religious minorities in Galicia, emphasizing that the only clear definitions of identity at the time were those pertaining to religion, and any attempt to establish affiliation with a specific minority group proved how vague such categories were and how many reservations they involved. In conclusion, McCagg states, "The intricate calculus of Hitler's Nuremberg Laws is witness to how much trouble even racists had in coming up with a satisfactory practical definition of who was a Jew."[100] In his letters to Kandel, the writer often distanced himself from Nuremberg's qualifications: "The chances of my surviving this war were negligible *a priori*, something like 1:100,000, which can be supported mathematically, indeed, by determining what percentage of my, let's say, ethnic group survived."[101] The poignant fragment concerning the scale of the unlikelihood of survival was summed up with a distanced view on the ethnic determinants applied to the Jewish population. Affiliation with the enormously diverse Jewish community depended on many factors that the Nuremberg Laws did not cover. In the practice of Nazi politics, such complications related to one's ethnic origin ceased to be relevant insofar as those inhabitants denounced by their neighbors as Jews became them. The complicated and disappointing relations between doctors and patients in *Hospital of the Transfiguration* reflect the tense situation of people imprisoned in the ghetto and dependent on the decisions of the Nazi authorities, but also on the attitudes of those from outside the ghetto wall. When considering the situation of a hospital, it is important to bear this dual perspective in mind and to look at the novel in a broader context.

The fate of patients of psychiatric hospitals and Jews—as Lem emphasizes several times in his prose—was connected by the language of Nazi propaganda, which described them as *Figuren*.[102] According to Giorgio Agamben, the term *Figuren*[103] ("figures, dolls, puppets") was used to describe the bodies of the victims of gas chambers and operations, while in Lem's novels, German commanders apply it to living people whom they already see as dead bodies and objects. The word also appears in accounts of witnesses in Claude Lanzmann's *Shoah*. The writer's use of the term *Figuren* is proof that he followed the publications of the Central Historical Jewish Commission[104] (although, of course, it is possible that he knew Nazi terminology from his own experience). *Figuren* appears in Leon Weliczker's memoir *Brygada śmierci* [Death brigade]. During the occupation, Weliczker lived in Lviv, where he was captured and imprisoned in the Janowska camp. There, he was forced to join Sonderkommando and ordered to cover up the traces of Nazi crimes. Weliczker also contributed to bringing to justice Johann Rauch,[105] commander of the Lviv ghetto, who was sentenced to death for his crimes and hanged in Kraków in 1949. In the diary written during the occupation and edited after the war, Weliczker reconstructs the peculiar parlance of German soldiers, who talked about alive prisoners as "figures," dead objects that might be "useful" for some time.

Also significant in the context of Lem's analogies between the treatment of mentally ill patients and the extermination of Jews are Grégoire Chamayou's conclusions regarding the status of "vile bodies":

> Vile bodies are convicts sentenced to death, galley slaves, prisoners, orphans, prostitutes, the mentally ill, patients of hospitals, paralytics, slaves and the dying, who for centuries have served as material in experiments that founded modern medical science.[106]

All those people were expelled from the social system; their legal protection was rescinded because they turned out to be a demographic and economic problem. Since the Enlightenment, therefore, similar arguments have been applied to them as in the Nazi T4 campaign, which, as Stefanie Coché notes, changed social practices with regard to patients in psychiatric hospitals, making the principal biopolitical criterion the protection of a "healthy" society against "threats" posed by people affected by mental disorders. Another argument was that the ill were unable to work, rendering them "useless" to the rest of society.[107] Thus, "vile bodies" are excluded from legal protection; they become objects—most frequently medical preparations[108]—which can be used in medical sciences. Therefore, the body becomes valuable for science and becomes (after such transformation) socially useful. Stefanie Coché also notes that such categories were extended to include other individuals that exhibited "inappropriate" behavior: the elderly, who at the time were frequently sent to psychiatric hospitals, but also, for example, wives who failed to perform household chores.[109]

The new man

The central issue in *Hospital of the Transfiguration* is undoubtedly the ethical attitude of doctors faced with violence against patients who do not understand their own situation. The tragic aspect of medical decisions, as well as the blatant betrayal of the idea of helping the sick, lead some of them to the climax of the novel, which, however, will not be followed by absolution of guilt. In the evening, doctors learn that the following day at dawn, the German army and the Ukrainian auxiliary units led by Obersturmfuhrer Hutka (whose superior is Dr.

Thiessdorff) will murder all the patients. The medics have various ideas on how to deal with the situation: release the patients into the forest, escape and leave the hospital without staff, offer a bribe, hide promising patients and burn their files. In the end, the majority decide on the latter solution. The problem concerns the selection of the "most valuable patients" (as Rygier's doctor described them) and whether they are going to survive in hiding for several hours. In the background, a question is posed that remains unanswered: "So we are supposed to make a selection?" An important aspect of the novel concerns the gradual and inevitable adoption of concepts from the language of propaganda, constructed on pseudo-scientific theories: over the course of the occupation, the Nazi way of thinking pervades the hospital. Lem addressed this aspect not only in this novel, but in *Hospital of the Transfiguration* is given a particularly dark tone: just as in the concentration camps, in the sanatorium the selection is carried out by doctors, and the tragedy of the situation is that doctors who openly protest against Nazi ideology are forced to do so. For this reason, their guilt will never be assuaged, and the crime committed in the sanatorium will leave a mark on their later life, as shown in the third part of *Time Not Lost.* I see here an echo of the ethical dilemmas associated with the activity of the Judenrat, the helplessness of the council against the war machine and the difficult situation of its members, forced to make tragic decisions.

On that critical evening, three doctors make decisions that are different to the rest of the group. Professor Łądkowski does not participate in the operation of hiding the sick, and he supplies himself with cyanide. Dr. Marglewski, for whom there is nothing more important than his own research,[110] escapes from the hospital in the evening, while neurosurgeon Kauters chooses "splendid isolation," just to declare himself as a person of German stock and start collaborating with German doctors (soon to be famous as a doctor injecting phenol). The novel's narrator focuses in particular on Kauters, a collector of unique anomalies and deformed body parts. In his apartment he keeps his collection of specimens in formalin: a cephalothoracopagus, a rare type of craniopagus parietalis, a teratoma specimen and a diprosopus, as well as a book bound in human skin. There are several instances in the novel when Kauters's description is reminiscent of Dr. Moreau from H. G. Wells's novel. Wells's book became an important point of reference for the description of the attitudes and mode of operation of Nazi doctors, and not only for Lem. Researcher Elana Gomel points out that *The Island of Dr. Moreau* (published in 1896) reflects an ideological trajectory that demonstrates the transformations of social Darwinism and eugenics.[111] From this perspective, a cruel scientist who vivisects animals because he wants to turn them into human beings becomes the New Man of Nazi ideology. The New Man is characterized by the fact that he can control nature and contributes to the better adaptation of the so-called Aryan race, disregarding any suffering this might entail.[112] Gomel quotes ample evidence that Nazi ideology completely revolutionized attitudes towards the body. From the researcher's point of view, it is Dr. Moreau that marks the beginning of thinking about evolutionary surgery, and since the Nazi New Man is entirely devoid of empathy, he can vivisect other people and act outside of ethical standards developed in medicine. The descriptions of the characters of Dr. Moreau and Dr. Kauters from *Hospital of the Transfiguration* converge at several points: these characters work away from scrutiny, so that no-one interferes in their experiments and collecting of unique anomalies; they are mysterious and secretive; they are reluctant to make closer acquaintances; they specialize in surgery, placing scientific knowledge above the welfare of patients. The only patient who dies before the German units appear in the sanatorium is the engineer Rabiewski. He was diagnosed with a tumor in the frontal lobe, and the prognosis was not good. Surgeon Kauters delays the operation, disregarding the obvious signs of suffering in the patient, who was placed in a special cage, preventing him from slipping down to the floor when his body is shaken by convulsions. This way, the doctor wishes to obtain a textbook example of an "acortical man" whose reflexes are supposed to resemble those of animals. The patient cannot be saved by surgery, and the doctor agrees to anesthesia only when Stefan pressures him. However, the surgeon fails to harvest Rabiewski's exceptionally large tumor for his collection of medical specimens, which infuriates him. The description of the procedure, as well as the prioritization of the scientific experiment over the welfare of the patient (the operation, which gave a shadow of a chance for recovery, is performed too late), is a clear reference to the medical tradition of experimenting on patients who have little to no chance of recovering. The first vile body, treated as an object of scientific experimentation, appears in the novel before the mass murder of patients. Dr. Kauters is ready to accept the ideological justification of his research, although what seems even more tragic is the fact that no-one stopped him from carrying out that scientific experiment on the patient.

The objectification of the body made in the name of the progress of science or ideology is an important topic in Stanisław Lem's entire oeuvre. In his realistic novels, the writer brings attention to how Jews are treated as non-humans, and in his science fiction prose, he depicts scientists objectifying aliens. At the same time, the narrator or the protagonist tries to defend those who are to be deprived of their ontological status as a living and intelligent being. Therefore, they often stand up for machines, which became hostages of humanity and do slave labor; they are now dummies (*Figuren*), which means that anything can be done to them. Moreover, Lem openly objects to the ideology of the New Man, and for this reason there are no supermen and heroes in his prose. Lem's typical protagonist suffers a more or less spectacular defeat because his bodily condition and randomness of his existence make it impossible for him to meet the heroic challenges, designed for a more permanent material and a predictable sequence of events. Lem's characters cannot complete their planned tasks because they are sweating, hungry, upset, sick, sleepy, paralyzed by fear, rusted or have had their fuel lines damaged. They are not suitable for tragedy; their defeat brings neither absolution nor consolation. Having lost, however, they rise up and take up new challenges, albeit without any faith in success.[113] Grotesque in their efforts, with numerous flaws, they are entangled in a series of random events that change their fate for the worse, and their self-image suffers a painful blow. Only such a perception of the human condition, as Lem seems to suggest, can prevent us from being seduced by the vision of a brave new world. The narrator and protagonist of *His Master's Voice* emphasizes, for example:

> I do not believe in human perfection, and people who have no quirks, tics, obsessions, the touch of some minor mania, or points on which they turn rabid – I suspect such people of systematic imposture (we judge others by ourselves) or of totally lacking character.[114]

Lem was particularly interested in writers who presented the human condition in a way akin to his own approach. In his letters, he often stressed, for example, how impressed he was by Saul Bellow's novel *Mr. Sammler's Planet*, the main protagonist of which is a Jewish survivor from Poland, watching contemporary New York through the prism of his earlier experiences. In his letter to the American translator, the writer noted that Bellow "is the voice of the 'losers,' life failures and defeats, the breaking of all spiritual bones, the wandering, the fears, the doubts."[115] Such a protagonist is an appropriate medium for the various human flaws, at the same time exposing the inner workings of the world of politics, science and family. Reproductions of paintings by Hieronymus Bosch made similar impressions on Lem:

> Bosch was a (brilliant, but this is another matter) painter of the bottomless human stupidity and unfortunate, self-flagellating human helplessness (which turns into anger) above all else.[116]

In *Hospital of the Transfiguration*, this is evident already on the level of the description of the character's appearance. It is not so much the bodies of patients that are of interest here as the physiognomy, tics and movement of doctors, their physiological existence and entanglement in the symptoms of patients.[117] At the beginning of the war, during the first meal together with the medical staff of the sanatorium, a newly arrived graduate of medical school is watching his colleagues. Dr. Rygier has a scar on his forehead, which creates a large indentation in the skull; Kuśniewicz has "a pimply face"; Kauters is thin, has flat feet and resembles the mummy of Ramses II. Dr. Marglewski is described as "strikingly but not unpleasantly ugly," because he has a harelip scar and a flat smile, while Professor Pajączkowski, head of the facility, resembled "a dove chick with his sparse, feathery beard through which the pink skin underneath was visible, was tiny, had wrinkled hands with a slight tremor, stuttered occasionally, slurped his coffee, and shook his head when he began to speak."[118] Dr. Krzeczotek, a friend of the novel's narrator, who shared his dislike of classes in the dissecting room at the medical school,[119] wears a shabby and not very clean "overcoat" and, as Stefan notes, not without irony, he

> felt confident in this hospital, like a one-eyed man among the blind. He was a gentle lunatic, a lunatic on a small scale, and so must seem uncommonly well-adjusted in this background of raving madness.[120]

In the background, spectacular symptoms of schizophrenia and other illnesses are outlined, progressing at a rapid pace because at that time there were no effective pharmacological means to manage or heal them. The novel mentions medication administered to the mentally ill in the 1940s and 1950s: scopolamine, morphine, barbiturates, bromine, insulin and cardiazole—used to cause shocks in schizophrenia. Symptoms of disease in patients are amplified by the behavior of lower-level staff, who use violence: pushing, beating or scalding with hot water. Patients are surrounded by doctors suffering from neuroses, manias and numerous neurological diseases, happily pillaging the hospital first-aid kit for sedatives and stimulants. Against the backdrop of these human imperfections, a German commander appears:

> A big German was standing at the wall, wearing a camouflage cape, dark goggles pushed up onto his helmet, and black gloves with embroidered labels. Patches of mud were drying on the folds of his cape. … Stefan's cheeks felt numb. He couldn't take his eyes off the German's sharp chin. His cold, sweaty fingers were clenched into fists. Those washed-out German eyes had seen hundreds of people strip naked at the edges of ditches, making meaningless movements as, understanding nothing, they tried to prepare their living bodies to tumble into the mud. The room spun – only the tall figure with the green cape thrown over his shoulders remained fixed. … [H]e had no idea who the German was. His cape had covered his insignia. He remembered nothing of his face, just the helmet and dark glasses. The man might as well have been a Martian, Stefan was thinking when the sound of light footsteps ended his reverie.[121]

This fragment best captures the confrontation between the body of Lem's typical protagonist, desperately trying to control his shivers, covered in cold sweat, with the ideal of the New Man—reminiscent of a dangerous inhabitant of a foreign planet, who does not identify with the fear of those at whom machine guns are aimed.

Operation Reinhardt

Operation Reinhardt entailed deporting hundreds of thousands of Jews from ghettos and concentration camps and murdering them in extermination camps, an important element of which was also the seizure of their property after their extermination. A significant portion of the crew that built the camps in Bełżec, Sobibór and Treblinka, and created an experimental program of mass murder in gas chambers, was made up of German personnel previously involved in the euthanasia program.[122] The chapter in *Time Not Lost* titled "Operation Reinhardt" does not refer to all the deportations organized in Lviv, because the events described there take place in mid-October, and the largest number of transports did not start leaving the Kleparów station and heading for Bełżec until March 1942, the operation reaching its peak in the second half of August. At that time, 50,000 Lviv Jews were murdered in the death camp with carbon monoxide.[123] The plot of this part of the novel *Among the Dead* concerns the final stage of the deportation of the Jewish population, which included almost all the remaining Jews, even those who had documents proving that their work was essential for the industry of the Third Reich.[124] Unlike in the case of Oskar Schindler's famous—and successful—endeavor in Kraków, employers in Lviv managed to protect only a handful of Jews working in factories and industrial plants from deportation to the camp. Despite the efforts of the entrepreneurs (by no means motivated by any noble purpose), lists with the names of Jewish workers were destroyed as a result of rivalry between the commanding officers in charge of the operation, and all the Jews were sent to the wagons.[125] Whereas Schindler's legend, built by Steven Spielberg, has been described by Dominick LaCapra as "'redemptive narrative' aligned with false mourning,"[126] Lem's vision is an example of a non-heroic narrative and portrays the humiliation experienced by the victims of mass murder.

"Operation Reinhardt" is a quasi-documentary chapter, in terms of character and autobiographical allusions (during the occupation, Lem worked for the Rohstofferfassung company, and one document detailed that he also worked in the Janowska camp[127]), reminiscent of dramatized testimonies published by the Central Jewish Historical Commission in the second half of the 1940s. The omniscient narrator presents an operation aimed against the few surviving Jewish residents of the city, outlining a wide range of viewpoints: the perspectives of the head of the Rohstofferfassung company, who employed Jewish workers; Dr. Wieleniecki, a Pole working at the German Institute of Forensic Medicine; Rohstofferfassung employees involved in the underground communist organization; the German command; the Ukrainian Pluwak, who uses the operation to bring a Jewish schoolgirl to his apartment; and finally Stefan Trzyniecki, taken for a Jew during a round-up and transported to Bełżec. Accompanying all these characters and their struggles is a throng of gawkers, Polish and Ukrainian Holocaust bystanders.[128] In the background, the activists from the underground group decide to organize help for the Jews rushed to the loading yard and try to save Jewish associates, although the outcome of their effort is not presented in the novel, which is filled with unfinished storylines and inconsistencies.[129]

One of the episodes in the chapter "Operation Reinhardt" involves an investigation into the murder of a German woman killed on the railway tracks, whose corpse was found near the site where the Nazis were loading Jews onto trains.

The criminal police, together with Dr. Wieleniecki, collect evidence of the crime at the station while the genocide continues around them, although they seem not to notice it. The results of the investigation indicate that the murderer is most probably an SS officer, but the hypothesis is rejected as it would be a heavy blow for the SS and the honor of the formation, while at the same time Jewish residents of the city are being beaten and sent to their deaths. Initially, Wieleniecki does not want to look at the victims around him:

> Four trucks stuffed with Jews were just arriving. Wieleniecki tried not to look. He lowered his eyes. He saw bundles, empty suitcases and trampled coats scattered in the passageway between the buildings, along the road the Jews were brought in.[130]

Nevertheless, on returning from inspecting the woman's body, the doctor inadvertently begins to watch the group of people being loaded onto the wagons:

> They all look the same: white faces, and instead of eyes – motionless spots. The first to walk was an old woman in a silk handkerchief, not tied, but held together under her chin with both hands, as if everything depended on it. Her head was high up, she tried to keep her back straight, which made a peculiar contrast with her fat, heavy body. Then he saw some familiar face. Half-deliberately, he tried to turn his eyes away, but it was too late.[131]

Wieleniecki's meeting with a lawyer he knows takes place in an atmosphere full of tension, between the crowd heading for the wagons and his supervisor, a Nazi commander, shaking the doctor to the core:

> The lawyer, walking on the edge of the group, approached Wieleniecki, who couldn't take his eyes off him. When the distance between them shrank to one meter, the lawyer moved his lips as if he wanted to say something, but could not find words. Wieleniecki, with Klopotzek practically on his heels, took off his hat as if in a greeting, but instead of putting it back on, he just kept walking, with his head uncovered.[132]

The lack of words and the respect demonstrated by taking off his hat suggest that at this dramatic moment the writer chose a well-known formula, namely Christian funeral customs. This respect is addressed to people who, though still nominally alive, are actually already dead, and at whom Wieleniecki finally decides to look, risking that he might recognize a familiar face, although he does not lose his privileged position as an employee of the Germans, entitled to leave the loading yard. The themes of lips moving silently and the inability to speak are present also in other post-Holocaust texts. In Hanna Krall's *The Subtenant*, the protagonist meets her cousins in London, where during a "polite English dinner" they converse about the last moments of those family members who had not emigrated from Poland before the war. Looking at family photos, the protagonist tells the story of her mother, who was forced to leave her brother in the city:

> "This is Uncle Szymon," she explained. "He will be running after the cart. Mother went back there after several days but everybody was gone. Since that time she often dreams about him as he runs and shouts. 'You know,' she says, 'I dreamt about him again. He was running and shouting something, but they could not hear the words, only his lips were moving.'"[133]

After such a dream, the mother feels that she needs to say a prayer for the dead. Silent lips utter the lament for loved ones and friends, abandoned and left behind. "Anguished memory," Langer notes, "in the testimony of surviving Holocaust victims, is inseparably identified with victims who did not survive, dividing the self between conflicting claims – the need and the inability to recover from the loss."[134] At the same time, the researcher stresses that in the case of memory contaminated with memories of the loss of loved ones, we cannot speak of guilt, as this category comes from a different social and cultural order than the world in which resistance and making choices was impossible, or more precisely—each choice led to inevitable death.[135]

In Lem's *Operation Reinhardt*, one particularly dramatic episode involves Stefan Trzyniecki, who returns from a meeting with Wieleniecki to his father's house. When it turns out that his father has left and it is not long until curfew, the young doctor goes to the station to wait until the morning in the third-class waiting room. The following day at dawn, in crumpled clothes, unshaven and unwashed, he walks to the city and notices that passersby look at him oddly. When Stefan asks a couple he meets for directions, they both walked past him in silence: "The woman, turning her head, looked him up and down with her fishy eyes."[136] However, another passerby warns him about a round-up and informs him that he should hide from the German patrol in the gateway. A group of youngsters[137] in the yard of the building where he has decided to wait out the operation turn against him and denounce him to the German soldiers, screaming: "Kike! Jew! Yid! The Yid's getting away! Yi-id!"[138] When Stefan is taken to the Schutzpolizei building, he "takes a look to the side: he sees the streets, the stone, the sunlit sidewalk, the trees and the couples walking leisurely."[139] The walking pace of the Polish and Ukrainian residents of Lviv and the bright streets contrast with the mental state of Stefan, who, despite documents confirming that he is "Aryan"—his Ausweis and Kennkarte – is loaded onto the train as a hiding Jew. When one of the Germans involved in the operation states that they have loaded 42 people into the car, another corrects him, using the word *Figuren* instead of "people." Instead of a Polish doctor, Stefan becomes a Jew escaping from the ghetto, and a "figure" instead of a human being. Every attempt at defending himself ends in a beating, and Stefan finally ends up at the yard, where a Jewish doctor tries to save him. The tragicomic nature of the attempt to save the so-called Aryan by his Jewish colleague, who is the only one aware of the mistake, demonstrates the arbitrariness of the division into those who may survive and those who will be sent from the loading yard to a death camp. Accidental contact with the machinery of death and humiliation means being stripped of all rights and handed a death sentence.

Among the Dead can be regarded as a novel which, as Michał Głowiński put it in his examination of similar relations concealed in post-war prose,

> tells terrible things about the attitude of the Polish society to the Holocaust. It does so nearly always indirectly, usually without any comments or explanations added for the sake of clarity, some things are simply taken for granted, in accordance with the common knowledge of reality.[140]

The attitude of the bystander, a silent witness to the annihilation of the Jewish nation, is the principal issue in Grzegorz Niziołek's *The Polish Theatre of the Holocaust.* As the researcher emphasizes,

> The key to establishing the position of a bystander is the moment when a certain group of people became *unpersons* for others, which means that their lives are no longer worth protecting and the norms of their own community no longer apply to them. The potential to shape such a social circumstance became an essential condition that made the Holocaust possible.[141]

Such a boundary between individual groups of people is particularly evident in the case of the situation of those suspected of being Jews and of Jews hiding on the so-called Aryan side. Under such circumstances, the mechanism is therefore very similar to those that constituted the category of "vile bodies."

In practice, the German definition of a Jew—formed by scientists affiliated with National Socialism—boiled down to the observation made by Klopotzek, who was in charge of the "displacement"—"he was good at it: the trembling eyeballs, the beard, the nose—a Jew, there's no denying"[142]—as well as the knowledge of a Catholic prayer and the "dick test," which, when combined—the prisoner had to pray and expose himself at the same time—built a grotesque scene of humiliation. Stefan's test turns out to be a failed, desperate attempt at salvation, as he still finds himself back at the yard and then in Bełżec. The naked bodies of people rushed into the chamber reinforce the significance of this scene, as that image underscores the humiliation of victims of mass murder, deprived of everything. In *Provocation*, written over 30 years later, Lem pointed out that the ritual of undressing the victims during the mass production of death could be considered the quintessence of Hitler's kitsch, which involved perpetrators copying the scenes they knew from depictions of the Final Judgment. Stefan is saved from the gas chamber by sheer coincidence and his own persistence, when his explanations begin to entertain the German commander guarding the entrance. Although the guard changes his mind and refuses to release Stefan, the door of the chamber is already locked, so, in order not to complicate the efficient operation, the SS man puts the naked doctor in a cell nearby. There, in the dark, it dawns on Stefan that he is in the room where the hair of the murdered women is stored:

> He instinctively raised his hands so as not to touch it, moaned and gasped. … In order not to look at it, he turned his eyes to the dusty windows, and then a distant, choral roar reached him from the outside.
>
> "What the … what …" – He mumbled, feeling his own lips as two thick, barely moving cylinders. The roar was incessant, distant, rising ever higher, with voices breaking like threads, and he stood there with his gaze stuck to the square of the sky; there, in the square window frame, a white cloud burning cold appeared slowly, surrounded by pure blue.[143]

The sensual closeness of the hair, neither dead nor alive, that surrounds Stefan's body, and the clear sky with the white cloud "burning cold," complete the dramatic scenery, accompanied by the moaning of victims murdered with carbon monoxide, suffocating for 20 minutes.[144] The hair is all that is left of the women, and although their screams, devoid of hope for salvation, are still ringing around the chambers, it is already no more than raw material that will soon fill German mattresses. Stefan becomes a witness not only to mass death but also to the whole production process, in which bodily matter is utilized and remnants are transformed into useful objects. The voices of the murdered will continue to haunt Lem's prose, because the lamentation of the dying, separated from their bodies, lasts longer than their slow death.

The third part of the trilogy, titled *Return*, contains few allusions to the occupation, and it is not until the end of the novel that the protagonist dreams during a train ride that:

> He was walking with his father and mother in the green hills scattered with cottages, under the blue sky. He held his parents' hands, even though he was taller than them. Among the hills, at the bottom, there was an ivory-colored town, as if carved out of bone, bizarre, with tiny buildings, with balconies shaped like coaches; supported by twisted columns, these houses bravely climbed the steepest slopes. There were many people walking around, boulders lay in the grass, cracked, gray, like stones in the Tatra mountains. Then, everyone started pointing to something. There, high up on the green mountain, stood a castle, similar to Wawel Castle, with a golden roof. Suddenly, it spat out parallel, crested streams of white smoke or steam.[145]

An idyllic picture of Lviv seen from one of the hills is surrounded by two synecdoches of death: a train ride and rising smoke. A fragment devoted to one of the most characteristic elements of the urban landscape is carefully concealed by likening it to Wawel Castle, although the name of the place appears in the sentence "*high* up on the green mountain, stood a *castle*." Putting the two words together, we get Highcastle.

Such minor stylistic techniques enabled the writer to write about occupied Lviv without provoking censors, or perhaps even following their instructions. During the Stalinist era, Lem's novel could not be published because the censors deemed the subject of the recent war too depressing for an era of optimism and reconstruction.[146] After the Thaw, however, ideological disputes between members of the party in the novel must have seemed jarring,[147] which is why *Time Not Lost* is not listed in the same category as works about ghettos, life in hiding and death camps. The collective imagination of that time focuses on other topographical traces, especially Auschwitz.[148] Lem made his book debut as a science fiction author shortly after he finished writing *Time Not Lost*, as *The Astronauts* came out in 1951. Subsequent books published at the turn of the 1960s and 1970s made him a classic author of this genre, but, in my opinion, he never stopped writing about Lviv. Descriptions of cities or city-like rock formations on other planets often resemble in Lviv's topography: a city situated among hills, dead, with burnt-out interiors or surrounded by mass graves. Even in the *Pirx the Pilot* series, the search in a dense cloud of moon dust is compared to moving through the maze of ruins in a destroyed city.[149] With each new title, the city becomes more and more spectral, and the explorers die there, go mad or are mutilated. Lem's story about Lviv goes beyond the mythical narratives of the city and adds an important theme to its forgotten past. The narrative in *Time Not Lost* reconstructs the story of the exterminated ghetto inhabitants, whom nobody wanted to remember anymore, while *Highcastle* reconstructs a private history, which makes it one of the few narratives that both Poles and Ukrainians accept as their own.[150] This is achieved at the cost of the almost complete erasure of the city's Jewish residents from the autobiographical essay.

Notes

1 In 1955–1975, Lem traveled for meetings with readers and scholarships to the USSR, Greece, France, Norway, East Germany, Germany, CSRS, Hungary and Italy. Based on passport documents of Stanisław Lem, IPN Kr 37/6738 and IPN Kr 49.

2 Naming "the Polish Lviv" as the place of birth could only be legitimized on the other side of the Iron Curtain, where it did not matter at all. For example, Milo Anstadt, Stanisław Lem's contemporary residing in Amsterdam, notes in his memoirs: "Place of birth: Lwów. Country ... Whenever I am filling a form, I always hesitate with this question. Poland? Ukraine? Russia? When I was born, Lviv was in Poland. Now it's in Ukraine. Without going into the formal validity of the answer, I write each time: Lviv/Poland." M. Anstadt, *Dziecko ze Lwowa*, Polish translation M. Zdzienicka, Wrocław 2000, p. 16.

3 The operation against Lem was codenamed "Astronauta."

4 Cf. for example, the scandal that broke out when the Speaker of the Sejm, Radosław Sikorski, stated that Vladimir Putin had offered Poland the partition of Ukraine. The event was the subject of heated debates for several weeks in autumn 2014.

5 G. G. Grabowicz, "Mythologizing Lviv/Lwów: Echoes of Presence and Absence," *Harvard Ukrainian Studies* 2000, vol. 24: *Lviv: A City in the Crosscurrents of Culture*, p. 313. In this article, the author focuses on the mythologization of Lviv, combining Polish and Ukrainian perspectives (from Bartlomiej Zimorowiec to Yuri Andrukhovych).

6 K. Zamorski, *O galicyjskich mitach* [in:] *Mit Galicji*, ed. J. Purchla, W. Kos, Ż. Komar, M. Rygier, W.M. Schwarz, Kraków 2014, p. 130–131.

7 Ibid., p. 130.

8 Cf. E. Wiegandt, *Austria felix, czyli o micie Galicji w polskiej prodzie współczesnej*, Poznań 1988; K. Zamorski, *O galicyjskich mitach*, p. 129–133.

9 On the subject of the myth of multiculturalism in relation to the Jewish city dwellers in Polish, Ukrainian and Jewish popular literature of the twentieth and twenty-first centuries, see Kotyńska, *Żydzi we Lwowie – Żydzi o Lwowie. Literacki obraz miasta*, series of electronic publications of the Center for Urban History of East Central Europe, no. 10, Lviv 2012; available online: <www.lvivcenter.org/download.php ?newsid =1079&fileno=3> [access: January 7, 2015]. Cf. K. Kotyńska, Lwów. O odczytywaniu miasta na nowo, Kraków 2015, p. 91–105.

10 J. Janicki, *Czkawka*, Warszawa 2000, p. 103.

11 Ibid., p. 33.

12 Ibid., p. 99.

13 For example, "Dad, Mojżesz G., until he was burned in Bełżec, had a shop with iron products on Słoneczna Street." Ibid., p. 19.

14 M. Semczyszyn, *Trasami pamięci. Lwowska przestrzeń historyczna w polskich, radzieckich i ukraińskich przewodnikach miejskich z lat 1900–2010* [in:] *Lwów: lustro. Obraz wzajemny mieszkańców Lwowa w narracjach XX–XXI wieku*, ed. K. Kotyńska, Warszawa 2012.

15 W. Wierzbieniec, "The Processes of Jewish Emancipation and Assimilation in the Multiethnic City of Lviv during the Nineteenth and Twentieth Centuries," transl. I.D. Kogut and P. Dabrowski, *Harvard Ukrainian Studies* 2000, vol. 24, p. 226.

16 Synagogues and temples were burned by the Germans in the first weeks of the occupation of the District of Galicia, often with people still inside. See T. Berenstein, *Eksterminacja ludności żydowskiej w dystrykcie Galicja (1941–1943)*, "Biuletyn Żydowskiego Instytutu Historycznego" 1967, no. 61, p. 5. On the burning down of the Lviv synagogue on Szajnochy Street with people still inside, see Janina Masłowska, report from Lviv [in:] *Życie i zagłada Żydów polskich 1939–1945. Relacje świadków*, eds. M. Grynberg, M. Kotowska, Warszawa 2003, p. 274.

17 On the Cori Gilod synagogue in Lviv, see O. Bojko, *Sinagogi L'vova*, L'vov 2008, p. 154–158.

18 Cited in: I. Lylo, "Jewish Lviv" (typescript courtesy of the author). Cf. also: T. Wozniak, *Galicja dziś*, transl. K. Kotyńska [in:] *Mit Galicji*, p. 134–138 and A. Polec, *Zapomniani – my Żydzi kresowi*, Olszanica 2006.

19 At this point, I would like to thank Taras Wozniak for the conversation and his explanations concerning the life of the Jewish minority in Lviv in the twentieth century. Based on the archives opened in the 1990s, a thematic issue of the magazine *Ji* was released, devoted to the pre-war Jewish residents of Lviv. See *Ji*, no. 51, 2008 – available online: < http://www.ji.lviv.ua/n51 texts/N5i-hebr.htm> [accessed January 7, 2015].

20 Ph. Ther, "War versus Peace: Interethnic Relations in Lviv during the First Half of the Twentieth Century," translated by J. Czaplicka, *Harvard Ukrainian Studies* 2000, vol. 24, p. 271. Ther reports that in 1959 Ukrainians accounted for 60 per cent of the city's population, Russians – 27 per cent, 4 per cent – Jews and 4 per cent – Poles.

21 *Teka Lwowska* at the Jewish Historical Institute contains numerous testimonies collected in response to an appeal to Lviv Jews made by the authorities in 1947, when evidence was collected for the trial of Heinz Weber and Robert Ulrich, arrested war criminals responsible for the liquidation of the ghetto and other crimes.

22 Andrzej Żbikowski points out that Polish historians who deal with Polish–Jewish relations during the occupation "focus mainly on events related to Warsaw and the

fate of the Warsaw Jewish community." Foreign sources, however, say much more about the situation in Łódź, Upper Silesia and Vilnius. A. Żbikowski, *A. Żbikowski, Antysemityzm, szmalcownictwo, współpraca z Niemcami a stosunki polsko-żydowskie pod okupacją niemiecką* [in:] *Polacy i Żydzi pod okupacją niemiecką 1939–1945. Studia i materiały*, ed. A. Żbikowski, Warszawa 2006, p. 437.

23 Anna Abakunova concludes her research on the representation of the extermination of Jews in Ukrainian public life as follows: "During the presidency of Viktor Yushchenko in Ukraine, the controversial subject of the OUN and the Ukrainian Insurgent Army (UPA) was raised in a debate on whether their members should be granted the status of national heroes. The Ukrainian academic community supported Yushchenko, but the subsequent research established that instead of heroes, they were actually killers of Jews. Ironically, therefore, the academics felt that there was no need to spend time and resources on research into the annihilation of the Jews, since Ukrainian history is full of no less tragic events, such as the Great Famine, and has its own heroes, such as the Cossacks, Taras Shevchenko and the partisans of World War Two. They preferred that the Holocaust continue to be studied solely by Jews, since Ukrainian Jews were not considered as their fellow citizens, so as such were expected to cope with own tragic national history on their own … . I am convinced that the average Ukrainian citizen does not even know the word 'Holocaust' and would not be able to say even a few sentences about the fate of Jews during World War Two." A. Abakunova, *Obecny stan badań nad Zagładą na Ukrainie*, "Zagłada Żydów. Studia i Materiały" 2014, no. 10, p. 913. Taras Wozniak emphasizes that Ukrainians should be responsible for the Jewish, Polish and Austrian cultural heritage. He notes, however, that he does not mean just the memory of the prosperity under the Austro-Hungarian monarchy, but also the emptiness left by the traumatic experiences of the first half of the twentieth century. T. Wozniak, *Galicja dziś*, p. 134–138.

24 "There was, however, another survivor community not yet spoken for: the Jews of the Soviet Union, the so-called Jews of Silence. … Real memory work in the Soviet Union was conducted in private; how and when we are only now discovering." D. G. Roskies, *What Is Holocaust Literature?* p. 200. On the contemporary situation in Russia, cf. the documentary film *Holocaust – Is That Wallpaper Paste?* dir. by M. Shakirov, Russia 2013.

25 This problem has been discussed in depth in Gabriele Lesser's article, see G. Lesser, *Pogromy w Galicji Wschodniej w 1941*, Polish translation E. Heyde [in:] *Tematy polsko-ukraińskie. Historia – Literatura – Edukacja*, ed. R. Traba, Olsztyn 2001, p. 103–126.

26 Martin Pollack stresses that the German-speaking world interested in Galicia focuses on the Jewish shtetl, Jewish literature and music, i.e. the exotic nature of Jewish life, which was irretrievably destroyed during World War Two; and that knowledge of the region is based on such works as novels by Joseph Roth or Martin Buber. "How can we explain the fact that so many people today feel something akin to a longing for a world so cruelly destroyed by their fathers and grandparents? It seems that nobody is bothered that this nostalgic image of Jewish Galicia, with its pious Hassidim, wise and miracle-working rabbis, has little in common with historical truth." Cf. M. Pollack, *Galicja to daleki, obcy kraj*, Polish transl. B. Andrunik. On the subject of the interests of American researchers of Galicia solely in this exotic aspect of Jewish life, see A. Woldan, *Literatura galicyjska*, Polish transl. B. Andrunik [in:] ibid., p. 214.

27 D. G. Roskies, *What Is Holocaust Literature?* The quoted fragment appears only in the Polish, revised version of the text: D. G. Roskies, *Czym jest literatura Holokaustu?* transl. M. Adamczyk-Garbowska. [in:] *Reprezentacje Holokaustu*. eds. J. Jarniewicz, M. Szuster. Kraków–Warszawa 2014 p. 31.

28 Ibid.

29 S. Lem, *Z żabiej perspektywy* [in:] the same, *Lube czasy*, ed. T. Fiałkowski, Kraków 1995, p. 110.

30 Idem, *Gdy ziemia dygoce* [in:] ibid., p. 117.
31 Jerzy Jarzębski stressed, for example, that enclosed spaces, rockets and places that can be associated with domestication do not ensure safety for the protagonists of Lem's novels and short stories. J. Jarzębski, *Kosmogonia i konsolacja* [in:] idem, *Wszechświat Lema*, Kraków 2003, p. 71.
32 During a trip to the Warsaw Jewish cemetery, Miron Białoszewski stops in front of the grave of a 5-year-old girl: "I read and note: – 'Born September 18, 5617, expired March 19, 5622.' According to the Jewish calendar – these future dates, mirabelle plums are nice, too ..." M. Białoszewski, *Kirkut* [in:] idem, *Szumy, zlepy, ciągi*, Warszawa 2014, p. 13.
33 G. Hryciuk, *Polacy w Lwowie 1939–1944; Życie codzienne*, Warszawa 2000, p. 60–61.
34 Ibid.
35 S. Lem, *The Conditional Reflex* [in:] idem, *Tales of the Pilot Pirx*, p. 63. The nuisance of using two time systems, one of which was completely useless in that geographical location, was the subject of Julian Stryjkowski's *Wielki Strach*.
36 On the changing of street names by the occupants, see G. Hryciuk, *Polacy we Lwowie 1939–1944. Życie codzienne*, p. 225.
37 L.L. Langer, p. 34.
38 Ibid., p. 66.
39 J. Madejski, *Deformacje biografii*, Szczecin 2004, p. 21.
40 K. Kotyńska, *Lwow. O odczytywaniu miasta na nowo*, p. 110.
41 Katarzyna Kotyńska discusses novels by Julia Prajs or Julia Brystiger. Ibid., p. 111–112.
42 Ibid., p. 109–111. Cf. also: K. Kotyńska, *Żydzi we Lwowie – Żydzi o Lwowie. Literacki obraz miasta*.
43 For example, Małgorzata Czermińska links *Highcastle* to the myth of Galicia, even though the writer was born and raised in the Second Republic of Poland, and Lem's memories, as the researcher points out, unlike many other autobiographical texts, do not concern family genealogy. These observations may indicate that Lem used the pre-existing model of a tale about Lviv. M. Czermińska, *Dom w autobiografii i powieści o dzieciństwie* [in:] *Przestrzeń i literatura*, eds. M. Głowiński, A. Okopień-Sławińska, Wrocław-Warszawa-Kraków-Gdańsk 1978.
44 K. Kotyńska, *Lwow. O odczytywaniu miasta na nowo*, p. 35, 42.
45 Ibid., p. 52.
46 M. Głowinski, *Mity przebrane. Dionizos, Narcyz, Prometeusz, Marchołt, labirynt*, Kraków 1990, p. 134.
47 Ibid., p. 150.
48 J. Sowa, *Fantomowe ciało króla. Peryferyjne zmagania z nowoczesną formą*, Kraków 2011, p. 453.
49 S. Lem, *Highcastle*, 57.
50 R. Sennett, *Flesh and Stone: The Body and City in the Western Civilization*, New York–London 1996, p. 15.
51 S. Lem, *Highcastle*, p. 82.
52 Ibid., p. 57.
53 *Time Not Lost* was entirely translated into Czech and German (in 1959 it was published in East Germany under the title *Die Irrungen des Dr. Stefan T.*). The first volume of the trilogy has been translated into English, Spanish, Turkish, Italian and Russian. Cf. D. Bilikiewicz-Blanc, J. Rzeszotnik, *Bibliografia przekładów (1954–2010)* [in:] *Lem i tłumacze*, ed. E. Skibińska and J. Rzeszotnik, Kraków 2010, p. 313, 378–379. Information found in the writer's archive by Wojciech Zemek suggests that in Czechoslovakia, the trilogy was also published in 1959, with a circulation of 11,500 copies (letter of October 12, 2014). In 1956 Lem wrote to Jerzy Wróblewski: "I am becoming more and more a writer for export. I already have contracts with the Czechs for all (4) books, no fee, of course, because financial issues have not been settled (for years) between our beautiful countries. Now the Germans also

want to translate *Time Not Lost* and *The Cloud* is coming out soon." Stanisław Lem, letter of April 26, 1956, unpublished, courtesy of Barbara and Tomasz Lem.

54 See K. Budrowska, *Literatura i pisarze wobec cenzury PRL 1948–1958*, Białystok 2009, p. 161–169. In 1946, Lem mocked the Press Control Office, which approved scientific books devoid of any cognitive value: "We believe that the Press Control screens should be set more universally than before. The pseudo-scientific rubbish is just as much, or perhaps even more harmful in terms of its impact than social or political nonsense." S. Lem, "O kopernikański światopogląd," "Życie Nauki" 1946, no. 11–12, p. 422. In the 1990s, Lem returned to the subject of censorship: S. Lem, *Dwie cenzury* [in:] idem, *Lube czasy*, p. 76–78.

55 W. Orliński, *Co to są sepulki? Wszystko o Lemie*, Kraków 2007, p. 51.

56 In his *Zegar słoneczny*, Parandowski uses very characteristic names of places and streets, which clearly point to Lviv as the subject of description (e.g. *Wały Hetmańskie, Akademicka, hotel George, Zamarstynów, kaplica Boimów, fabryka wódek Baczewskiego, katedra św. Jura, Łyczaków, plac Kilińskiego, kopiec Unii Lubelskiej*). In Lem's *Time Not Lost* there are mainly allusions to names or descriptions of the appearance of buildings.

57 Izabela Domaciuk analyzed the names that map out the topography of Lviv in the second part of *Time Not Lost*, although she did not set them in a broader interpretative context that would include history, deciding, for example, that the prison on Dębickiego Street is not a proper noun, while it is clear that Lem is playing a game with the censors; the name is reminiscent of the prison on Łąckiego Street, a site of both Soviet and German crimes, which is why its real name could not appear in the novel. Cf. I. Domaciuk, *Nazwy własne w prozie Stanisława Lema*, Lublin 2003, p. 18–32.

58 Cf. E. Zielińska, *Idealizacja Lwowa w esejach wspomnieniowych Jerzego Janickiego* [in:] *Lwow: lustro. Obraz wzajemny mieszkańcow Lwowa w narracjach XX–XXI wieku*, p. 155.

59 I have borrowed the name from Timothy Snyder, who applies it to the area "from central Poland to western Russia, through Ukraine, Belarus, and the Baltic States." T. Snyder, *Bloodlands: Europe Between Hitler and Stalin*, 2010, p. vii–viii.

60 G. Hryciuk, *Przemiany narodowości i ludnościowe w Galicji Wschodniej i na Wołyniu w latach 1931–1948*, Toruń 2005, p. 236. According to the researcher, the most reliable data indicate that 610,000 Jews died in the District of Galicia in 1941–1944.

61 "After the liberation of Lviv by the victorious Red Army on July 21, 1944, it turned out that only several hundred Lviv Jews (823 people, meticulously counted by the chairman of the Provisional Jewish Committee in Lviv, Dr. David Sobel, based on the applications submitted to the Committee) survived in Lviv. F. Friedman, *Zagłada Żydów lwowskich*, Wydawnictwo Centralna Żydowskiej Komisji Historycznej, Łódź 1945, text available online: < http://www.mankurty.com/fridpl.html> [accessed October 17, 2015].

62 G. Hryciuk, *Przemiany narodowości i ludnościowe w Galicji Wschodniej i na Wołyniu w latach 1931–1948*, p. 331.

63 A. Wylegała, *Obraz "Innych" w narracjach biograficznych lwowskich Polaków* [in:] *Lwów: lustro. Obraz wzajemny mieszkańców Lwowa w narracjach XX–XXI wieku*, p. 61. On the subject of the separation of Jews in the structures of officially existing organizations (e.g. in the Polish Association of Former Political Prisoners and Nazi Prisoners and Concentration Camps) see Z. Wóycicka, *Przerwana żałoba. Polskie spory wokół pamięci nazistowskich obozów koncentracyjnych i zagłady 1944–1950*, Warszawa 2009, p. 105–109, 126–135.

64 S. Lem, *Chance and Order, The New Yorker* 59 (January 30, 1984), p. 88–98.

65 J. Błoński, *Biedni Polacy patrzą na getto*, Kraków 2008, p. 86. The first version of this article makes no reference to *Highcastle*. Cf. J. Błoński, *Autoportret żydowski (1981)* [in:] idem, *Kilka myśli co nie nowe*, Kraków 1985, p. 117.

66 Julian Stryjkowski (born 1905) escaped from Lviv after the German troops entered the city, and survived the occupation in the USSR.

67 There are indications that the parents of Lem's mother had links with the Yiddish culture, in all likelihood; however, the Lem family did not maintain close relations with them. In a letter to Michael Kandel, Lem wrote in English (although his letters were usually in Polish): "Any link with yiddish is improbable, since, even in the spirit of Nuremberg laws I am a Jew." S. Lem, *List z 13 kwietnia 1973* [in:] idem, *Sława i fortuna. Listy do Michaela Kandla 1972–1987*, Kraków 2013, p. 137–138. On the methodological problems associated with the post-war classifications of ethnic minorities and the dangers arising from ignoring the identification of the persons concerned, see A. Rykała, *Przemiany sytuacji społeczno-politycznej mniejszości żydowskiej w Polsce po drugiej wojnie światowej*, Łódź 2007, s. 9–13

68 S. Lem, *Chance and Order*. English Wikipedia cites this fragment, concluding that Stanisław Lem was brought up Roman Catholic, cf. <https://en.wikipedia.org/wiki/Stanis%C5%82aw_Lem> [access: September 15, 2015]. Information about his Catholic education was also published on Polish-language Wikipedia.

69 In his biography of the writer, Wojciech Orliński makes an interesting and reliable attempt to verify the information Stanisław Lem shares in these two interviews. Fragment of the typescript courtesy of the author.

70 Kurt I. Lewin, less than 4 years younger than Lem, wrote about anti-Semitism in Polish schools in Lviv: "I was a good student at school. Externally, I began to resemble others. But only externally. More and more, I was staying away from my colleagues. It was at school that I first came across anti-Semitism. That was the first time I heard it shouted in my face: 'You dirty Jew.' My soul rebelled, and because I was belligerent in nature, I beat my classmate, a Pole, bloody. I organized self-defense for my Jewish classmates against the 'superior race.'" K. I. Lewin *Przeżyłem. Saga Świętego Jura spisana w roku 1946 przez syna rabina Lwowa*, Warszawa 2006, p. 13.

71 Copy of the school-leaving certificate of Stanisław Herman Lem. He received "very good" marks in Judaism studies and in all other subjects, both at the end of the second grade and school-leaving exams.

72 The March Constitution contained the following provision: "Instruction in religion is compulsory for all pupils in every educational institution, the curriculum of which includes instruction of youth under eighteen years of age, if the institution is maintained wholly or in part by the state, or by self-government bodies. The direction and supervision of religious instruction in schools belongs to the respective religious communities, reserving to the state educational authorities the right of supreme supervision." Dz. U. [Journal of Laws] of 1921, no. 44, item 267, art. 120.

73 J. Błoński, *Biedni Polacy patrzą na getto*, p. 85. On Lem's reluctance to write about his Jewish roots, see J. Jarzębski, *Lem i Mrożek w dziwnym świetle lat sześćdziesiątych* [in:] S. Lem, S. Mrożek, *Listy 1956–1978*, Kraków 2011, p. 10.

74 J. Błoński, *Biedni Polacy patrzą na getto*, p. 86.

75 Particularly difficult in interpreting Lem's attitude towards his Jewish roots are fragments of his conversations with Stanisław Bereś.

76 W. Bartoszewski, *Mój przyjaciel pesymista* [*Stanisław Lem*] [in:] idem, *Pisma wybrane 2002–2012*, selection, ed. A. K. Kunert, vol. 6, Kraków 2012, p. 363. The Nobel Prize was a recurring theme of discussions in Lem's context. In his correspondence with Kandel, translator of *The Cyberiad* into English, the writer stated ironically: "Nobel Prize? Mind just how many people would flip their lid! – a) the whole SFWA – plus a part of Fandom; b) 85% of the members of the Zw. Literatów Polskich [Polish Writers' Union]. Would that be justified to pay the price of such a massacre in exchange for rewarding one guy, no matter how deserving?" S. Lem, *List z 7 grudnia 1972* [in:] idem, *Sława i fortuna. Listy do Michaela Kandla 1972–1987*, p. 113.

77 "[M]y very first novel was a realistic one, which I wrote perhaps in order to rid myself of the weight of my war memories – to expel them like pus. But perhaps I wrote this book also in order not to forget; the one motive could well go together with the other." S. Lem, *Chance and Order*.

78 S. Lem, *Mówi głos ciemności* [in:] idem, *Wejście na Orbitę*, Kraków 1962, p. 108.
79 Ibid., p. 108.
80 See B. Shallcross, *The Uncanny Soap: Zofia Nałkowska and the economy of the Holocaust*, Polish transl. K. Maciejewska, "Teksty Drugie" 2007, no. 5, p. 67.
81 Ibid., p. 69.
82 The Central Office for Control of Press, Publications and Performances and the Ministry of Culture and Art blocked the first works Stanisław Lem submitted for publication: *Wywiad i atomy*, *Kula czasu* (book not yet found), *Areanthropos* [The Man from Mars] and the novel *Hospital of the Transfiguration* (released only in 1955 as *Time Not Lost* after two more parts were added). K. Budrowska, *Literatura i pisarze wobec cenzury PRL 1948–1958*, p. 148–168.
83 J. Jarzębski, *Skalpel i mózg* [afterword to:] S. Lem, *Szpital Przemienienia*, Warszawa 2008, p. 182.
84 Following the suggestion of Izabella Galicka, daughter of Karol Mikulski, it was concluded on the Polish Radio broadcast devoted to *Hospital of the Transfiguration* that Lem's novel refers to the events that took place in the hospital in Gostynin. See the broadcast of November 22, 2010: *Oddał życie za swoich pacjentow*, available online: <http://www.polskieradio.pl/7/178/Artykul/277151,Oddal-zycie-za-swoich-pacjentow> access: October 18, 2015].
85 Footnote in Jan Józef Szczepański's diary indicates that the landscape of *Hospital of the Transfiguration* is reminiscent of the landscape of Przegorzały (Lem used to visit Halina and Roman Husarski there, but Tomasz Fiałkowski does not provide the source of this information, nor does he present any detailed explanation.) J.J. Szczepański, *Dziennik 1945–1956*, Kraków 2009, p. 339, footnote 7.
86 Cf. T. Nasierowski, *Zagłada osob z zaburzeniami psychicznymi w okupowanej Polsce. Początek ludobojstwa*, Warszawa 2008.
87 Janina Masłowska, account from Lviv [in:] *Życie i zagłada Żydów polskich 19391945. Życie i zagłada Żydow polskich 1939–1945. Relacje świadkow*, p. 275. I did not find any confirmation in the testimonies given by doctors who worked in Kulparków during the occupation. See the account of Hipolit Latyński, Doctor of Psychiatry, "Informacja o ilości przyjętych do szpitala chorych i zmarłych w latach 1941–1943." Archiwum ŻIH, sygn. 301/1000: "The psychiatric hospital in Kulparków, by coincidence, avoided the fate of Chełm (although there were some such designs there, too) in the sense of a violent, barbaric liquidation, but it did not avoid a slow liquidation, through deliberate malnutrition, as a result of which only 260 of about 2000 patients from June 1941 survived until January 15, 1943, while others, suffering from starvation swelling, died as a result of exhaustion."
88 Letter courtesy of Barbara and Tomasz Lem.
89 On the interchangeability of the terms "Moorish" and "Turkish" concerning the discussed architectural style, see E. Bergman, *Nurt mauretański w architekturze synagog Europy Środkowo-Wschodniej w XIX i na początku XX wieku*, Warsaw 2004, p. 16, 19.
90 S. Lem, *Hospital of the Transfiguration*, p. 39.
91 "I don't like post-war Warsaw (and I don't know the pre-war Warsaw, because I hadn't left Lviv until the war except for Yaremche and Vorokhta)." Stanisław Lem to Prof. Władysław Kapuściński, letter from December 24, 1978, depository of the Museum of Literature in Warsaw, ref. no. 3740. Yaremche and Vorokhta are spas located in the Eastern Carpathians.
92 There was no Moorish synagogue in Lviv; the last Tempel synagogue to be built (1845) was built in the Palladian style. E. Bergman, *Nurt mauretański w architektury synagog Europy Środkowo-Wschodniej w XIX i początku XX wieku*, p. 37.
93 "The most interesting, decorative synagogue-type dome in the former Polish territory can still be seen today in the former Israelite Hospital in Lviv. It is covered with seledine slate, with geometric patterns of yellow tiles." Ibid., p. 72.
94 According to Irena Szajowicz, a hospital for the tortured and exhausted victims of the Janowska camp was established on the grounds of the old Jewish cemetery,

because that was the only location approved by the German authorities. Irena Szajowicz, account from Lviv [in:] *Życie i zagłada Żydów polskich 1939–1945. Relacje świadków*, p. 287.

95 The area of the Jewish district was changed by successive decrees of the German authorities, but their execution encountered numerous problems, so it lasted from October 1941 until March 1942, when resettlement processes were already associated with deportation to the death camp (cf. F. Friedman, *Zagłada Żydów lwowskich*). A schematic plan of deportation from the Jewish quarter to the ghetto is featured on the map in the Archives of the Jewish Historical Institute in Warsaw: "Przesiedlenie Żydów we Lwowie, plan getta," sygn. 245/50 (November 13, 1941). "The ghetto was to consist of three sections of streets, the second and third of which were to be designated 'a residential area for Jews who, as craftsmen or professional workers, would receive … a stamped identity card.'" T. Berenstein, *Eksterminacja ludności żydowskiej w dystryktu Galicja (1941–1943)*, p. 17.

96 E. Kuryluk, *Norma – zabobon – getto – "eutanazja." Pożegnajmy raz na zawsze drzwi bez klamek* [in:] *Zagłada chorych psychicznie. Pamięć i historia*, ed. T. Nasierowski, G. Herczyńska, D. M. Myszka, Warszawa 2012, p. 448.

97 M. Zaremba, *Wielka trwoga, Polska 1944–1947. Ludowa reakcja na kryzys*, Kraków 2012, p. 134; cf. also on this subject: A. Żbikowski, *Antysemityzm, szmalcownictwo, współpraca z Niemcami a stosunki polsko-żydowskie pod okupacją niemiecką* [in:] *Polacy i Żydzi pod okupacją niemiecką 1939–1945. Studia i materiały*, ed. A. Żbikowski, Warszawa 2006, p. 433.

98 T. Snyder, *Bloodlands: Europe Between Hitler and Stalin*, p. 8–20.

99 T. Berenstein, *Eksterminacja ludności żydowskiej w dystryktu Galicja (1941–1943)*, p. 3–4, 19.

100 W. O. McCagg, *A History of Habsburg Jews 1670–1918*, Indianapolis 1992, p. 6.

101 S. Lem, *List z 28 października 1976* [in:] idem, *Sława i fortuna. Listy do Michaela Kandla 1972–1987*, p. 510.

102 This term appears in the context of mentally ill people in *Hospital of the Transfiguration* and, in reference to Jews in the second part of *Time Not Lost*, in the chapter *Operation Reinhardt*.

103 G. Agamben, *Remnants of Auschwitz: The Witness and the Archive (Homo sacer III)*, transl. by Daniel Heller-Roazen, New York 1999, p. 51.

104 Grzegorz Niziołek noticed the correspondence between the description in *Brygady śmierci* and Stanisław Lem's *Provocation* written in the 1980s. References to this historical text can also be found in the author's early works. Cf. G. Niziołek, *Polski Teatr Zagłady*, Warszawa 2013, p. 96–99.

105 Cf. for instance: A. Morawiec, *Wstęp* [in:] L. Weliczker, *Brygada śmierci (Sonderkommando 1005)*, Lublin 2012, p. XVIII.

106 G. Chamayou, *Les Corps vils. Expérimenter sur les êtres humains aux XVIIIe siècle et XIXe siècle, Éditions la Découverte, 2008*, quotation based on the Polish edition, *Podłe ciała. Eksperymenty na ludziach w XVIII i XIX wieku*, trans. J. Bodzińska, K. Thiel-Jańczuk, Gdańsk 2012, p. 5.

107 S. Coché, *Praktiken der Einweisung von Patienten in die Psychiatrie im Dritten Reich, der BRD und der DDR 1941–1963/Practice of referring patients to psychiatric institutions in the Third Reich, East Germany and West Germany 1941–1963*, paper presented at the international conference "Medicine in occupied Poland in the shadow of Nazism," held on October 10–12, 2014 in Poznań.

108 Stefanie Coché states that as a result of the selection of children and adolescents "unfit for learning," 300 preparations of child's brain were collected in one of the clinics. Ibid.

109 Ibid.

110 Marglewski worked on a theory that was intended to prove that behind every brilliant discovery there was a disease: "Balzac – a hypomaniacal psychopath, Baudelaire – a hysteric, Chopin – a neurasthenic, Dante – a schizoid, Goethe – an alcoholic,

Hölderlin – a schizophrenic." Lem criticized this type of pseudo-scientific theory in an article published in "Życie Nauki." – S. Lem, *Psychologizm i realizm*, "Życie Nauki" 1947, p. 213–216. Perhaps this figure constitutes – in a grotesque way – a polemic with the concept of *schizophrenia paradoxalis socialiter fausta* proposed by Eugeniusz Brzezicki, whose lectures Lem attended during his medical studies at Jagiellonian University.

111 E. Gomel, *From Dr. Moreau to Dr. Mengele: The Biological Sublime*, "Poetics Today" 2000, no. 21:2, p. 393.

112 Ibid., p. 393–394.

113 Maciej Michalski analyzed Lem's typical protagonist in the context of existential philosophy: "He is usually aware of his limitations. His mediocrity, frequent reflexive and intuitive actions, both determine his strength and expose typically human defects and weaknesses. In this sense, he is a parabolic hero – universal, ordinary, barely outlined." M. Michalski, *Egzystencjalny wymiar twórczości Stanisława Lem* [in:] *Stanisław Lem: pisarz, myśliciel, człowiek*, ed. J. Jarzębski, A. Sulikowski, Kraków 2003, p. 107.

114 S. Lem, *His Master's Voice*, p. 133.

115 Idem, List z 5 listopada 1976 [in:] idem, *Sława i fortuna. Letters to Michael Kandel* 1972–1987, p. 518.

116 Idem, *List z 2 września 1976* [in:] idem., p. 490.

117 In *His Master's Voice* there is one such self-referential commentary on the way of describing the bodies of eminent scholars, who were previously known only from their works: "To observe how pure thought or lofty detachment sweats, blinks, digs in its ear, how it manages, with varying success, its own machinery, which, supporting the soul, so often gets in the soul's way – this has always been for me an iconoclastic treat, malicious through and through." Ibid., p. 133.

118 S. Lem, *Hospital of the Transfiguration*, p. 42.

119 Ibid., p. 32.

120 Ibid., p. 41.

121 Ibid., p. 177–179.

122 Cf. Y. Arad, *Belzec, Sobibor, Treblinka. The Operation Reinhard. Death Camps*, Indiana University Press 1999, p. 14–22.

123 R. Kuwałek, *Obóz zagłady w Bełżcu*, Lublin-Bełżec 2005, p. 9.

124 "The November operation lasted five days. First of all, she touched working Jews who trusted their work IDs and stamped registration cards and were not hiding at all." Dawid Kahane, report from Lviv, transl. from Yiddish by A. Bielecki [in:] *Życie i zagłada Żydow polskich 1939–1945. Relacje świadków*, p. 273: "On the yard, a nightmarish night again. More people than ever before. All those sent by companies to the camp several days ago, with the assurance that they would save themselves that way, have now found themselves there. Most of them were from Kremin and Wolf (Rohstofferfassung)." Irena Szajowicz, account from Lviv [in:] ibid., p. 290.

125 After the liquidation of the ghetto in Lviv, a Judenlager (Julag) camp was set up in its place, where people employed in German companies were housed in special apartments. Julag was liquidated on June 1, 1943, but before that several thousand young and healthy people had been selected and sent to the camp. T. Berenstein, *Eksterminacja ludności żydowskiej w dystryktu Galicja (1941–1943)*, p. 25–26.

126 A. Lowenstein, *Shocking Representation: Historical Trauma, National Cinema, and the Modern Horror Film*, Columbia University Press 2005, p. 6. Cf. J. Hirsch, *Postmodernism, the Second Generation, and Cross-Cultural Posttraumatic Cinema* [in:] idem, *Afterimage: Film, Trauma and The Holocaust*, Temple University Press 2004, p. 6.

127 "The warfare, and above all the German occupation, made it impossible for me to continue my studies at the Faculty of Medicine in 1941–1944. During that time, I was forced into hard physical labor in the garage of a German company and partly in the Janowska camp." Jagiellonian University Archives, registration card for first-time applicants for admission to the University, WL II 387, punkt 9. According to

the annotated edition of Janina Hescheles's memoirs, in June 1943, "already after the liquidation of Julag began, [the Rohstofferfassung company] was moved to the Janowska camp, and most of the workers were shot." J. Hescheles, *Oczyma dwunastoletniej dziewczyny*, Warszawa 2015, p. 64, footnote 21.

128 On the situation of the witness and the bystander, see G. Niziołek, *Polski teatr Zagłady*, p. 69.

129 On the subject of the circumstances in which both novels were written, see S. Lem, *List z 14 października 1975* [in:] idem, *Sława i fortuna. Listy do Michaela Kandla 1972–1987*, p. 420.

130 S. Lem, *Czas nieutracony*, Kraków 1957, p. 305.

131 The scene of old women being rounded up and led to death would metaphorically return in *Memoirs Found in a Bathtub*: "One door bounced back open, revealing a large room full of old women in shawls and high-buttoned shoes. Their voices blended into one complaining and quarrelsome sound as we passed.
'What was that?' I asked.
'Busybodies,' said the cremator. 'We keep them in reserve. This way, please.'
And he pushed me forward. I got a good whiff of his cheap hair tonic, and the smells of ink and soap." S. Lem, *Memoirs Found in a Bathtub*, p. 140. Repeated in this scene are both the description of surprise at the sight of old women with different headgear and the haste of the observer, accompanied by a dangerous guide – "the cremator."

132 S. Lem, *Czas nieutracony*, p. 306–307.

133 H. Krall, *The Subtenant/To Outwit God*, transl. J. Anders, Northwestern University Press 1992, p. 37.

134 L.L. Langer, *Holocaust Testimonies: The Ruins of Memory*, p. 75.

135 Ibid., p. 138–139.

136 S. Lem, *Czas nieutracony*, p. 311.

137 On the subject of groups of children that attacked Jews in Lviv, see M. Zaremba, *Wielka trwoga, Polska 1944–1947. Ludowa reakcja na kryzys*, p. 226.

138 S. Lem, *Czas nieutracony*, p. 312.

139 Ibid., p. 313.

140 M. Głowiński, *Oczy donosiciela*, "Zagłada Żydów. Studia i Materiały" 2014, no. 10, p. 858–859.

141 G. Niziołek, *Polski Teatr Zagłady*, p. 69. Dawid Kahane reported on the attitude of Lviv residents watching the liquidation of the ghetto: "On Friday, August 21, I took a business assignment to the community on Starotandetna Street. I wanted to see what was happening on the other side of the bridge, what the operation looked like. Everywhere the same images, everywhere the same ruins, except for the Aryan population, who came from the city to watch the German work." Dawid Kahane, account from Lviv [in:] *Życie i zagłada Żydów polskich 1939–1945. Relacje świadkow*, p. 271. Cf. A. Żbikowski, *Antysemityzm, szmalcownictwo, współpraca z Niemcami a stosunki polsko-żydowskie pod okupacją niemiecką*, [in:] p. 445–446, 474.

142 S. Lem, *Czas nieutracony*, p. 318.

143 Ibid., p. 326.

144 Cf. R. Reder, *Bełżec*, Kraków 1999, p. 49.

145 S. Lem, *Czas nieutracony*, p. 632.

146 On the subject of exceptions related to the presence of the subject of the Holocaust in socialist-realist prose, see S. Buryła, *Zagłada Żydów w prozie socrealistycznej*, "Midrasz" 2008, no. 11, p. 26–30.

147 J. Jarzębski, *Skalpel i mózg* [in:] S. Lem, *Szpital Przemienienia*, p. 181. Even Jan Józef Szczepański, preferred *The Magellan Cloud*, published in parallel to the trilogy, to *Time Not Lost*. J.J. Szczepański, entry dated January 15, 1956, *Dziennik 1945–1956*, Kraków 2009, p. 592.

148 In 1950, the process of "Stalinization" of historical memory in Poland was completed, which coincided with the opening of the State Museum in Oświęcim, whose permanent exhibition served the authorities as an instrument of Cold War

propaganda. Z. Wóycicka, *Przerwana żałoba. Polskie spory wokół pamięci nazistowskich obozów koncentracyjnych i zagłady 1944–1950*, p. 21. Snyder also brought attention to the selective memory of the Holocaust sites. Cf. T. Snyder, *Bloodlands. Europe between Hitler and Stalin*, p. xix–xx.

149 S. Lem, *The Conditioned Reflex* [in:] idem, *Tales of Pirx the Pilot*, p. 42.

150 Larisa Andriievska, translator of *Highcastle*, stresses that the accusations of typically Polish perspective, usually voiced by extreme right-wing parties, were rare in the Ukrainian reception to the book. The book was very popular, not just in Lviv; it was also placed third as the book of the year in the essay category (2002). The edition of *Highcastle* was very thorough and the publishing house emphasized its *genius loci*, which fit the profile of books on the history of Lviv published there. For this reason, for example, the Ukrainian edition was illustrated with photographs from Lem's former home. As far as the Ukrainian publishing market is concerned, at that time the circulation of *Highcastle* was considerable and amounted to 13,000 copies, with a new release in the works at the moment. The translator stresses that "*Highcastle* is always available in Ukrainian bookstores, at least in Lviv, where Lem is a cult writer: 'the most famous Lvivian in the world.'" Letter from Larissa Andriievska dated September 30, 2015.

2

THE SPLIT

Multiple portrait

Who is Stefan Trzyniecki, the protagonist and narrator of Stanisław Lem's first novel, *Hospital of the Transfiguration*, and the two other volumes of the *Time Not Lost* trilogy? Commentators point to many autobiographical allusions in the series, and it is Trzyniecki that they see as the writer's alter ego. However, this protagonist is one of the most complex characters in Lem's prose, and any attempt to make his biography more coherent encounters various problems when individual information about his life is confronted with the political and social background of the war and post-war years.

Details of Trzyniecki's life during the war seem particularly inconsistent. In the third volume, entitled *Powrót* [Return], a short summary of the hero's experience during the occupation reconstructs his peregrinations through a number of camps: first Bełżec, then Auschwitz, and finally Leitmeritz. This is a turning point in the descriptions of Trzyniecki's biography that could mark the beginning of the search for the split, or rather multiplied, autobiography. If Stefan Trzyniecki had been sent to Bełżec, even if he had worked in the Sonderkommando, he would not have survived, as it was a death camp.[1] It is also very unlikely that from there he was sent to Auschwitz. Shortly after the war, all information about the camp in Bełżec was reconstructed based solely on the testimony of one of the only two prisoners who had managed to escape and survive the war—Rudolf Reder, whose memoir was published in Krakow in 1946. The other prisoner, Chaim Hirszman from Janów Lubelski, was shot dead by members of an underground Polish organization in March 1946 in Lublin, on the day he gave his testimony about the camp.[2] The descriptions of the camp and individual buildings in Lem's novel openly draw on Reder's publication,[3] which contains detailed accounts and schematic maps. It was from that book that

DOI: 10.4324/9780367855642-3

Lem took information about Jewish divisions working in the camp, about rooms where women's heads were shaved and where the hair was stored, or about pulling gold teeth from victims' mouths.[4] Stefan Trzyniecki is not one of the two survivors of Bełżec, his character does not serve to reconstruct the fate of witnesses, so why did Lem put him in a death camp for two weeks and—breaking the rules of probability—save him from suffocation? In this case, the interest in the camp must have been personally motivated, given what happened to the writer's family and friends, as all but his parents died in Bełżec or Lviv. Another factor that contributed to such a strange turn of events in the novel was certainly censorship. *Return* was written in 1950, which, according to Zofia Wóycicka, was the peak of the Stalinization of historical memory in Poland, marking the moment when Auschwitz became an instrument of Cold War propaganda.[5] The camp in Bełżec, on the other hand, where the Lviv Jews perished, was one of the quickly forgotten sites of martyrdom:

> While Stutthof and Gross-Rosen could still count on the interest of local branches of PZbWP [Polish Society of Former Political Prisoners], areas of former death camps, Chełmno, Bełżec, Treblinka and Sobibór, were absent from the map of Polish martyrdom sites at that time, visited only by those who sought gold and valuables.[6]

The efforts of Jewish organizations to commemorate those places where almost exclusively Jewish people were killed ultimately failed, and soon the political attention of all victims' associations focused on Auschwitz and Majdanek.[7] The authorities of the People's Republic of Poland returned to the issue of the Bełżec camp in the 1960s, when investigations into SS officers suspected of having worked there began in Germany. In March 1967, Polish police also launched an investigation in connection with those trials, and their report gives the number of people murdered in the camp: 600,000.[8] In the typed manuscript, the number of victims is followed by the phrase, "mostly Jewish population"; symptomatically, the comment was crossed out with a pen by an unknown editor.[9]

Time Not Lost, especially its two parts, *Among the Dead* and *Return*, written at the turn of 1949–1950, are novels that uniquely document the changes in historical politics in Poland in the second half of the 1940s. They feature two opposing trends, reinforced—as can be predicted—by the Main Office for the Control of the Press, Publications, and Public Performances. On the one hand, Lem's individual memory of the occupation in Lviv and the need to commemorate the crimes committed by Germans and Ukrainians in the ghetto, in the Janowska camp, at Kleparów station and in Bełżec are clearly discernable. On the other hand, also present is the martyrologic and heroic narrative described by Wóycicka, associated with the need to legitimize the new government, based on the myth of "an international anti-fascist resistance movement, allegedly led by party comrades."[10]

Lem's trilogy is also a carefully camouflaged story about life on the so-called Aryan side—hiding, escaping from the ghetto, which involves constant thinking about those who stayed and whose fate the writer himself and his parents could have shared. The most important challenge Stefan faces is an accusation of being a Jew. Throughout the trilogy, an important role is played by the theme of the face seen in a mirror and reflected in someone's eyes: "He thought I was a Jew. That had happened before,"[11] Trzyniecki explains to himself the allusion of one of the conspirators. "Looks like a Jew, thought Stefan and froze because it was his own reflection in the mirror."[12] "She then stared at his face until he remembered that he looked like a Jew. He thought that hairdressers glanced at him oddly."[13] After the war, the hospital staff, such as one of the interns who "took Stefan for a Jew," were unfriendly to him.[14] At a ball, a medical student associated with the Polish Home Army tells him openly: "You're a Jew, I know."[15] In a conversation with his friend Pościk, Stefan confides to him:

> the doctor you saw in the staff room, the young one, thinks I'm Jewish. ... you know, sometimes I can sense the same glances as during the Occupation. All that is still going on. It's like – not hate exactly, you know, but like they're not looking at a human being. You don't know it.[16]

The image of the protagonist's own face is multiplied in those reflections and superimposed on subsequent images, but the denial of his Jewish ancestry does not appear until Operation Reinhardt, when Stefan is brought to the collection point and transported to Bełżec. Then, already on the train, he thinks, "it's so good that I'm not Jewish, it's so terrible,"[17] and the absurdity of this remark is that he is already on his way to a death camp in a cattle wagon.

The alternative biography[18] leads to a split narrative, although the novel does not once state that Stefan is hiding on the so-called Aryan side. In a way, the "resemblance to a Jew" obliterates the most important implications of Jewish ancestry, leading to a multiplication of denials. In the case of figures hiding on the so-called Aryan side, the method of recounting their war experiences by transferring them to others can be found, for example, in Artur Sandauer's *Zapiski z umarłego miasta* [Notes from the dead city], an autobiography which, as soon as it approaches the period of hiding, smoothly turns into a parabiography of a fictional character, Mieczysław Rosenzweig. A similar technique involving "white" and "black" lives appears in Hanna Krall's *The Subtenant*. The splitting of "Polish" and "Jewish" biographies is accompanied by a narrative distance as autobiographical themes are attributed to other characters, which often boils down to writing about one's experiences in the third person. In her interpretation of *The Subtenant*, Inga Iwasiów emphasized that while fragments concerning this split can be interpreted as self-referential,

> the theme of the novel is to construct an identity that chooses clichés – patriotic, national, political, private – in order to demonstrate that the apparent otherness, multiplied by the experience of the Holocaust, becomes part of the personality of the one who takes on the task of telling the story.

> Literature is therefore an identity work … . The message is that otherness is our identity. Innocence filled with memory.[19]

Grzegorz Niziołek explains this process in psychoanalytic terms, stressing that "as a result of trauma, one feels one's own experience as the experience of another."[20] Langer approaches this problem from a different perspective, pointing out that the "divided self" is created in the confrontation of the accounts of former victims with the contemporary ethical system, when the witness

> instinctively realizes how uncongenial is the principle of being that he himself has expressed: "All that mattered is to remain alive." This is too primitive a morality for the society he now inhabits, hence the birth of his divided self.[21]

Functioning in alternative space–time continua and confrontation with listeners who never experienced occupation causes a shock, leading to an identity fracture.

Particularly important in Lem's trilogy is the Polish-sounding surname ending in *-ski*, which becomes an effective method of social mimicry for many survivors, both during the war and in post-war times. Apart from his name, Stefan Trzyniecki is also descended from landed gentry, and even the impoverishment of his family perfectly fits the image of his "typically Polish" background. Despite meeting the family at the funeral and the wake in the family estate, there is much to suggest that Stefan confronts the observed rituals and behaviors with a different tradition. In the opening scene of *Hospital of the Transfiguration*, during the funeral Trzyniecki looks at the open coffin and marvels at:

> the pains taken over the appearance of the corpse, the dressing of the deceased, the pillow placed under the head, the box as resistant as possible to the forces of nature. No, such actions betrayed a dark and uncomprehending faith that the dead endured, a faith in that gruesome, horrifying living existence in the narrow confines of the coffin, apparently preferable, in people's instinctive opinion, to complete annihilation and union with the earth.[22]

The awkwardness that the protagonist feels during the Roman Catholic ceremony is in harmony with his thoughts on funeral customs. Indestructible caskets symbolize a different, atypical perception of death, one that requires explanation, while in the background there are elements of Jewish rituals, such as "complete union with the earth." This fragment evokes many associations with the funerals of Jews who died of natural causes on the so-called Aryan side and were buried according to the Christian rite.

Autobiographical allusions in the trilogy are also found in the character of engineer Szymon Druk.[23] Like Druk, Stanisław Lem worked for Rohstofferfassung, a company run by Wiktor Kremin, and in 1943 hid on the so-called Aryan side. On the basis of the notes Barbara Lem made in the 1980s based on her husband's recollections,[24] supplemented with documents I found, we managed to partially reconstruct the life of the writer and his family during the occupation and clarify the dates. I quote them below, with modified syntax, indicating the sources.

After the Germans entered Lviv on July 2, 1941, the Jews, as alleged perpetrators of a communist crime in Brygidki, were rounded up, brought to prison and ordered to take out the bodies of prisoners murdered by the retreating Red Army, including Jews. Actively participating in the pogrom were Poles and Ukrainians, who pointed out Jews to the Germans.[25] Dead bodies were dragged out of the prison basement through windows and laid out on the grass. Then Lviv people approached them and identified the bodies of their loved ones. Stanisław Lem worked in the basement, and the stench of decaying corpses was so overpowering that the Germans avoided going downstairs. On the internal prison courtyard, Jews were beaten mercilessly while they were bringing out the corpses. During the beating, a German propaganda crew came with a camera and filmed both the corpses and people who were pulling them out.[26] The beating stopped for a while. The Jews who worked with the corpses were shot and new ones replaced them, rounded up into the courtyard by Ukrainian volunteers.[27] In the evening, the gates to the prison were opened and the Jews who had been detained to carry the bodies were released. In these events, 3,000 Jews were killed, although according to some sources there were up to 7,000 victims.[28] In the second pogrom, the so-called Petlura pogrom, which lasted from July 25 to 27, 1941, Stanisław Lem's uncle, Dr. Gecel (Marek) Wolner, a prominent laryngologist, was killed.[29]

After those events, Stanisław Lem spent a week in his parents' apartment waiting for his first "Aryan papers."[30] In the autumn of 1941, Stanisław Lem's parents, who lived in the ghetto, were expelled from their apartment by the Germans, and they moved in with Uncle Fryc,[31] who lived at 7 Bernsteina Street.[32] After the move, Stanisław Lem wore a white armband with a six-pointed star on his right arm,[33] as ordered by the occupiers, which seems to indicate that his Aryan papers were not entirely reliable. We do not know what name he used. After several months, Uncle Fryc and his wife were deported to the death camp in Bełżec.[34] Stanisław Lem's parents stayed in the apartment along with Seweryn Kahane, who had already lived at that address before the war. While it has not yet been possible to establish the degree of kinship between Seweryn Kahane and Stanisław Lem,[35] it is known that for some time they were hiding together, along with the so-called Viennese woman, probably Kahane's life partner. Seweryn Kahane presided over the Jewish Committee in Kielce just after the end of the war and was one of the first victims of the Kielce pogrom. He was shot in the back by the Polish uniformed services in the building on Planty Street.[36] There is only one registration card preserved in the archives of the Jewish Historical Institute, which indicates that circa 1945 he was 35 years old and, like Fryderyk Lehm, worked as a lawyer.[37] Perhaps he was the son of Uncle Fryc's second wife.

According to Rafael Blumenfeld, Seweryn Kahane came to Kielce together with a Home Army partisan unit and started working for the survivors immediately after the liberation of the city.[38] Although the matter is difficult to resolve categorically, the first scene of *Hospital of the Transfiguration*, i.e. the funeral, may refer to Kahane's death, although this intuition is based solely on one sentence, namely the remark that the coffin came from Kielce.[39]

Stanisław Lem worked as a car mechanic's assistant at Wiktor Kremin's company. Before he got that job, the Jews employed there searched the clothes brought from concentration camps for hidden valuables, which were then transported to Germany. Eliyahu Jones reports that Kremin's company was involved in the processing and disposal of all waste and its collection from garbage cans throughout the city. They were looking for glass, scrap metal and other raw materials, and workers had a special label sewn onto their clothes: the letter R (*Rohstoff* means "raw material").[40] According to Kurt I. Lewin, "The Rohstoff ID card was one of the most reliable documents and, in a way, it was honored by the Gestapo."[41] The Rohstofferfassung company had two Fiat trucks on the grounds of the Eastern Fair, used to transport old and new cars, ammunition, cannon balls, smoke bombs and anti-tank mines retrieved from under the snow. At that time Lem was contacted by an anonymous man from the underground organization (he only gave his first name) and introduced to the fundamental principles of conspiracy. Lem showed him his hiding place under the first step above the garage, where he hid mechanical parts and German avionics from Russian planes. The writer accepted an order from the conspirator to supply explosives. The intermediary came in the evenings and carried away gunpowder and flak ammunition in an old briefcase; he refused to accept bayonets, magazines for Degtyaryov machine guns and cartridge discs. In all likelihood, Kremin took money for employing Jews. Presumably, Stanisław Lem's workplace was paid for by his father through intermediaries.

In the autumn of 1941, Stanisław Lem's documents were forged, based on an authentic Armenian baptismal certificate under the name "Jan Donabidowicz." He also received a forged Kennkarte. As Donabidowicz, Lem lived (at least at first) on Zielona Street at the Podłuski family's home. It is not entirely certain whether the date is correct because according to Dawid Kahane's account from the German occupation of Lviv, "Aryan papers" did not become popular in the city until the summer of 1942. In addition, the set of documents consisted of a certificate of residence, an old Polish identity card, a special certificate of Aryan ancestry, a baptismal certificate and a registration of residence certified by the police.[42] Perhaps, then, Lem managed to purchase some of those documents; they could also have been brought from other areas of the General Government or he might not have received them until the end of 1942, which would mean that he spent over a year in the ghetto.[43] Mass escapes to the so-called Aryan side started only after the August operation.[44] At the end of 1942, all Jews were taken from the Rohstofferfassung company, so Stanisław Lem must have left earlier or was one of the handful who were transferred to the Janowska camp. He remembered that during the liquidation of the ghetto, Jews were hiding in tombs in the Janów cemetery, located near the railway station, while Germans threw grenades inside. In the autumn of the same year, Lem was unexpectedly evicted from the apartment by the person with whom he was hiding. Most probably, it was a place located near the Lychakiv cemetery.[45] Since he was not allowed into the apartment, he had to pass through the city center after curfew. Under such dramatic circumstances, he decided to go to his parents, who were initially hiding with their friend. Even before the liquidation of the ghetto, Stanisław Lem's parents moved (without him) to the house of a woman they knew and from there to an apartment near Kazimierzowska Street. They were hiding there until the end of the occupation, paying for their stay. Jones estimates that in Lviv the number of people hiding on the so-called Aryan papers did not exceed 2,000.[46]

After the Red Army re-entered Lviv, Lem's parents moved to Sykstuska Street. At the turn of 1944–1945, Stanisław Lem returned to medical studies and was accepted into the second year. At that time, he already worked as a volunteer at the Department of Normal Physiology at the Lviv Medical Institute. In a statement by the director of the department, Professor Anatol Markovich Vorobyov, we read that during his time there Lem investigated the issue of infrared radiation as an indicator of the central nervous system. He also initiated experimental research on "Potential of generating a galvanic conditional reflex in a frog."[47] He received a scholarship in the amount of 150 rubles per month for his excellent achievements in science.[48] After the end of the academic year—on June 25, 1945—when it was already certain that Lviv would not remain within the borders of Poland, the Lem family decided to leave for Krakow.[49] Expatriation took place in July 1945,[50] less than a month before the Krakow pogrom in which police and military officers participated.[51] It is estimated that one person died during that event.[52] In post-war Krakow, the safety of the Jewish population was constantly threatened; beatings, looting and murders were common; Jews were not employed; and some churches continued to spew anti-Semitic propaganda.[53]

Let us return to Lem's prose and multiple autobiographical traces. In the second volume of *Time Not Lost*, an entire chapter is devoted to Rohstofferfassung:

> The company employed almost exclusively Jews. The vast majority of them were poor people collecting waste from garbage cans, while the minority – crème de la crème of local Jewry, former merchants, factory owners, lawyers and councilors. According to their work cards, they were ragbaggers and received minimum wages, but in reality they paid Kremin for protecting them, and they paid him so lavishly that it was mostly this source that lined the director's pockets.[54]

In addition to a detailed description of the company's activities and its internal hierarchy, the part of the story devoted to episodes featuring Szymon Druk reconstructs Lem's memories of hiding in Lviv, as he indirectly mentions in his unpublished letter of April 17, 1967 to an unknown addressee:

> In the second volume … the figures of occupation-era profiteers were inspired by real people I used to know, albeit barely and from afar, in Lviv in [19]41–42. The character of Pluwak is based on a real person I hardly knew, while the tenement described in this volume is a variation on the subject of the house in which I lived for some time during the occupation ([19]43).[55]

In the novel, both Poles and Ukrainians living in the tenement blackmail the family of a Jewish lawyer, taking furniture, paintings and carpets out of his apartment.[56] In June 1941, one of the residents—Jan Pluwak, mentioned in the letter, a French teacher in a girls' grammar school (*gimnazjum*)—decided to change his name to Ivan and started collaborating with the Germans. At some point he decided to hide his pupil, a Jewish girl; there is a vague allusion that he was sexually abusing her.

At that time, the engineer Druk was sent by Zawoyski, captain of the Home Army, to the apartment of the Poprzeski family, but the latter quickly realize that they are hiding a Jew and are highly displeased about it. In Druk's room there is also a conversation between Zawojski's liaison officer, Zawieja, and the engineer in hiding, who decides to join the conspiracy. Surprised, Zawieja replies: "'But you can't. The J … no, well, the Israelites aren't … well, not at the moment. Our 'Konar' wasn't really in favor of that at all, but, uh, he, um,' he cleared his throat because they weren't allowed to talk about it."[57] This fragment sheds some light on the issues associated with the Home Army's assistance during Lem's hiding on the so-called Aryan papers, as well as on the principles of his involvement in the organization.[58] In the archives of the Holocaust Museum in Washington DC there are memoirs of a Jewish resident of Lviv who, after escaping from the ghetto and later from the Janowska camp, wanted to join the Home Army partisans. Marcel Lubash offers an account of his cooperation with Captain Kazimierz Tomasik from the Home Army. The captain agreed to accept Lubash into the organization, but given that 25 per cent of the Home Army members were anti-Semites, according to the estimates of the commander, Lubash could not work in the underground on the same principles as the rest, that is, in four-person groups, because if one of the remaining conspirators found out that he was a Jew, they could have killed him. Captain Tomasik decided that Lubash would work alone and provide information about Poles and Ukrainians collaborating with Germans.[59] In his memoirs, titled *Mój przyjaciel pesymista* [My friend the pessimist], Władysław Bartoszewski mentions that during the German occupation Lem was helped by the Home Army, or rather by his schoolmates who had joined the organization.[60] In the case of Szymon Druk, the hero of *Among the Dead*, the support from the Home Army is limited to finding him an apartment, for which he has to pay himself, and when the underground network is exposed and Zawoyski and Zawieja are arrested, Druk is left without assistance or help. After a piece of artillery hits the tenement, the engineer is thrown out of the building with the other residents and his story ends with a question from a German officer: "Bist du ein Jude?!" which determines his fate.

Between doctor Stefan Trzyniecki and engineer Szymon Druk, there is a story playing out about an accidental rescue and chances of survival. When a young Jewish man is murdered, Trzyniecki is sent to the camp in Bełżec and later transferred to Auschwitz, where he pretends to be a graphologist in front of one of the commanders, thus saving his life. Both men would have died in the historical reality, but in the novel Trzyniecki is saved by chance.

Multiple portrait—supplement

Biographical allusions distributed among several protagonists can also be found in *His Master's Voice*, if we read this science fiction novel as a *roman à clef* and take into account the writer's own interpretative guidelines in his correspondence with Michael Kandel. The explanations of Lem's novel are presented by Lem to the translator in brackets and insertions, as well as in the margins of his principal reflections on translating texts into English. In a letter from 1972, the writer explained:

> I have a lot of sympathy for Hogarth. To have no illusions is a crushing thing, so he faked this place a little. And Baloyne is a famous Polish critic and a friend of mine, who recognized himself right away …[61] There are other people enciphered there because I found it amusing. Rappaport isn't, him I invented from scratch.[62]

Hogarth, a character who neither holds any illusions nor too much trust in the world, reappears in Lem's correspondence a year later, this time in more detail: "I am an extremely cruel and unpleasant person through and through, not unlike Professor Hogarth, only I know how to contain it."[63] The accuracy of this description of the literary character is confirmed by Fredric Jameson, according to whom the narrator of *His Master's Voice* is one of the most realistic characters in Lem's prose, with considerable psychological complexity and at the same time the most repulsive of all the writer's creations.[64] The ambivalence between the sympathy for Hogarth and his recognition as the protagonist of a cruel and unpleasant character generates interesting tension, although this is not the only thing on which Lem focuses. In a letter dated January 24, 1974, the writer answered Kandel's question about how people acted in the face of death during the war. General reflections soon turned into a description of his personal circumstances, when the writer was afraid for his parents and certain that his closest family would perish during the occupation. Lem confessed that he had had little hope for survival because he had been aware of the mortality rate and pointed out that he had suffered from a kind of disability, namely an inability to self-deceive, which had had a terrible effect on his mental state at the time. As an antidote to his fear, he used two things: a weapon and poison he carried with him at all times.[65] If we project these reflections onto the protagonist of *His Master's Voice*, Hogarth's annoying penchant for constantly challenging his interlocutors, who try to see a shadow of a chance for a more successful outcome, deluding themselves with hope and looking to the future with optimism, lends this character an autobiographical quality.

Jerzy Jarzębski described *His Master's Voice* as "seemingly one of Lem's most personal books."[66] The scholar also explored scattered biographical themes in other protagonists, naming, aside from Hogarth and Rappaport, Kris Kelvin from *Solaris* and Golem. However, he did not analyze what he called "the game of masks" because he was interested in other aspects of those works.[67] Helena Eilstein, a philosopher that Lem held in high regard, considered *His Master's Voice* to be the best of the writer's books to date, and when discussing the subject of self-identification with Hogarth, she emphasized, "There is no doubt that any of the characters in his earlier books were given so much of the author's own blood."[68] And N. Katherine Hayles pointed out the importance of the novel's first chapter, which resembles a biography and plays with the generic convention.[69]

His Master's Voice was written two years after *Highcastle*, and is therefore a valuable addition to some of the themes that do not fit the theme and chronology of the memoir essay.[70] The introduction emphasized by Hayles is not only a presentation of the writer's views on his philosophy, but also an ironic game with critics of Lem's work, as the disappointed author puts down yet another biographical volume because his biographer "as if frightened by his own acumen, then returned – inconsequently – to the accepted version of me as the persistent, modest genius, and even trotted out a few of the old-standby anecdotes about me."[71] Of course, it is also the writer's own doing that readers of books about him encounter the same anecdotes over and over again, and then start to repeat them themselves, because he answered many questions about his personal life with funny stories. By the way, it is worth noting that this habit could have helped the writer and his family at a time when, in the 1960s, he was under surveillance from the security service, and informants infiltrating the Krakow branch of the Polish Writers' Union had to admit that Lem restricted his contacts to only a handful of trusted friends and close family, so it was difficult to obtain relevant information about him.[72] Let us return to Hogarth and his bitter disappointment that "remain[s] completely unknown."[73] The distress after reading yet another volume of biography ends with a fragment analyzed by Hayles, i.e. a game with the convention of a personal document, when the narrator emphasizes that he knows little about himself, "The one described, however, possesses nothing more than hypotheses on the subject of himself, hypotheses that may be of interest as the products of his mind but that do not necessarily serve as those missing pieces."[74] For this reason, the story about his participation in the Project to decode the signal from the stars is—as he puts it himself—nothing but "the story of an ant." The introduction also includes the most important declarations of worldview that allow us to identify Hogarth with the writer. From self-accusation of negative character traits and dislike of their own body, which can also be found in

Highcastle, through philosophy of chance ("I know that Chance fashioned us, put us together as we are."[75]), to the confession which he later repeats in his correspondence: "My pessimism is based on personal experience."[76] The most ironic part of the introduction to the recollections of working on the Project is writing about oneself as a genius. As Istvan Csicsery-Ronay noted in an interview with the writer, in the mid-1960s Lem's protagonists change, marking the moment when he became interested in the intellectual genius and the limits of theoretical speculation. According to the scholar, this is evident in the case of mathematicians such as Hogarth or Golem XIV. Although Csicsery-Ronay admitted that there were undoubtedly purely literary reasons for such authorial decisions, he also asked the writer whether the geniuses in his prose were not related to writing autobiography. In response, Lem pointed out that the issues raised in those works required characters who would be able to face such difficult intellectual challenges, and then modestly admitted that literary figures could be smarter than their creators.[77]

The question of searching for the author's portrayal a *roman à clef* is complicated when one considers the significance of another protagonist, one that appears in a research unit from another world and with a baggage of experience different from that of other characters. In a letter to his translator in May 1972, Lem stressed that Rappaport's character was completely invented, but in December of the same year he wrote in parentheses:

> Dr. Rappaport's adventure is *my* adventure, from Lviv 1941, after the German army entered – I was to be shot; and aside from the addition about calling out a volunteer, everything else is consistent … with the evoked fiction of reincarnation imagined *ad hoc*, I simply tried to ease my last few moments, in order, as they say, to keep a stiff upper lip in the face of death. But as you can see, it was such a clear lie to me that there was not even an attempt to call upon God's help. I mean, *Non serviam*, and nothing else.[78]

The intuition of the translator, who saw Saul Rappaport—a refugee from East-Central Europe—not only as an allusion to scientists born in the former Austro-Hungarian Empire and working in Los Alamos, but also the autobiographical background, marks out an interpretative path leading from Lem's identification with Hogarth to the projection of his own experiences of the occupation onto Rappaport, including the entry of German troops into Lviv and being forced to carry decaying corpses in Brygidki prison.

There is an inaccurate date in the novel (1942 instead of 1941), probably due to the censor's intervention, as the writer could not write that the story concerned prisoners murdered by the NKVD (The People's Commissariat for Internal Affairs; in Russian, Narodnyj komissariat wnutriennich dieł) in Lviv. During that event, the protagonist is not 19 years old, as was the case with Lem, but 30, and as the narrator emphasizes, "the Holocaust having claimed his entire family. He never spoke about it, except one evening."[79] The entire testimony is conveyed in indirect speech, so paradoxically it is not told by Rappaport himself, but by Hogarth:

> He was pulled off the street, a random pedestrian. They were shooting people in groups, in the yard of a prison recently shelled and with one wing still burning. Rappaport gave me the details of the operation very calmly. The executing itself could not be seen by those herded against the building, which heated their backs like a giant oven; the shooting was done behind a broken wall. Some of those waiting, like him, in his turn, fell into a kind of stupor; others tried to save themselves – in mad ways.
>
> He remembered a young man who, rushing up to a German gendarme, howled that he was not a Jew – but howled it in Yiddish, probably because he knew no German. Rappaport felt the insane comedy of the situation, and suddenly the most precious thing to him was to preserve to the end the integrity of his mind, which would enable him to maintain an intellectual distance from the scene around him. However, he had to find – he explained this to me objectively and slowly, as to a man from "the other side" who could not be expected to understand anything of such experiences – some value external to himself, a prop of some sort for his mind. Since that was altogether impossible, he decided to believe in reincarnation.[80]

This is probably the most complete testimony about the events of the occupation to be found in Lem's entire oeuvre. The identity split is present on the successive levels of the mediated narratives. If Hogarth is the voice of the writer and Rappaport tells him his own story, which he tries to understand already as a man on the "other side," then this is a narratively recreated situation described by Langer, who analyzed the ruins of memory and the narrative efforts of survivors to make the existential split cohesive. In this context. Hogarth and Rappaport can be seen as characters from alternative times, thus depicting the tension generated by the humiliated memory, which is "driven by the need to share its contents and its conviction of the impossibility of doing so."[81] Hogarth is a recognized genius of high esteem, respected by scientists and open to other disciplines, expert in science and philosophy, and his wartime experience remains unknown. Rappaport, on the other hand, is a victim of wartime violence, trapped in the past, telling emotionlessly and in great detail the story of what he had witnessed and experienced. Describing this mechanism of contaminated memory, Langer uses the term "impromptu self," which

> emerged from the camp situation [and] does not continue to evolve and adapt beyond its perimeters. It loses its raison d'être with the moment of so-called liberation, though as we have seen, it lingers in consciousness as an orphaned incubus long after its apparent demise.[82]

Also revealed in the quoted fragment of the novel is the typical mistrust of the former victim concerning the possibility of conveying the horror of that time and the feelings accompanying the confrontation with inevitable death, a form of "uncompensating recall,"[83] one that does not bring relief. The same uncertainty is found in the story of a Jew who shouts to a German gendarme in Yiddish that he is not a Jew. The "insane comedy" evoked by the protagonist is meant to save Rappaport himself from paralyzing fear, because such gallows humor did not so much reduce the experienced horrors as reduce them subjectively, requiring a different perspective, and thus a kind of escape from the execution site. Therefore, it was an attempt to see events that could not be emotionally assimilated from the perspective of someone else.[84]

The horrific scenes of beatings, torture and mutilation of fellow prisoners are rationalized by Rappaport, whose story is told by Hogarth:

> In that moment Rappaport understood even this: the subordinates had to behave that way; they were hiding from the victims in the hatred of them, but the hatred could not be produced in themselves except through acts of brutality. They had to batter the Jews with their rifle butts; blood had to flow from lacerated heads and crust upon faces, because it made the faces hideous, inhuman, and in this way – I am quoting Rappaport – there did not appear, in what was done, a gap through which horror might peer, or compassion.[85]

The blurring of the similarity between the perpetrators and the victims is therefore necessary to carry out a war crime. The exposed vulnerability of the body and its susceptibility to injury can, as Judith Butler emphasizes, awaken a sense of common destiny and compassion.[86] Humiliated, massacred bodies, faces devoid of individual features, become only objects, objects to be eliminated. In this fragment the narrative frame is also clearly outlined. The phrase "I am quoting Rappaport" serves to create a distance from the story, but also from the one who experienced this violence. The identity split, the separation from the victims and the third-person narration seem to be a necessary condition for telling the story at all. Analyzing the tension between autobiographical confession and literary fiction, Andrzej Zieniewicz stressed that

> authors need the literary nature of representation, in the sense of invention, because it is only with literary tools that the torn historical substance of biography and pre-biography can be reinforced; this is what is needed to create the mass that archaeologists use to fill in the missing chunks in the reconstructed vessels (from the era before they were broken).[87]

The commander of the firing squad, the personification of the Nazi New Man, occupies a separate place in the reported history of Rappaport:

> But the young deity in the silver-braided uniform required neither these nor any other contrivances to act perfectly. He stood in a slightly elevated

> place, the white handkerchief applied to his nose with a movement that had something in it of the refined duelist. He was the master of the house and the commander, in one person. In the air floated flakes of ash, driven by the heat that pulsed from the fire; behind the thick walls, through the grated windows without panes, flames roared, but not a single ash fell on the officer or on his white handkerchief.[88]

Amidst decaying corpses, burnt bodies, beaten and murdered Jews forced to carry the dead, the impeccable uniform evokes respect even among the victims, but at the same time the figure of the commander seems unrealistic. Just as in the scene from *Hospital of the Transfiguration*, where the trembling Stefan Trzyniecki is confronted with a German commander who glares at him menacingly, the feelings of victims murdered by elegant soldiers are depicted. The commander did not need to torture prisoners because he had deeply internalized the belief in the inhuman status of the murdered Jews:

> He knew that we comprehended human speech but that nevertheless we were not human; he knew this quite well. Therefore, even if he had wanted to explain things to us, he could not have. The man could do with us what he liked, but he could not enter into negotiations, because for negotiation you must have a party in at least some respect equal to the party who initiates it, and in that yard there were only he and his men. A logical contradiction, yes, but he acted exactly according to that contradiction, and scrupulously. The simpler ones among his men did not possess this higher knowledge; the appearance of humanity given by our bodies, our two legs, faces, hands, eyes, that appearance deterred them a little from their duty; thus, they had to butcher those bodies, to make them unlike people's. … This sort of explanation is usually received metaphorically, as a kind of fable, but it is completely literal.[89]

The war is based, as Butler proves, on depriving an entire population of its human status. The victims of the lost potential for mourning cannot be destroyed because they had already been lost ontologically, so if they are killed, "[their] loss is no loss."[90]

The unexpectedly smooth execution is interrupted:

> In the presence of such perfection, Rappaport managed to forget about himself, when suddenly the gate opened and in drove a film crew. Various orders were given in German, and the gunshots immediately ceased. Rappaport did not know then – or later, when he told me this – what had happened. Perhaps the Germans intended to film a pile of corpses, to use the footage in a newsreel depicting the enemy's actions (this took place near the Eastern Front). The slain Jews would be shown as the victims of the Bolsheviks. That may have been the case; Rappaport, however, offered no interpretation; he only related what he saw.[91]

Rappaport's objective description includes not only accounts of the recording of a propaganda film, but also political allusions, clear to those in the know. Undoubtedly, the arrival of the film crew was linked to Rappaport's survival, as it interrupted the slaughter, deemed unsuitable for the propaganda film—media representations of warfare do not serve to document one's own crimes. At the same time, Lem included two historical narratives that should not have appeared in the Eastern Bloc in the 1960s. The piles of corpses in the film were victims of the NKVD, and some of the victims of brutal Soviet murders were Jews, although German propaganda, using Ukrainians and Poles, produced a story about the responsibility of Jewish residents for the death of political prisoners. Since several thousand Jews died in the Brygidki pogrom, it cannot be ruled out that they were shown in the film as victims of the Bolsheviks. As Gabriele Lesser emphasizes, the prison operation in Lviv was extremely brutal, even against the background of the 35 other pogroms that accompanied the entry of German troops into Eastern Galicia:

> Film shots of the bloody pogroms on "Bolshevik Jews" were featured in German film chronicles, some of them also in the General Government. The aim of those films was to confirm and reinforce existing prejudices against "Jewish-Bolshevik criminals."[92]

Although NKVD officers were responsible for the crimes in Brygidki, and the discovery of the bodies of prisoners was followed by the murder of randomly captured Jewish residents of Lviv, the propaganda film blamed the Jews for all the crimes, and all that was meant to reinforce the conviction of their inhuman brutality.

Then, the filmed victims of torture, waiting in line to face the firing squad, were unexpectedly released:

> It was dusk when the large gate was set ajar and, staggering in the cold evening air, the group of those left alive ran out into the empty street.
>
> They dared not flee at first, but no one showed any interest in them. Why, Rappaport could not say. He did not attempt to analyze what the Germans did; they were like fate, which one did not have to explain.[93]

Thus, the deliverance does not bring them joy, but marks them with a paralyzing certainty that their lives depend on the whim of others and that their rescue was decided by "blind chance." This mechanism was explained by Butler, who stressed that war involves creating and distributing precarity, and that it introduces fear into everyday life, sometimes killing members of a population whose lives have been written off, and sometimes letting them live. In the introduction to her book *Frames of War*, she argues that in conditions of precarity, life does not need to be wiped from the face of the earth, as violence has already made a lasting and profound impact.[94] When faced with such forces, one begins to believe that ethical norms are insignificant and that social bonds are unstable.

The ghetto

The chapter of the novel *Among the Dead* from the *Time Not Lost* trilogy, entitled "Bukiet astrów" [A bouquet of asters], recounts the situation of the Lviv ghetto, a place that disappeared from the map of Lviv after the liquidation, and later, as a result of the historical policy of the People's Republic of Poland, vanished from the Polish collective memory. There is no point looking for the ghetto in the Ukrainian or Soviet memory either.[95] In Lem's novel, activists of the communist underground organization listen to a girl who summarizes the occupant's orders to create a Jewish district, talks about liquidations, cites the numbers of those imprisoned and killed and reports how much the ghetto inhabitants know about death camps. In this fragment, the protagonist harshly criticizes the attitude of Judenrat as an institution that "satisfies all the cravings of Germans demanding old silverware, valuables, paintings, antiques."[96] The girl describes how grenades made of burnt-out light bulbs are constructed in the ghetto, in preparation for an armed uprising.[97] Another chapter mentions the fact that the uprising did indeed break out, but it only lasted two days because the Germans set fire to that part of the city.[98] When reporting to his party colleagues,

> Wieleniecki said that after the fighting stopped, many people went to the ghetto area when the cordons were removed, but there was nothing to see there. There's nothing left. No houses, no streets. Even the rubble was almost gone. The buildings, mostly wooden, burnt down, the foundations were demolished by landmines. They're all dead.[99]

The final liquidation of Julag, a labor camp organized as a secondary ghetto, began in June 1943. Statistical data provided to the superiors by the SS and police commander Frederick Katzmann indicate that even though 12,000 people were registered in the ghetto at that time, about 8,000 more were hiding in various holes and bunkers. While the Germans searched the ghetto grounds, almost 3,000 corpses of people who had committed suicide by swallowing poison were found in basements. Katzmann also had to submit a report on the losses on the German side, according to which Jews shot seven German soldiers, stabbed one and wounded twelve; two soldiers went missing and five more suffered grave injuries.[100] The protagonist of *Time Not Lost*, while unaware of such statistical data, stresses that the ghetto inhabitants were killed in a fight, not murdered, pointing to the forgotten uprising, rarely mentioned in historical documents, as well as the armed resistance of the residents of Lviv, who were burned alive. Later, the communist activists reminisce about the Treblinka Uprising, which is said to have been stirred up by one of the heroes of the Lviv Ghetto Uprising. Particularly interesting in that fragment is the heroization of the Jewish suffering, a story of resistance by Jewish fighters that is rarely encountered in literature, although it is worth remembering that in the late 1940s the policy of the new authorities focused on emphasizing the importance of the resistance movement associated with communists, thus avoiding the problem of showing the real suffering and humiliation experienced by the victims.[101]

Lem would later employ a different tone to describe the ghetto in the final part of *Highcastle*, written in the mid-1960s:

> It is amazing that I am at all able, straining against the current of time with my memory, to restore innocence to such words as Janów, Zniesienie, Piaski, Łąckiego, to which the years 1941 and 1942 gave such evil meaning, when the streets from Bernstein's and past the theater, toward Słoneczna and beyond, one day were empty, silent, their windows open and curtains moving in the wind. The walls, courtyards, balconies – deserted, and in the distance appeared, then disappeared, the wooden fence of the ghetto. I saw the far, scattered buildings outside the city, then only rubble overgrown with grass.[102]

In the autobiographical essay, the ghetto is mentioned only on the margins of the story about the late 1930s and the grotesque (in hindsight) military training for secondary-school students in case of an armed conflict. The fragment hidden in the story of childhood and adolescence reconstructs the topography from before the catastrophe of the occupation, with Bernsteina Street, where his Uncle Fryc lived, the Jewish theater and the market square, as well as places associated with the Steinhaus Milling Machine factory before the war, which would soon become synonymous with execution and burial (Janów and a nearby sandy ravine). Just as in the chapter of *Among the Dead*, the Jewish district designated by the Germans is emptied of its inhabitants, who were deported to a death camp. What is characteristic about Lem's narrative is the breakdown of the sensual experience of the Holocaust into images, smells and sounds.[103] The descriptions of the ghetto's appearance are not accompanied by a cacophony of sounds and the smoke of fire; just as in several other novels, desperate cries for help and the groans of the dying come from behind the walls, and there is a cloying smell hanging in the air.

The depiction of the subsequent fate of people deported from the ghetto appears in the trilogy—in the last part titled *Return*—as a report of a participant in events who tries to face the images of thousands of people walking towards the "bathhouse." Stefan Trzyniecki tells Anna that:

> those who were led straight from the ramp to the furnace had only one way to manifest their humanity, namely their stench. What can a hero do in a naked crowd led to a slaughter? Thousands of shaved heads, one next to the other, like dirty eggs. They went up in smoke, and I saved one man.[104]

Underpinning this fragment is also the theme of courage and resistance—thanks to the position in the camp—against German orders, although at the same time it resonates with the feeling of disgust, nausea caused by the repulsive stench of maltreated bodies, dirt and the sweet, suffocating smoke. Stefan's confession harmonizes with the letter Lem sent to the editorial office of the magazine *Tygodnik Powszechny* in 1948, criticizing the enthusiastic reviews of the film directed by Wanda Jakubowska. The writer pointed out that the plot of the film says more about political struggle and war taking place in the background of camp reality than about the life of an individual there or about the difficulties of survival and death. After sharing many critical comments on how to construct the plot, Lem emphasizes:

> I admit that during the film I felt my throat close twice: the first time when the train with a transport of Jews arrived, and the second – when I saw the faces of old women standing silently in a row. In silence. It was those infinite masks of torment that gave me a taste of *catharsis*, not the scene of burning the camp doctor with a red-hot iron.[105]

Perhaps this fragment of the film inspired the image of old women waiting in silence to be transported to a death camp that I described earlier. Lem adds that the camp in Auschwitz has yet to have a real portrayal on film, and as an example of an adequate approach to the subject of the camp, he points to Tadeusz Borowski's short stories.[106] Borowski's works would also serve as a point of reference for Lem 20 years later, when in a letter to the translator he stressed that the addressee should read the prose of the author of *Kamienny Świat* [A world of stone], and intertwined the story presented in his short stories with the autobiographical theme:

> With the exception of my parents, my whole family was killed by the Germans (mainly gas – death camps). And so I think it is our DUTY to read Borowski. I have never visited the museum in Auschwitz, nor do I intend to – I know all that firsthand. But Borowski – well, that is a must.[107]

The murder of his family and the rescue of his parents were rarely the subject of the writer's reflections, although there is no doubt that throughout his life, the most important figure for him was his father.

Father

Commentators on Stanisław Lem's prose agree that for him, chance was one of the most important subjects. Philosophy of chance, probability calculation and statistics not only determined the cognitive horizons of the author's entire oeuvre, but also had a significant impact on the structure of his novels and short stories, dismantling narrative patterns and literary conventions. Undoubtedly, the disruption of the cause-and-effect principle of the plot determines its attractiveness, and sudden turns make it possible to expand the field of activity of the protagonists, which, of course, is quite important in science fiction prose. Lem often spoke as a literary critic, and in his reviews he also referred to popular literature, pointing out the simplifications and patterns that enable mass production of such type of works. *The Chain of Chance*, *The Investigation* or *Skonocony kryminał* [A botched crime story] are attempts to go beyond the limitations of the crime story convention and break down its central characteristic, namely the cause-and-effect principle. In his 1960 column *O powieści kryminalnej* [On crime fiction], Lem criticized the assumption underlying the plot structure of novels about a murder investigation, in which a meticulously planned crime can be carried out without disruption. The writer pointed out that novels of this type do not take into account the fact that people's plans are rarely fully realized because the outside world constantly averts them, modifies them and prevents them from being executed, largely due to "blind chance."[108] After analyzing the Sherlock Holmes series and Chandler's detective stories, the writer cites the following example:

> The Occupation, for example, gave a large number of people in Poland (too large ...) an opportunity to experience such moments, whether as future victims or conspirators .... Anyone who has been in a similar situation knows from their own experience how seemingly clear situations (I am talking about their structure, not about the horror) can be made vague, or even turned upside down by some insignificant blind chance: a quarrel in the background distracts a German officer in charge of shootings for a second or two, but by that time the one who was meant to be next has already passed the critical point of the execution line; someone wants some cold borscht, goes home from the basement during an air raid – and survives, while the whole family are killed after the shelter collapses in a grenade explosion .... In eschatological situations, the immanent, so to speak, tragicomic nature of human fate likes to manifest itself.[109]

Unexpectedly, the column about crime fiction transforms into a story about the occupation, accidental survivors and unsuccessful conspiracy operations, and ends with a point about tragicomic fate of people in the face of final situations. When these conclusions are applied to the plots of Lem's fiction, one can see the trajectories of random coincidences, minor failures and physical imperfections that make up the adventures of the protagonists he created. The tragic comedy of their exploits concerns carnality and materiality, because in comedy terms it is the body that becomes indestructible, not universal values: "In comedy, the fact of survival," Grzegorz Niziołek emphasizes, "becomes not so much an object of affirmation as a cause and, at the same time, object of merciless ridicule."[110] In his reply to Kandel's question about the writer's worldview, Lem reflected on the translator's suggestions:

> Nihilism? In my books? You may have some secret point there. I would call it – futility … caring about the decor, which seemingly contradicts it. To say horrible things innocently enough, as if playing and offering even seemingly unsophisticated "jests."[111]

Thus, jokes and japes conceal the vanity of human actions caused by the unpredictability of fate.

In Lem's prose, more or less fortunate coincidences are interlinked with traces of the writer's autobiography and the fate of his family. The accidental saving of his father from being shot during the Great War and the equally unlikely deliverance of his family during the occupation lend Lem's philosophy of chance an existential quality. One of the principal examples of the use and transformation of these themes is the review of a non-existent book, published in the volume *A Perfect Vacuum* and titled *Cezar Kouska: "De Impossibilitate Vitae"; "De Impossibilitate Prognoscendi."* The fictional book is devoted to coincidences that make the birth of Benedict Kouska possible. In contrast to mythical stories, it is not the miraculous signs that herald the birth of the hero; the life of the protagonist of the invented book is constantly hanging by a thread because it is the result of a coincidence and consequences of some ill-advised decisions of his future parents, who may not have liked each other or survived World War One. The story of how the author of the fictional book was born contains some important details from Lem's own life, including a family anecdote about a chance meeting of his parents and about his father being drafted to the Austrian army as a doctor during the Great War. The way to their marriage was paved by random incidents, mainly including the diseases of other candidates, such as rheumatism, indigestion, whooping cough and hernia, which robs this digressive narrative of its romantic atmosphere. Irony of fate and tragicomic mood are the main themes of this pseudo-biographical story about a family tree, inspired by Samuel Lehm's story[112] about how he was about to be shot by a Russian soldier at the end of the war, but a hairdresser he knew, who happened to be passing by, saved him from execution.[113]

The father of the author of *The Star Diaries* was the prototype of several characters in Stanisław's prose. Unlike Lem's mother, who, it seems, never understood her son's life choices, including his desire to become a writer,[114] his father was a constant point of reference in Lem's reflections on the past, medicine and ethics. At the same time, biographical information about his father offers an insight into the life of Stanisław Lem before the war and during the occupation. Samuel Lehm attended the Imperial-Royal Fourth Grammar School in Lviv, where the language of instruction was Polish.[115] He then studied at the Medical Faculty of the University of Lviv and graduated at the age of 30 in 1909. In 1912 he took up the position of assistant in an otolaryngological clinic. Initially he practiced medicine at 14 Rzeźnicka Street, where he lived together with his father, Hersz Nussen Lehm,[116] and his mother Sara Lea (nee Bick).[117] The Chief Rabbi of Lviv also lived on the same street as the Lehm family. Hersz Lehm was a *senzal*, or a broker, and had eight children: Józef (b. ca. 1862), Chaje (b. 1863), Elke (b. 1866),[118] Frojem or Efrain (b. 1869),[119] Basche (b. 1872),[120] Mechcie (b. 1877), Samuel (b. November 1, 1879) and Anna (b. 1884).[121] In *Highcastle*, we find scarce traces of family contacts, namely anecdotes about Uncle Fryc, Uncle Mudek or the husband of Aunt Hania (Chaje? Anna?), an aunt living on Jagiellońska Street, or cousins Mietek and Stefan. Lviv birth records transported to Poland are cataloged according to birth dates, so it is extremely difficult to carry out genealogical research and determine how many people from Lem's family lived in Lviv before the war. The only anecdote about the future writer's father's side of the family concerns some unknown relative. In a letter to Kandel, Stanisław Lem recounted the following story:

> As a medical student and then as a novice writer, I often told my wife that I expected a letter from a notary from the US, notifying me of an enormous inheritance, because some time ago, even before the last world war, a distant relative (who disgraced my father's family), was given a ship card and sent off to the States – and since he was a piece of work, he must have made a fortune there ... For years I would repeat this joke so often ... it was almost an obsession.[122]

Little is known about the fate of Samuel Lehm's family members, with the possible exception of Jan Marian Hescheles's cousin, Marian Hemar,[123] whom the writer himself saw only once in his life, when he was a teenager and Hemar visited his parents in the company of Hanna Ordonówna.[124] I have cited the names of Stanisław Lem's relatives also in order to demonstrate the scale of the tragedy that struck his loved ones. Even if Lem's parents did not stay in touch with all of his father's siblings, information about their fate must have become particularly important during the occupation, especially since most of them and their children were likely sent to the ghetto in Lviv or its vicinity. After all, Lem wrote in *Highcastle* that he had not experienced the death of close relatives before the war.

The manuscript of the biography of Dr. Samuel Lehm, written up by him after the war and attached to his job application, contains the information that his mother Salomea Lehm died in 1920 and his father Herman died a year later, that is in the same year Stanisław Lem was born (he was given his middle name after his grandfather). According to Samuel Lehm, his brother Józef died of natural causes in Lviv in 1941 at the age of 79, while Fryderyk was murdered by the Germans in 1942.[125] Berta Hescheles née Lehm was murdered in 1941 during a German operation against the elderly.[126] The fate of the rest of the family remains unknown.

Stanisław Lem's parents got married on May 30, 1919, in Lviv. The witnesses to the wedding of Samuel Lehm and Sabina Wolner (born on October 15, 1892) were Izak Enser and Paul Buxdorf, and the ceremony was officiated by Samuel Guttman, rabbi of the progressive synagogue (Tempel).[127] Two years later, on September 12, Stanisław Herman Lem was born. The baby was delivered by

Erna Baronowa, a midwife.[128] Benjamin Lehm, probably the brother of the deceased grandfather, became the spiritual mentor of the child.[129] The apartment on 4 Brajerowska Street did not belong to the Lem family;[130] it is uncertain when exactly they moved to that address, but it must have been associated with the opening of the doctor's private laryngological practice.

Samuel Lehm belonged to a generation that chose to assimilate with Polishness. After 1880, Jewish residents of Lviv changed their previous tendency to educate children in religious or German schools. By the end of the nineteenth century, most Jewish students attended Polish schools. Assimilation meant leaving behind those aspects of Jewish life that did not fit with the spirit of modernity, and it involved a critical attitude towards religious schools (*cheders*), ridicule towards Hasidism and disregard for the Yiddish language. Only the growth of nationalist moods among Poles, their distrust of the Jewish residents of the city and pogroms that followed the regaining of Polish independence interrupted that assimilation process. The void left after pro-assimilation tendencies were quashed under the pressure of the anti-Semitic movement was filled with Zionism.[131] Larry Wolff offers a different explanation of the shift towards Zionism, highlighting the legal problem associated with the 1867 constitution in the Habsburg state, which was meant to protect the political rights of every nation. Constitutionalists at that time were contemplating whether Jews should be considered a nation:

> Since nationality was determined by language, and since the Habsburg census carried out every ten years did not include Yiddish, Jews often chose the Polish language. This helped to build a vision of the Polish majority in Galicia – a fictional one, although there was, of course, a Polish-language Jewish newspaper, *Ojczyzna* [Homeland], which in the 1880s called on Galician Jews to assimilate culturally with Poles. However, in a political system based on political competition between different national groups, Galician Jews ultimately had to take an interest in Jewish nationalism.[132]

It is significant that most Zionist documents and studies in that area were published in the Polish language because the movement was not initiated by Jews from traditional communities, but by a generation that had undergone Polish assimilation.[133] The generation growing up before World War One remembered vividly the prosperous period of the Austro-Hungarian monarchy, but following the war—according to Timothy Snyder—"would not enjoy comparable levels of prosperity during the rest of their lives."[134]

The few surviving documents indicate that the post-war years were difficult for the young doctor and his family, and it was only his private medical practice that afforded them a better standard of living. In the inter-war period, Samuel Lehm supported the Jewish populace of Lviv and took an active part in its life, including supporting the Jewish community with generous donations.[135] Together with his brother Fryderyk, he was also a member of the Society of Rygorozants (founded in 1868), the aim of which was to help Jewish youth gain higher education through material and organizational support (among other things, the Society maintained a Jewish students' dormitory).[136] Lehm did not teach at the university; in 1912 he was an assistant at the otolaryngological outpatient clinic in Lviv and worked with Professor Antoni Jurasz.[137] As an assistant, he earned little, and most of his salary in the inter-war period was the "cost-of-living allowance." The young doctor must have been struggling at the time, as evidenced by the fact that he applied for (and received) a loan.[138]

Apart from his medical practice, Samuel Lehm was involved in research and took an active part in the Lviv Otolaryngological Society, where he presented cases of upper respiratory tract pathologies, namely congenital laryngeal defects, and was particularly interested in rhinoscleroma, a condition endemic to the region of Volhynia and Białystok. Rhinoscleroma is a chronic disease with a very severe prognosis, leading to facial deformities.[139] Often the only procedure that made it possible for patients to breathe was a tracheotomy. Since the bacterial etiology of this disease had not been yet discovered, Lehm, together with Marian Panchyshyn, tried to treat it with X-rays (initially it was believed that rhinoscleroma was caused by cancer).[140] The acquaintance with Panchyshyn sheds light on the complicated social relations in Lviv in the years following the Great War. Panchyshyn was a member of the Ukrainian patriotic intelligentsia; he became dean of the Faculty of Medicine at the Secret Ukrainian University,[141] and after the Polish rule was consolidated, he called for peaceful coexistence and collaborated with Polish and Jewish doctors. At the same time, he secretly organized a Ukrainian underground university when students of Ukrainian descent were refused admission to the medical faculties in Lviv as a measure of retaliation for the civil war in 1918–1919.[142]

In 1937, Samuel Lehm was diagnosed with heart disease (*angina pectoris*). During the occupation, he escaped from the ghetto together with his family and hid on the so-called Aryan side. On July 17, 1945, the Lems were displaced from Lviv and decided to settle in Krakow. Despite his advanced age, heart disease and several years of starvation, Lem's father took up a job in a hospital and supported the whole family.[143] In May 1946, Lehm applied for financial assistance to the Society for the Protection of Jewish Health (also known under the acronym TOZ), which operated as part of the Central Committee of Polish Jews. The aid was addressed to doctors, as well as widows and orphaned children of doctors, who were unable to work.[144] In the questionnaire, Samuel Lehm wrote that before the war he had been a *primarius* at a Jewish hospital and a long-time member of the TOZ. The granted funds were to be used for the purchase of medical equipment, clothes and linens. In his application he wrote that he was living with his family in a single room, and during the war he had lost his life's work.[145] The aid was granted to the Lem family because of the doctor's poor health, which prevented him from taking up employment.

His health was deteriorating year by year, so he took more and more time off, and it is evident from his test results and the opinions of doctors that neither his heart nor the consequences of starvation during the occupation could be cured.

In an unpublished letter to Professor Władysław Kapuściński, Stanisław Lem reminisced about the life of his family after their expatriation to Krakow:

> My father worked in a hospital until the last day of his life – in the morning of that day he was in the infirmary as usual, I bought him some figs, they had just appeared in shops, and I went to my wife … and there I got a phone call: he died suddenly, he went to send a letter to the post office – right next to our house at that time. By the way, Father had been given a "hard" diagnosis of *angina pectoris* in 1937, after that, he smoked "Egyptian" cigarettes, lighter on nicotine, always carried nitroglycerine on his person and was told to avoid intense emotions (occupation, however …).[146]

He died in 1954.

Maria Orwid remembered Lem's father as a distinguished gentleman transferred to post-war Krakow from another era: "I remember perfectly well that Lem senior was a wonderful gentleman from the Young Poland era, with a black *fontange* on his shirt."[147] Similar information can be found in *Highcastle*: "My father's tie was soft in texture and black in color; it looked like a sash and was tied like an ascot."[148] The *fontange* was worn instead of a tie at the turn of the nineteenth and twentieth centuries, so in the mid-1940s, after two wars, it must have seemed astonishing to the young woman, who was planning to emigrate to Israel at the time. This incongruity of Samuel Lehm's way of life is most likely described in *Return*, the third part of *Time Not Lost*:

> The father, whose best years had been anchored in the Austro-Hungarian monarchy years and who sipped coffee every morning from a mug decorated with Franz Joseph's sideburns, understood nothing, nothing at all. He looked at Stefan with reproach whenever there seemed to be the slightest trace of approval for the changes taking place in Poland in his words.[149]

The figure of the father is a recurring theme in Lem's prose, both in old, wise doctors and in people suffering from *angina pectoris*; the writer also dedicated *Hospital of the Transfiguration* to him. At the very beginning of the novel, Stefan Trzyniecki's father gives his son incomprehensible advice, and the protagonist puts it down to the elderly gentleman's quirks:

> What was and is gone, it is no more, as if it never was at all. It's like a cake you ate yesterday, you've nothing left of it. That is why you can make a past that you did not have, if you only believe in it, it will be as if you've really lived it.[150]

This sentence reflects the emotional state of resettlers and survivors in the years immediately after the war, when nobody was interested in their experiences from the occupation era (e.g. Maria Orwid emphasized that the subject was never discussed after the war), and there were constant pogroms, looting and violence.

The image of the father is also sent into the space of the Solar Ocean, when Kelvin is persuaded to transmit his own brain waves in order to try to make contact with the mysterious alien. Although his colleagues urge him to think about the sublime things, hopes and efforts of humanity, the protagonist first evokes affection for his deceased wife and then thinks about the tragically deceased Giese,[151] "the father of the Solarist studies and the Solarists":

> I was not visualizing the nauseating mud-eruption which had swallowed up the gold-rimmed spectacles and carefully brushed moustache. I was seeing the engraving on the title-page of his classic work, and the close-hatched strokes against which the artist had made his head stand out – so like my father's, that head, not in its I features but in its expression of old-fashioned wisdom and honesty, that I was finally no longer able to tell which of them was looking at me. … I momentarily forgot the Station …. Recent memories were obliterated by the overwhelming conviction that these two men, my father and Giese, nothing but ashes now, had once faced up to the totality of their existence, and this conviction afforded a profound calm which annihilated the formless assembly clustered around the grey arena in the expectation of my defeat.[152]

The specter of the father's figure does not evoke fear and is linked to a sense of stability and "reliability" of the world; it guarantees safety, but also reminds us of death. Lem was writing *Solaris* convinced that he would die soon. In 1974, he wrote to Kandel:

> I have died twice in my life – once a long time ago, when I was to be squashed like a cockroach – during the German occupation – and the second time circa 1960. That second period was more important. At that time I suffered ailments which, according to the best medical knowledge, are caused by coronary artery disease (*angina pectoris*).[153]

Traces of the symptoms of this disease appear in the novel itself: "As though from a distance, I heard the beating of my heart. I summoned up all my remaining strength, straining every nerve, and waited for death. I went on waiting …";[154] "I dropped off several times after that, and each time an anguished start jolted me awake. Panting, exhausted, I pressed myself closer to her; my heart gradually growing calmer";[155] "I woke up, and drew down great gulps of air."[156] The spirit of the father, who died of the same disease, fills the melancholic interior of the space station, and the feelings for him conveyed to the Solaris ocean will save the protagonists from phantoms.

In the autobiographical *Highcastle*, the figure of Samuel Lehm returns in dreams, hidden in the deepest layers of memory, which—as the narrator emphasizes—sparingly and defiantly suggests images from the past and retains them in several frames:

> While writing this book, between one rainy Zakopane day and another, I dreamed of my father. Not indistinct and of indeterminate age, as I see him when I am awake, but in a specific moment, alive. I saw his gray eyes behind his glasses, eyes not yet weary, and the trimmed mustache and small beard, and his hands with short fingernails – the always scrubbed hands of a doctor – and his gold ring grown thinner with wear. The folds of his vest, the coat pulled a little to the right by the weight of the laryngologist's mirror. … All this is inside me, an inaccessible host of memories, sequences of minutes, hours, days, weeks, years – and nothing can enter there except dream, whose movement I have no control over. Stryjski Park is in there somewhere, all in snow, and my father walking on a path between dark trees, his freezing hands in the pockets of his overcoat, while I, on skis for the first time, can hardly move y legs, imagining myself a king of infinite space.[157]

Writing down memories triggers images from the past, returning, even though the world and the people who inhabit it are gone and will never return. The only place of their residence turns out to be the memory of the writer, and even he does not have full access to it. The care of the father and his constant presence by his son's side are invoked in the essay repeatedly, although time blurs the features of his face. Father figures in Lem's prose become guides for several protagonists; they are also among the few characters that are not ridiculed. In *Highcastle*, self-depreciation affects only the narrator, teachers and colleagues, and the ironic distance and grotesque of individual characters do not concern the father. This principle is extended to all fiction and father figures that feature there.

Angina pectoris and a doctor from another era

In the works written before Samuel Lehm's death, fear of coronary heart disease is a fixed feature. In the first part of *Time Not Lost*, Stefan Trzyniecki's father suffers from breathing problems, and his son, alarmed by his aunt, comes to the city to see what the prospects are of healing his heart, and meets his father's doctor:

> Doctor Marcinkiewicz had an office of glass and white walls. There was a Solux lamp and three quartz ones, whose presence may have been connected with the resettlement of Jewish doctors in the ghetto. Every third word he said to Stefan was "Doctor," but Stefan felt nevertheless that he was not being taken seriously. Their dislike was mutual. Marcinkiewicz gave Stefan an unadorned description of his father's condition: really just a simple case of angina pectoris, except that the pain was weak and not radiating. The changes in coronary circulation, however, were bad news, as

> bad as could be. He unrolled an electrocardiogram on the polished desktop and began explaining it, but Stefan interrupted him angrily.[158]

Trzyniecki's father in *Hospital of the Transfiguration* resembles the mad patriarch-inventor from *Cinnamon Shops* by Bruno Schulz, absorbed by subsequent manias, and not a sensible doctor like Samuel Lehm, whose views are more like those of his uncle Ksawery (this applies especially to the attitude of his uncle in the second part of the trilogy and his concern for Stefan's fate). In the quoted fragment, chances for a cure are slim, and there is an allusion to the property of Jewish doctors being seized by their Polish colleagues.

Doctor Machewicz from the third part of the trilogy, who works with Stefan in a gynecological hospital, also suffers from ischemia of the heart. In the book, written in 1950, there is a scene when Machewicz suddenly leaves the operating theater to take medication and stop an attack of dyspnea and pain.[159] The dramatic description of the attack and the anecdote about the doctor who, despite being unable to breathe, did not interrupt the operation, indicates an acute fear for the health of the author's father, also working in a hospital. At the same time, the novel stresses the gap between pre-war doctors and the new generation of physicians employed in state institutions. Doctors working in the hospital in the second half of the 1940s are incompetent, career- and profit-oriented, they drink on duty and molest nurses. It is only at the end of the novel, on the last pages, that the situation changes—most likely a result of the censor's intervention—and the positions are taken over by new doctors, who cooperate with the party and are full of good intentions.

The theme of an old doctor who does not fit in with the new times returns in other novels. For example, one of the most interesting characters in *Return from the Stars* is a doctor who turns out to be both a historian and a very old man. Bregg is referred to him because he specializes in the history of space medicine, so he is the only one who knows the secrets of the body and the condition of a human being experiencing Einstein's space–time paradox:

> Soon the doctor entered. He looked as though he had stepped out of a family portrait in my father's study. He was short but not slight, gray-haired; he wore a tiny white beard and gold-rimmed glasses – the first glasses I had seen on a human face since I landed. His name was Dr. Juffon.[160]

It is to this doctor that Bregg tells the story of his lost companions and explains that his return cannot be associated with heroism, because by losing subsequent colleagues, the participants of the expedition become

> a group of mortally frightened, desperate animals. ... Each saved himself the best way he knew how. Think about it, doctor. Here I sit before you. I've rented myself a villa, I've bought an old car; I want to learn, read, swim; but I have all that inside me. That space, that silence, and

> how Venturi cried for help, and I, instead of saving him, went into full reverse![161]

The visit, which was supposed to concern the protagonist's state of health, suddenly turns into a therapy session. If *Return from the Stars* is to be read as a novel about the so-called "small stabilization," then the peaceful and carefree existence presented there is constantly haunted by the nightmare of the Holocaust. The dialogue with the doctor is at the same time a conversation with a historian, with a person who remembers the past and can imagine the scale of Hal Bregg's personal losses. "In spite of efforts to escape it," stresses the researcher of the ruins of memory, "this corrosive reality retains a contemporary as well as a contemporaneous thrust. The fate of the 'others' clings tenaciously to the present, harassing efforts to reestablish a normal identity for those who have survived the disaster."[162] During the protagonist's conversation with the doctor, there is a subtle autobiographical allusion because Bregg states that he is 40 years old, but the physician explains to him that he can subtract a year due to the hibernation, and it was in 1960 (when Lem completed *Return from the Stars*) that the writer turned 39. A conversation with the father-like doctor is intended to convince Bregg to try to adapt to modern times, even if none of the people around him understand his past and although they underestimate the heroism that has enabled him to survive in a dangerous space. Just as in *Time Not Lost*, the father figure from *Return* encourages us to cut ourselves off from the past and build a new life despite painful experiences. Juffon cannot give absolution to the protagonist because he is aware that Bregg had to act in extremely difficult conditions, violating the ethical foundations of today's world, and he could not foresee the consequences of his actions. Therefore, he so frequently feels like a "Neanderthal" amongst people who are unable to identify themselves with his past. In their conversation, Juffon is constantly intertwining the future with the past:

> If you were someone else, I would be silent, but you deserve the truth. You are alone. A man cannot live alone. Your interests, the ones you have returned with, are an island in a sea of ignorance. I doubt if many people would want to hear what you could tell them. I happen to be one of the interested ones, but I am eighty-nine years old.[163]

To which Bregg replies:

> And that indifference, now – if you must know – affects me only on account of the ones who were left behind.[164]

Then follows the protagonist's significant confession that he is "like a guilty conscience that no one wants,"[165] and he explains to one of the old men who remembers the expedition that neither bodies nor remnants can be found in space, so they could not bring the corpses of their companions back. At the same time, remorse related to the death of a colleague forms such a general reflection: "Because each one of us was priceless, human life had the highest value where is could have none, where such a thin, practically nonexistent film separated it from annihilation."[166] *Return from the Stars* features such interjected sentences, and their universality, or rather the meaning that can be applied to historical events, interferes with the seductive power of the convention of a science fiction novel. Perhaps this is the only way to tell the story of the loneliness of visitors from "another world," which means not only those who survived the Holocaust, but also those who survived and were immediately displaced afterwards. The alien nature of the space and the way new inhabitants speak, the breakdown of the social tissue and the loneliness caused by the death of all one's relatives reflect the emotional atmosphere of that period. Bregg's conversation with the doctor who resembles his father, examining the protagonist in a conventional way, listening to his lungs and heartbeat, makes him start to recognize his own situation better and cease to feel resentment that no one is interested in his experiences.

I have placed Lem's *Return from the Stars* in the category of prose associated with so-called Small Realism, because the principal problems include settlement with the past and emigration. In the background of the novel there is an egalitarian, "betrized" society, where violence was combated with violence, and although Bregg comes from "another world," he decides to focus on everyday life and gradually accepts ordinariness and a non-heroic lifestyle. This is an extremely interesting novel, if we look at it from the point of view of the theme of emigration. In the finale, the protagonist decides against embarking on yet another expedition into space, which reflects the atmosphere of tension in Poland of that era, when Lem's friends decided to leave. That time (the novel was written circa 1958) was marked by the largest wave of emigration of the Jewish minority from Poland.[167] Grzegorz Niziołek notes that the studies on the so-called "Thaw" that ended the Stalinist period usually emphasize the image of the cultural and political breakthrough and the courage of protesting workers, but rarely mention the rise of anti-Semitism, which forced many Jews to emigrate.[168] Dawid Kahane, Chief Rabbi of the Polish Army, who officiated funeral ceremonies after the Kielce pogrom, was under surveillance by the Security Service. In his file, there are, among other things, notes concerning speeches to the Jewish community that the rabbi made at Seders. "Polish Jewry is condemned to complete and unavoidable assimilation," reads the summary of the agent's report of May 3, 1949. "The lack of rabbis, yeshivot, Jewish scholars, etc. accelerates the assimilation process."[169] Although in this work I try not to quote the Security Service files based on surveillance or exploiting third parties,[170] I consider this fragment important because it demonstrates that the authorities of the People's Republic of Poland from the very beginning followed a deliberate policy of thwarting the development of Jewish communities, while at the same time ordering silence about the Holocaust and thus forcing the Jews to emigrate. It was clear to the Jewish communities that the lack of support from the state along with the Iron Curtain cutting off the organizational structures would make it impossible to preserve Jewish identity for all those who would stay in Poland. In 1949–1950, following temporary permission to emigrate to Israel, nearly 30,000 Jews left Poland. On the wave of the Thaw emigration, in a growing atmosphere of anti-Semitic incidents, 47,000 Jews left the country (the largest number departed in 1957), thus marking the period of the largest Jewish emigration from Poland.[171] In this context, *Return from the Stars* becomes an extremely important document of the era, devoted to a narrative ignored in official syntheses. Unfit for the new society, Bregg tries to understand the world around him and decides not to continue his intergalactic voyage.

Later, in his autobiographical essay titled *Highcastle*, written several years after *Return from the Stars*, the figure of the father occupies the central place, and the attempt to recreate the realities of contemporary life is referred to family history, which evokes the memory of the deceased. The first lost object described in *Highcastle* is the doctor's library, viewed from the perspective of a child. German and French laryngology books, never read by the narrator, would have the power to restore the image of Samuel Lehm and help to understand him:

> I would give a great deal now to know what my father kept there, what he read, but the library was swallowed whole by the chaos of war, and so much happened afterward that I never asked. And thus the child's version – primitive, false, really no version at all – remains the final one for me, and this applies not only to those books but also to a multitude of things, some of them dramatic, which were played out over my head.[172]

Thus, we learn about the occupation and emigration from the one phrase: "so much happened afterward"; all we know about pre-war pogroms, harassment and aggression is that the child was protected from them. The books could remind the medically educated writer-narrator of the history of medical techniques of the inter-war era and reconstruct the work of his father, whose death seems to be the most painful loss in the entire autobiographical story. Thus, *Highcastle* can be seen as an attempt to fill the floating gap that emerged when, as Jan Assmann emphasizes, "communication memory is extinguished and cultural memory institutions have not yet been formed."[173] This gap is directly related to the death of parents, whose memories of past generations are lost forever. In Lem's essay, there is no shadow of hope for an institutional cultural memory of the tragedy of World War One and life under the Austro-Hungarian monarchy. In the writer's correspondence with Kandel, however, the opposite problem emerges: the permanence of things, as their long duration is a challenge to the fragility of biological existence:

> My parents left me their wedding rings, now extremely thin after being worn for many decades. When I look at them, I am reminded of a fragment of *The Magic Mountain*, where Mann writes that man vanishes and disperses like a fog, leaving behind nothing but objects.[174]

In *Highcastle*, family memorabilia were annihilated; one has to imagine them in order to be able to recall them from memory and reconstruct their relations with family members. Emigration, after all, means losing everything.

Parallel worlds

In Lem's work, the theme of refugees is manifested in various ways; it is inseparably connected with expeditions to other galaxies and time dimensions, or with subsequent scientific discoveries. The scientist Rappaport from *His Master's Voice*, called by the narrator "a refugee from a country of victims,"[175] was described from the perspective of the narrator, Peter E. Hogarth:

> From his European wanderings he preserved a certain habit that I found amusing: he operated on the principle of *omnia mea mecum porto*, as if instinctively prepared for the necessity of another flight at short notice. That was how I explained the fact that in his suitcase he had a kind of "survival kit," complete with coffeepot, sugar, and crackers.[176]

I have already discussed autobiographical allusions associated with Rappaport; his story forms an ostensibly separate narrative, and it seems that it has little in common with the main theme of the novel, which concerns secret research on cosmic matter. In an American center situated in the desert, scientists are working on deciphering the "signal from the stars." This is an allusion to Los Alamos, where in 1942 a nuclear research center was established (Stanisław Ulam, an emigrant/exile from Lviv, worked there).[177] In this context, Rappaport's short tale becomes not so much a separate, insignificant story, but one that focuses on the main theme of the novel, as through a lens, in which work on solving a scientific problem transforms into research on long-range weapons and heralds the annihilation of all humanity. Returning in the quoted fragment is, as Ewa Wiegandt put it, "an aura of a classical Galician *gimnazjum*,"[178] namely a Latin quote that conceals the emotionality of the story. *Omnia mea mecum porto* means not only "all that is mine, I carry with me"; this maxim is also used to emphasize that "our true wealth is our internal value." In the context of the novel world, the second meaning is an ironic travesty of refugee traumas. Latin aphorism collapses outward suffering into a banality and, at the same time, it contains—like a "great platitude" in Theodore W. Adorno's view, analyzed by Aleksandra Ubertowska: "an element of risk and transgression, leading to the undermining of orders and rules of representation that establish the premises of 'false objectivity' which, in the face of the 'unimaginable,' reveals its epistemological limitations."[179] In Lem's novel, the aphorism by Bias of Priene helps cover the suffering of the protagonist and narrator, and the reference to the Mediterranean culture and to the tale of a philosopher who persuades people to leave the country so that as many of them as possible avoid death during warfare, universalizes this kind of experience. Both protagonists eat the "survival kit" from a displaced person's suitcase and drink alcohol, convinced that the world will soon end and that total war will break out.

The refugee theme can also be found in Lem's earlier novel, *Return from the Stars*, whose protagonist returns from a space voyage to his hometown; as a result of Einstein's time paradox, however, it is now 127 years later, so he finds neither his loved ones nor home. The opening paragraph is rather upsetting: "I took nothing with me, not even a coat. Unnecessary, they said. They let me keep my black sweater: it would pass. But the shirt I had to fight for."[180] New clothes constantly make the protagonist feel distant, not to mention that he travels on the "new" Earth without any luggage and he has no idea where he should go, so he decides to stay in a hotel. If one were to forget the standard question asked when interpreting science fiction, namely what the world will look like in such a long perspective, and in doing so attempted to read the novel against its literary genre, one could wonder not so much from *where*, but from *when* narrator Hal Bregg comes. Bregg compares airports to bookcases, sends telexes, rents a suburban villa that reminds him most of the old world, marries a woman who is similar to his female friends from before the expedition, and when his colleagues go on a "voyage" again, he, having accepted his life during a mountain trek, decides to stay on "Earth." References to the pre-war era become obvious when the protagonist watches a period drama at the cinema:

> Right away I was delighted by the costumes; the scenario was naturalistic, but for that very reason I enjoyed myself, because I caught a great number of mistakes and anachronisms. The hero, a handsome swarthy man with brown hair, came out of his house in a dress suit ["tailcoat" in the original Polish version] (it was early morning) and went by car to meet his beloved; he even had on a top hat, but a gray one, as if he were an Englishman riding at the Derby. Later, a romantic roadhouse came into view, with an innkeeper like none that I had ever seen – he looked like a pirate; the hero seated himself on the tails of his jacket and drank beer through a straw; and so on.[181]

The tailcoat, the innkeeper, the Derby and the top hat are hardly evocative of the late 1950s, even if they set the film in the United States or England. The narrator finds it funny that the brown-haired man wears a tailcoat in the morning to drink beer at an inn. There are more references to the pre-war era; for example, in the world of the future, the greatest achievement is overcoming the law of gravity, which was accomplished thanks to the development of theoretical mathematics, including topology, so important for the pre-war Warsaw and Lviv schools. The novel mentions, for example, the name of Georg Cantor, the author of set theory. Hugo Steinhaus came into contact with his works during his studies in Göttingen before World War One,[182] and in *Return from the Stars*, it was the development of Cantor's concept that radically changed the technology.[183] Fragments of pure mathematics, a discipline that, according to the protagonists, dominates all other disciplines, are followed by information about a journey to a place 23 light years away, so if the lecture by mathematician Roemer is to be treated as an encouragement to do calculations on one's own (not topological by any means), subtracting this number from the date when the novel was written lands us in the second half of the 1930s. Thus, perhaps, we get an answer as to *when* the protagonist-narrator of *Return from the Stars* comes from, and the references to the tailcoat and top hat seem more comprehensible in such a time context.

Treatise on oblivion

The attempt to describe the history of adolescence in Lem's *Highcastle* reminds us, especially in self-referential fragments, of the contemporary reflection on the status of historiographic research. The story of Lviv can be seen through the prism of thinking about "the space of experience" proposed by Reinhart Koselleck. Hayden White explains this concept as "warehouse of archived memories, ideas, dreams, and values which we go to as a kind of 'old curiosity shop' in search of intimations of where we came from."[184] In the case of Lem's recollections, this is, in my opinion, growing up in the shadow of World War One and the unknown history of a family living at the time of the Austro-Hungarian monarchy.

Highcastle is only seemingly chronologically organized, suggesting narrative order. The mosaic-like structure consists of crumbs of lost objects, to which specks from tombstones are glued. All this creates a fuzzy image with blurred lines and several points marking out particular episodes. Often the narrator's patience with those details is put to the test, and he gets irritated by individual elements. Dissatisfied with his work, he withdraws and violates the intricate structure by inserting extensive self-referential sections.

In *Highcastle*, Lem compares memory to a pot filled with trinkets, glass slivers from a broken kaleidoscope, describes it as "capacious void" and "the soul's desk." In the following paragraphs, Lem uses more dangerous juxtapositions and contrasts memory with testimony, and the process of recollection with the work of a detective "following the clues of a crime."[185] The crime committed by the narrator of *Highcastle* is presented in the introduction to the volume:

> I wished to let the child speak, stepping back, not interfering in any way – and instead I exploited him, robbed him, emptied his pockets, notebooks, drawers, to boast to the adults what promise he showed, and how even his little faults were virtues in embryo. I turned my theft into an attractive road sign, practically into a whole highway. … I commented, I interpreted, I spoke too much. And spoke of secrets and toys that were not mine – for I no longer have secrets and toys – and I built a tomb for that young boy and placed him in it, a meticulous, calm, factual tomb, as if I were writing about someone made up, someone who never lived, and who with will and

> planning could be fashioned according to the rules of aesthetics. It was not playing fair. You do not treat a child that way.[186]

From the beginning, the metaphor of memory in this fragment is one of violence and looting, and finally of murder—after all, the introduction ends with a reference to the corpse of a child, and the rest of the essay tells retrospectively the story of how the murder happened. Thus, the ironic distance in *Highcastle* alludes to the writings of Witold Gombrowicz,[187] and the introduction and individual chapters related to reminiscing about school refer to the prologue and the first part of *Ferdydurke*, pointing to a temporary multiplication of the narrative subject, who is both a child and a "forty-year-old" going to school, a loner-inventor and a Holocaust survivor, a resident of Krakow and a refugee. The bitterness of irony harmonizes with the ambiguous, vague allusions to two occupations, which Lem could not discuss in the 1960s. In the fragment devoted to the splitting of adulthood and childhood, he writes, for example, that "[his] childhood once took up [in Polish lit. "was blurred in-between"] more than a dozen calendars, progressing through all the dates in black and red,"[188] which may mean working days and holidays usually marked with these two colors, but it may also indicate—especially in the context of smearing and the possibility of disappearing or wiping out—the two forces: Fascist and Stalinist with their separate calendar systems. Robbing a child of things forever lost is an important metonymy of expulsion, and the narrator himself confesses that "When the photographs and portraits are lost, our complete defenselessness against time becomes apparent."[189] A photograph, which could have the status of a holy relic in a post-catastrophe world, is, as Susan Sontag points out, "a thin slice of space as well as time,"[190] so the loss of all the photographs is therefore associated with the loss of stability, of points of support in the past, as well as the impossibility of working through mourning. Sontag points to the strong relationship between photography and death:

> As the fascination that photographs exercise is a reminder of death, it is also an invitation to sentimentality. Photographs turn the past into an object of tender regard, scrambling moral distinctions and disarming historical judgments by the generalized pathos of looking at time past."[191]

Highcastle lacks such comforting, sentimental clichés, and historical judgments must remain on the sidelines of stories, in allusions and digressions, since there are no material traces of the past to help overcome the time gap and focus attention on family anecdotes.

The meanderings of the narrative point to transgressive places of memory, where time orders, literary allusions and grotesque juxtapositions, known for example from *The Cyberiad* (1965), appear in one sentence, destroying the hierarchy of events and concealing reluctantly recalled incidents. In the fragment about early childhood, the narrator mentions acts of self-harm:

> For a while I liked hanging myself and collected the necessary rope, though of course I didn't go all the way. And I would torture myself; for example, tie a string around my finger to make it "go to sleep," or tie myself to a doorknob, or hang upside down on a rope ladder (I had one), or press a finger into my eye socket to see double. But I never stuck peas and beans in my nose or ears, well aware of the bad consequences of that – my father was an otolaryngologist, after all. I don't know where I got the idea, but for quite a while I considered the foot, particularly a bare foot, to be the most indecent part of the human body. Once I got into a terrible fight about this with my cousin Mietek, who was two years older (he perished in Warsaw, like Stefan)."[192]

How to paraphrase this fragment? Which information is more important? Testimony of the death of cousins or children's games? How to arrange the interpretative accents? Grotesque descriptions of the struggle with one's own body are intertwined with an ironic distance to psychoanalysis and fetishism, which is one of a number of allusions to Schulz's stories, although they conclude—as befits a writer with medical education—with a rational diagnosis, bringing the double vision that accompanies inflicting pain through "press[ing] a finger into [his] eye socket"—childhood memory sets in motion further sequences, which, in a way, invalidate the events from before the war. The parenthetical phrase "he perished in Warsaw, like Stefan" evokes another difficult historical theme, alluding perhaps to one of the two uprisings or a street round-up. The motif is abandoned and the paragraph concludes with the grotesque line, "nothing of the foot idea survived, and I did not become in any way a fetishist."[193] Cancelling the horror of war by means of erotic allusions erases the traces of the tone of mourning and helps escape from the descriptions of deaths that Lem witnessed or knew about in detail. All the evoked relatives die outside the frame of the narrative, and the information about them is expressed in short declarative sentences. The writer consistently avoids descriptions of cruelty, murder and the macabre in his fiction, and, as in ancient tragedy, prevents drastic events from being presented by having them only reported by protagonists or a doctor performing an autopsy.

"The Legacy in the Form of Absences"[194]

Like Jacob in Schulz's stories, the growing boy in Lem's tale becomes a guardian of imperfect matter, defective equipment and damaged dishes. He accumulates them, collects them, takes care of them:

> There was something I collected for its own sake, and persistently, for a long time: electrical-mechanical junk. To this day I have a special feeling for broken bells, alarm clocks, old radio coils, telephone speakers, and in general for objects derailed, worn out, [in Polish: drifting] abandoned, and

> which are given for the last time a chance to exist, with a pitiful vestige of respectability, at a flea market behind a theater."[195]

In *Highcastle*, a camouflaged tale about history that cannot be told is breaking through the history of things. Lem writes about objects "in general ... derailed"—unnecessary, redundant, "drifting," to be thrown out, while it is still possible to give them a chance "to exist, with a pitiful vestige of respectability." The narrator does not argue like Jacob and the Demiurge about the ontology of imperfect matter, but talks about the common fate of people and things, drawing attention to the blind chance that determines their survival or annihilation.

Things play an important role in every chapter of *Highcastle*. The father is seen through the contents of the pockets or the furnishings of the study, just as Uncle Fryc and the aunts are described through their apartment. Descriptions of characters extrapolated to the space of studies and living rooms are also an important feature of Lem's fiction. The old-fashioned *milieu* technique in his prose makes it possible to speak of issues dangerous to articulate in the People's Republic of Poland, and, therefore, to touch on topics that are unacceptable for the censor. Such an indirect narrative strategy avoids labels and unambiguous ideological classifications of individual protagonists, pointing to their internal inconsistencies.

Focusing the narrative on the history of things lost during the occupation is an important political move, as it eliminates deliberations about the perpetrators and makes it possible to eschew the necessity of accusing ethnic, national, linguistic or religious groups of specific crimes, the multitude of which overwhelms modern historiography.[196] Lem writes from the position of someone who was "Jewish," pretended to be "Aryan" and finally became an "asylum seeker"[197] in Krakow, when his Polish citizenship bothered the newly established authorities in reorganizing the post-Yalta world, according to which ethnic homogeneity would guarantee a stable social system. History of objects eliminates hatred and accusations from Lem's prose. As a result of these attempts to conceal the later history of the city, in the writer's tale synagogues and Orthodox churches disappear from the Lviv landscape, while the Armenian Cathedral and the cart with halva sold by a Greek vendor remain.

The temporal multidimensionality of the subject in *Highcastle* and his constant movement as a commentator of events are contrasted with the stability of the apartment and the city: "Space is, after all, solid, monolithic; it contains no traps or pitfalls. Time, on the other hand, is a hostile element, truly treacherous, I would even say against human nature,"[198] stresses the narrator at the end of the chapter on early childhood. Spatial imagery of the time inhabiting the individual floors of the tenement house leads to the conclusion that "I was somehow convinced that tomorrow was above us and yesterday below – a yesterday that did not dissolve into nonexistence but continued, abandoned, somewhere under my feet."[199] The image of the underfloor past is overlaid with the memory of a fire in the tenement and the fear of a child who puts his hand to the floor to check whether it is heating up from the flames. If we put together those images of the underfloor past and fire, the history of childhood in Lviv will reveal its tragic dimension, without the possibility of changing the ending—the past repeats and reproduces itself in an alternative reality, it is a fragile parallel world, indicating the vulnerability, randomness and possible destruction of each version of the world.

Notes

1 Yitzhak Arad notes that Mina Astman and Malka Talenfeld from Żółkiew (Zhovkva) and a dentist named Bachner from Krakow escaped from Bełżec and managed to return to their hometowns, but none of them survived the war. Arad cites the testimony of Rudolf Reder and mentions Chaim Hirshman. Y. Arad, *Belzec, Sobibor, Treblinka. The Operation Reinhard. Death Camps*, Indiana University Press 1999, p. 264–265.
2 D. Libionka, *Wstęp* [in:] *Obóz Zagłady w Bełżcu w relacjach ocalonych i zeznaniach świadków*, ed. D. Libionka, Lublin 2013, p. 9. The researcher describes Bełżec as "the least known death camp of the operation 'Reinhard.'" (ibid., p. 10).
3 A third survivor from Bełżec emigrated to the United States and did not testify until the 1990s.
4 R. Reder moved to Krakow after the war, but I have been unable to establish if he knew the Lem family.
5 Z. Wóycicka, *Przerwana żałoba. Polskie spory wokół pamięci nazistowskich obozów koncentracyjnych i zagłady 1944–1950*, Warszawa 2009, p. 27.
6 Ibid., p. 270.
7 Ibid., 270–271.
8 Contemporary data indicate 435,000 casualties.
9 J. Wnuk, "Charakterystyka obozu zagłady w Bełżcu" [typescript], IPN Lu 432/5/ On the process of commemorating the victims of the death camp in Bełżec, see J. Małczyński, *Drzewa "żywe pomniki" w Muzeum – Miejscu Pamięci w Bełżcu*, "Teksty Drugie" 2009, no. 1/2, p. 208–214.
10 Z. Wóycicka, *Przerwana żałoba. Polskie spory wokół pamięci nazistowskich obozów koncentracyjnych i zagłady 1944–1950*, 174–175.
11 S. Lem, *Hospital of the Transfiguration*, transl. W. Brand, Orlando 1991, p. 105.
12 S. Lem, *Czas nieutracony*, Kraków 1957, p. 268.
13 Ibid., p. 287.
14 Ibid., p. 515.
15 Ibid.
16 Ibid., p. 625.
17 Ibid., p. 321.
18 The issue of the identity fracture of Lem's protagonists was brought to the attention of Maciej Michalski, although he considered it in the context of existential philosophy: "The problem of identity together with the problem of consciousness is one of the most important in Lem's work, and at the same time the most important existential theme and a starting point for the analysis for philosophers of existence. For Lem's heroes, individual identity often becomes problematic, even though the characters in his works are usually ready, already found and actually do not undergo any evolution, changes in personality and character." M. Michalski, "*Egzystencjalny wymiar twórczości Stanisława Lem*" [in:] *Stanisław Lem: pisarz, myśliciel, człowiek*, ed. J. Jarzębski, A. Sulikowski, Kraków 2003, p. 109.
19 I. Iwasiów, "Powieść w obiegach. Lata osiemdziesiąte i kontynuacje" [in:] *Prywatne/publiczne. Gatunki pisarstwa kobiecego*, ed. I. Iwasiów, Szczecin 2008, p. 179. On

the subject of "telling one's life as someone else's" in other texts concerning the Holocaust, see A. Ubertowska, *Aporie, skandale, wyrwy w tekście. Etyka opowieści o Zagładzie*, "Teksty Drugie" 2002, no. 1–2, p. 136.

20 G. Niziołek, *Polski teatr Zagłady*, Warszawa 2013, p. 103.

21 L.L. Langer, *Holocaust Testimonies: The Ruins of Memory*, New Haven, 1991, p. 68.

22 S. Lem, Hospital of the Transfiguration, p. 6.

23 Paweł Majewski believes that aside from Trzyniecki, the character of Wieleniecki has the most of Lem's autobiographical features, although he neither justifies this claim nor supports it with examples. P. Majewski, *Lem fantastyczny czy makabryczny? O możliwym źródle pisarstwa nie-realistycznego*, "Przegląd Filozoficzno-Literacki" 2009, no. 1, p. 127.

24 Document sent by Barbara Lem on March 20, 2014.

25 Cf. E. Jones, *Żydzi Lwowa w okresie okupacji 1939–1945*, Łódź 1999, p. 57–61.

26 A fragment of this propaganda film is available online at: <https://www.youtube.com/watch?v=9dDONW2EU3Y> [accessed June 24, 2014].

27 Cf. E. Jones, *Żydzi Lwowa w okresie okupacji 1939–1945*, Łódź 1999, p. 47.

28 Cf. *Kronika 2350 dni wojny i okupacji Lwowa 1 IX 1939 – 5 II 1946*, zebr. G. Mazur, J. Skwara, J. Węgierski, Katowice 2007, p. 205–206.

29 M. Redner, "Żałobne wspomnienia o życiu i męczeńskiej śmierci lekarzy-Żydów w lwowskim getcie" [typescript], IPN Bu 2323/10. Tatiana Berenstein emphasized that during the pogrom several thousand Jewish intellectuals of Lviv were killed. T. Berenstein, *Eksterminacja ludności żydowskiej w dystrykcie Galicja (1941–1943)*, "Biuletyn Żydowskiego Instytutu Historycznego" 1967, no. 61, p. 6. The writer made a short mention of his uncle in *Highcastle:* "when my allowance wasn't enough, I would either touch my uncle – my mother's brother and a physician like my father – or concoct some scheme. This uncle – I called him by his first name, almost as if he were a schoolmate – had occasional fits of generosity, which didn't please my parents." S. Lem, *Highcastle. A Remembrance*, transl. M. Kandel, Krakow, 2017, p. 117.

30 The account from the period just after the Brygidki incident was presented by Kurt I. Lewin, who, like Lem, survived the pogrom: "When the door opened and I went inside, black specks started drifting through my field of vision. It took a long time before I came to myself. At first, they all ran up to me, but they staggered back immediately. I stank of the corpses. Bent down, I looked at the floor with unseeing eyes. They brought me a basin of water with Lysol. I mechanically took off my clothes, washed and changed without saying a word to anyone. We went to sleep. I was lying on the couch in the bedroom. The Brygidki images never left me for a moment. In a nightmarish half-dream, I saw piles of twisted dead bodies, a sea of human blood." K.I. Lewin, *Przeżyłem. Saga Świętego Jura spisana w roku 1946 przez syna rabina Lwowa*, Warszawa 2006, p. 63–64.

31 Fryderyk Lehm was a lawyer and lived in Bernsteina Street before the outbreak of the war. A remembrance of him was also included in *Highcastle*.

32 Address based on *Ilustrowany informator miasta Lwowa, ze spisem miejscowości wojew. lwowskiego na rok 1939*, ed. J. Brunelik, Lwów 1939. On the same street, at number 12, the Jewish Religious Community had its seat, in whose cellars several hundred Torah scrolls were stored during the first months of the German occupation. Dawid Kahane, account from Lviv [in:] *Życie i zagłada Żydów polskich 1939–1945. Relacje świadków*. M. Grynberg, M. Kotowska, Warszawa 2003, p. 267.

33 Cf. *Kronika 2350 dni wojny i okupacji Lwowa 1 IX 1939 – 5 II 1946*, p. 211, 230; T. Berenstein, *Eksterminacja ludności żydowskiej w dystrykcie Galicja (1941–1943)*, p. 6–7, 14.

34 The first transport from Lviv reached Bełżec on March 17, 1942. Fryderyk was about 72 years old in 1942. See R. Kuwałek, *Obóz zagłady w Bełżcu*, Lublin-Bełżec 2005, p. 24 for more information about transports to the camp.

35 According to the information provided by Stanisław Lem to Barbara Lem, Seweryn Kahane was Fryderyk Lehm's son-in-law. Letter from Barbara Lem dated March 20, 2014.

36 See B. Szaynok, *Pogrom Żydów w Kielcach 4 lipca 1946 roku*, introduction: K. Kersten, Warszawa 1992, p. 45. *Tłum ruszył po dziesiątej. Pogrom kielecki – kalendarium wydarzeń*, "Gazeta Wyborcza" July 6–7, 1996, p. 11.
37 This document was found in the archives of Agnieszka Reszka, head of the Jewish Historical Institute Archives. Letter of July 8, 2015.
38 Based on a letter from Manny Bekier, chairman of The Kieltzer Society in New York, dated January 5, 2015. Filip Friedman recalls, however, that the Lublin and Kielce regions were characterized by a strong guerilla movement, which Jews could join. Cf. F. Friedman, *Zagłada Żydów lwowskich*, Łódź 1945.
39 S. Lem, *Hospital of the Transfiguration*, p. 2.
40 E. Jones, *Żydzi Lwowa w okresie okupacji 1939–945*, p. 96. In his account, Kurt I. Lewin recalls that the employees of the Rohstofferfassung company also wore an additional green band above the star of David, with the inscription *Nutzjude* ("useful Jew"), which provided a sense of security. K.I. Lewin, p. 87.
41 K. I. Lewin, p. 108.
42 Dawid Kahane, account from Lviv [in:] *Życie i zagłada Żydów polskich 1939–1945. Relacje świadków*, p. 266. Lewin stresses that obtaining these documents was not difficult if one had several thousand zlotys and knew a reliable source. K.I. Lewin, p. 106.
43 In Lem's biography Wojciech Orliński puts forward a hypothesis that he escaped from the ghetto between February and April 1943 at the latest.
44 Cf. K.I. Lewin, p. 105–106.
45 At the request of the writer's family, for the sake of the third party, I have decided not to disclose the person's identity.
46 E. Jones, *Żydzi Lwowa w okresie okupacji 1939–1945*, Łódź 1999, p. 183.
47 Translation of the certificate issued by Professor Anatoly Markovich Vorobyov, Archiwum UJ, WL II 387, card No. 7.
48 Ibid. card No. 3.
49 A version of Barbara Lem's notes supplemented with documents, made available courtesy of the author in a letter of March 20, 2014.
50 Archiwum ŻIH, "Rejestr Centralnego Komitetu Żydów w Polsce: Żydzi ocalali," cf., S. Lem, "Przystań na Wiślanej" [in:] idem, *Lube czasy*, ed. T. Fiałkowski, Kraków 1995, p. 122. Maria Orwid recalls that she left Lviv with her mother as soon as possible, and the first transports left the city in February 1945. Cf. M. Orwid, *Przeżyć ... I co dalej? Interview with K. Zimmerer, K. Szwajca*, Kraków 2006, p. 71. In 1946, displaced transports from Lviv were included in train operations, which consisted in catching Jews headed to Poland and throwing them out at the station or between stations, which often ended in death for the repatriates. Cf. M. Siek, A. Bańkowska, A. Jarzębowska, *Morderstwa Żydów w latach 1944–1946 na terenie Polski na podstawie kwerendy w zbiorze 301 (Relacje z Zagłady) w Archiwum ŻIH*, "Kwartalnik Historii Żydów" 2009. On the subject of attacks on Jews in Krakow, also after the pogrom, see M. Zaremba, *Wielka trwoga, Polska 1944–1947. Ludowa reakcja na kryzys*, Krakow 2012, 216–217, 228.
51 A. Cichopek, *Pogrom Żydów w Krakowie 11 sierpnia 1945 roku*, Warszawa 2000, p. 81.
52 Ibid., p. 87.
53 A. Cała, *Ochrona bezpieczeństwa fizycznego Żydów w Polsce powojennej.* Komisja Specjalna przy Centralnym Komitecie Żydów w Polsce, Warszawa 2014, p. 92.
54 S. Lem, *Czas nieutracony*, p. 217.
55 A letter dated April 17, 1967. Made available courtesy of Barbara and Tomasz Lem.
56 The looting in Lviv is a frequent theme in post-war testimonies: "The greed and shamelessness of those villains knew no bounds. They often took the last pillow from under people's heads, the only clothes from the closet, the last shirt. They took the last groszes out of their pockets or hiding places, any watch they could get. They pulled pictures from the walls, kitchen utensils, even those most miserable, and even children's toys. During the winter, they took fuel from the cellars, down to the last

lump of coal." "Żałobne wspomnienia o życiu i męczeńskiej śmierci lekarzy-Żydów w lwowskim getcie" [typescript], IPN BU 2323/10.

57 S. Lem, *Czas nieutracony*, 353–354.

58 Dariusz Libionka, who found examples of rejection of Jews' efforts to join the Polish underground, elaborated on the subject of the instructions issued by the Home Army/Union of Armed Struggle to exclude representatives of the Jewish minority from the organization. The researcher also pointed out that the inclusion of Jews in the Polish underground was rare and random. D. Libionka, "ZWZ-AK i Delegatura Rządu RP wobec eksterminacji Żydów polskich" [in:] *Polacy i Żydzi pod okupacją niemiecką 1939–1945. Studia i materiały*, ed. A. Żbikowski, Warszawa 2006, p. 109–111.

59 "Wspomnienia Marcela Lubasha z czasu II wojny światowej. Zbiór mikrofilmowanych kopii relacji osób, które przetrwały Holocaust na terenie III Rzeszy i okupowanej Europy, pozyskanych z Muzeum Holocaustu w Waszyngtonie," IPN BU 2721/ [testimony in English].

60 The account of Władysław Bartoszewski contains many mistakes, partly explained in footnotes in the new edition. I try to correct mistakes in the main text, reconstructing the writer's biography. W. Bartoszewski, "Mój przyjaciel pesymista [Stanisław Lem]" [in:] idem, *Pisma wybrane 2002–2012*, sel., ed. and footnotes A. K. Kunert, vol. 6, Krakow 2012, p. 361.

61 Baloyne is Jan Błoński, whose ironic, friendly portrayal can be found in several fragments of the novel, e.g. "He is a person that physically you could make two of, and intellectually – four, at least. Baloyne is and, I think, will always remain greater than his achievements, because it very rarely happens that in so gifted a man all the psychical horses pull in the same direction." S. Lem, *His Master's Voice*, p. 54.

62 Idem, *List z 30 maja 1972* [in:] idem, *Sława i fortuna. Listy do Michaela Kandla 1972–1987*, Kraków 2013, p. 52. According to Tomasz Lem, Wilhelm Eeney is Janusz Wilhelmi – head of cinematography of The People's Republic of Poland. Letter sent on September 14, 2015.

63 S. Lem, *List z 8 sierpnia 1973* [in:] ibid., p. 154.

64 F. Jameson, *Archaeologies of the Future: The Desire Called Utopia and Other Science Fictions*, London–New York 2005, p. 108.

65 S. Lem, *List z 24 stycznia 1974* [in:] idem, *Sława i fortuna. Listy do Michaela Kandla*, p. 188. In his account, David Kahane emphasized that "Potassium cyanide was such a popular poison, so popular among Jews that there was no Jewish house where this article would not be found." Dawid Kahane, account from Lviv [in:] *Życie i zagłada Żydów polskich 1939–1945. Relacje świadków*, p. 263.

66 J. Jarzębski, "Przypadek i wartości. (O aksjologii Stanisława Lema)" [in:] idem, *Wszechświat Lema*, Kraków 2003, p. 187.

67 Idem, "Literackie przygody uniwersalnego Rozumu. (O eseistyce Stanisława Lema)" [in:] ibid., p. 166–167.

68 N. Pospieszalska [Helena Eilstein], *"Głos Pana," czyli zwierciadło z nieba*, part 2, "Nurt" 1969, no. 8, p. 34. 1969, no. 8, p. 34. On Lem's admiration for the magazine edited by Helena Eilstein and Leszek Kołakowski (*Studia Filozoficzne*) see I. Csicsery-Ronay, Jr., *Twenty-Two Answers and Two Postscripts: An Interview with Stanisław Lem*, transl. by M. Lugowski, "Science Fiction Studies" 1986, vol. 13, p. 243. In an unpublished letter to Jerzy Wróblewski, Lem explained, without losing an ironic distance: "I wrote to you from the heart, because it's you, my friend, that sixty-year-old mathematician is myself. Just a bit of a loner, a freak, a little twisted; he wanted to write more intimately at first, and then, you know, he probably got over it, and this is why he stands out a little from the rest." S. Lem, letter to Jerzy Wróblewski dated January 1, 1969, courtesy of Barbara and Tomasz Lem. In the quoted fragment, I have corrected obvious typos in the original.

69 K.N. Hayles, "Chaos as Dialectic: Stanisław Lem and the Space of Writing," [in:] *Chaos Bound: Orderly Disorder in Contemporary Literature and Science*, p. 122.

70 Cf. N. Pospieszalska [Helena Eilstein], *"Głos Pana," czyli zwierciadło z nieba*, part 2, "Nurt" 1969, no. 8, p. 34.; J. Jarzębski, *Bóg, diabeł, listy z kosmosu* [afterword to:] S. Lem, *Głos Pana*, p. 234.
71 S. Lem, *His Master's Voice*, p. 4.
72 Four secret collaborators were used in this case, although they failed to obtain any information. However, the case was not closed until July 1976. IPN Kr 010/11912.
73 S. Lem, *His Master's Voice*, p. 4.
74 Ibid., p. 5.
75 Ibid., p. 18.
76 Ibid., p. 23.
77 I. Csicsery-Ronay, Jr., *Twenty-Two Answers and Two Postscripts: An Interview with Stanislaw Lem*, p. 245.
78 S. Lem, *List z 7 grudnia 1972* [in:] idem, *Sława i fortuna. Listy do Michaela Kandla 1972–1987*, p. 111–112.
79 Idem, *His Master's Voice*, p. 62.
80 Ibid., p. 80.
81 L.L. Langer, *Holocaust Testimonies: The Ruins of Memory*, New Haven, 1991, p. 85.
82 Ibid., p. 144
83 Cf. ibid., p. 83.
84 Cf. Ch. Ostrower, "Humor as a Defense Mechanism during the Holocaust," *Interpretation: A Journal of Bible and Theology* 2015, vol. 69, no. 2, p. 195.
85 S. Lem, *His Master's Voice*, 64.
86 J. Butler, *Frames of War: When is Life Grievable?* London 2009, p. 14.
87 A. Zieniewicz, *Pakty i fikcje. Autobiografizm po końcu wielkich narracji (szkice)*, Warszawa 2011, p. 21.
88 S. Lem, *His Master's Voice*, p. 64.
89 Ibid., p. 80–81.
90 J. Butler, *Frames of War*, p. 24.
91 S. Lem, *His Master's Voice*, p. 65–66.
92 G. Lesser, "Pogromy w Galicji Wschodniej w 1941 r." [in:] *Tematy polsko-ukraińskie. Historia – Literatura – Edukacja*, ed. R. Traba, Olsztyn 2001, p. 107.
93 S. Lem, *His Master's Voice*, p. 65.
94 J. Butler, *Frames of War*, preface, p. 1ff.
95 In Ukrainian texts, the history of Lviv Jews is usually mentioned in the context of the underground network organized by Metropolitan Archbishop Andrey Sheptytsky and his brother Klymentiy to rescue the Jewish population. For example, Philipp Ther argues that many representatives of the Ukrainian and Polish intelligentsia risked their lives to save the Jewish residents of Lviv, and that the waves of Polish and Ukrainian anti-Semitism were exclusively linked to the brutal politics of Nazi Germany. Ph. Ther, "War versus Peace: Interethnic Relations in Lviv during the First Half of the Twentieth Century," transl. J. Czaplicka, *Harvard Ukrainian Studies* 2000, vol. 24, 268–269.
96 S. Lem, *Czas nieutracony*, p. 338. During the occupation of Lviv, Germans demanded three contributions, including one a month before the final liquidation of the ghetto. The Lviv Judenrat was blackmailed by the German army, which imposed a contribution and took hostages at the same time, and their lives were to depend on the timely payment of the amount indicated. However, the first deposit of the imposed contribution failed to save any of the hostages. The Commission of the Jewish Council saved many people from death during the gradual liquidation of the ghetto. Cf. for instance: F. Friedman, *Zagłada Żydów lwowskich*.
97 Filip Friedman points out that attempts to organize underground life and resistance in the ghetto were made only after the 1942 deportations. According to his account, in 1943, conspiratorial military training for Jewish youth began and an underground newspaper was published. "There were no organizations that could provide the Jews with weapons and, if necessary, with armed support. A small number of

weapons (pistols, hand grenades) were purchased by illegal Jewish organizations from Hungarian and Italian soldiers." Friedman admits that during the final liquidation of the ghetto in June 1943, the Jews put up armed resistance against the Germans, who finally set the ghetto buildings on fire. F. Friedman, *Zagłada Żydów lwowskich*. On underground life and Jewish partisans see also: Irena Szajowicz, account from Lviv [in:] *Życie i zagłada Żydów polskich 1939–1945. Relacje świadków*, p. 289.

98 S. Lem, *Czas nieutracony*, p. 382.

99 Ibid.

100 T. Berenstein, *Eksterminacja ludności żydowskiej w dystrykcie Galicja (1941–1943)*, p. 29. Cf. A. Żbikowski, „Raport Fredericka Katzmanna i zagłada ludności żydowskiej w dystrykcie galicyjskim" [in:] *Akcja Reinhardt. Zagłada Żydów w Generalnym Gubernatorstwie*, ed. D. Libionka, Warszawa 2004, p. 136.

101 Cf. on this subject: Z. Wóycicka, *Przerwana żałoba. Polskie spory wokół pamięci nazistowskich obozów koncentracyjnych i zagłady 1944–1950.*

102 S. Lem, *Highcastle*, p. 133.

103 Bogusława Latawiec, for example, drew attention to the "autonomous world of sounds" in Lem's prose. B. Latawiec, *Kosmos i medycyna*, "Odra" 1976, no. 7–8, p. 44.

104 S. Lem, *Czas nieutracony*, p. 645.

105 Idem, *Jeszcze "Ostatni etap,"* "Tygodnik Powszechny" May 16, 1948, p. 14.

106 In his column *Poza granicami pojmowania* [Outside the limits of comprehension] in the mid-1990s, Lem emphasized: "I was saddened by the disputes that broke out because of the Auschwitz anniversary, all that rope-pulling, mutual accusations of Judaism or Polonization of the camp museum. There should be silence over the graves. Perhaps it is impossible to bring justice to the visible world, as Conrad told us, in this segment of history. It is difficult to administer justice where crime and evil have gone beyond the final limit of human comprehension." S. Lem, "Poza granicami pojmowania" [in:] idem, *Lube czasy*, p. 18.

107 S. Lem, *List z 10 listopada 1972* [in:] idem, *Sława i fortuna. Listy do Michaela Kandla*, p. 107.

108 Idem, "O powieści kryminalnej" [in:] idem, *Wejście na orbitę*, p. 69.

109 Ibid., 69–70.

110 G. Niziołek, *Polski teatr Zagłady*, p. 302. Niziołek summarizes the main theses of Alenka Zupančič's *The Odd One In. On Comedy* (2008).

111 S. Lem, *List z 1 lipca* 1972 [in:] idem, *Sława i fortuna. Listy do Michaela Kandla*, p. 62.

112 Archival documents indicate that from 1904, the name of Samuel Lehm should be spelled without the letter *h*. However, in address books, documents related to his professional career and his publications, it is always spelled "Lehm" (as in the case of Fryderyk Lehm). While it is difficult to explain why *h* reappears, I use it because it was consistent in the documents I have found. Cf. Archiwum Główne Akt Dawnych, birth records of the Jewish community of Lviv from 1879, book No. 533, p. 206, item 1048.

113 S. Lem, "Chance and Order," transl. F. Rottensteiner, *The New Yorker* 59, January 30, 1984, p. 88–98.

114 "For years my Mother kept telling me that I didn't have 'any real, serious job,' just those 'books and books.' (She's stopped since)." S. Lem, *List z marca 1975* [in:] idem, *Sława i fortuna. Listy do Michaela Kandla*, p. 218.

115 The first and last name of Samuel Lehm as a pupil of the 7th grade of the grammar school (*gimnazjum*) is listed in the 1898 register: *Sprawozdanie dyrektora c.k. IV Gimnazjum za rok 1898*, Lwów 1898, p. 100; cf. M. Gayak-Toczek, *Męskie gimnazja państwowe we Lwowie w latach 1772–1914*, "Acta Universitatis Lodziensis. Folia Litteraria Polonica" 2010, no. 13, p. 352.

116 Hersch Nussen born c. 1843, son of Mojżesz Lehm and Chane Jitte [no last name given].

117 Sara Lea born c.1845, daughter of Abraham Wein and Fajga Bick. In the register of births of the Jewish community of Lviv from 1879. (I egzemplarz, Archiwum Główne Akt Dawnych, księga nr 533, s. 206, poz. 1048) the mother's name was corrected – from Wein to Bick.

118 There is a different spelling of the parents' names next to her name: Hermann Lehm, Sara Weinwald.

119 Fryderyk, "Uncle Fryc," had a son, Edward (born 1903), whose mother was Sara Jetti Bohrer/Altman.

120 Mother of Marian Hemar, wife of Izak (Ignacy) Mendel Hescheles. She got married on February 14, 1897, at the age of 25. Cf. *Księgi metrykalne gmin wyznania mojżeszowego z terenów tzw. Zabużańskich, 1789–1943*, Archiwum Główne Akt Dawnych, zespół 300, księga nr 1806, s. 25–26.

121 Birth records of the Lviv community until the beginning of the twentieth century have been indexed as part of the Jewish Records Indexing Poland project. Information about the project and the database can be found at www.jri-poland.org. On the website of Archiwum Główne Akt Dawnych (Central Archives of Historical Records), at www.agad.gov.pl/inwentarze/Mojz300xhtml, there is an inventory of Jewish birth records, along with scans of cards from the books. I would like to thank the staff of Archiwum Główne Akt Dawnych in Warsaw for this information.

122 S. Lem, *List z 6 sierpnia 1975* [in:] idem, *Sława i fortuna. Listy do Michaela Kandla*, p. 399–400.

123 In December 1936, the official permission to change the name of Hescheles to Hemar was given, and it was then noted that Marian Hemar was baptized in the Reformed Evangelical Rite in June 1936. *Księga urodzin izraelickiego okręgu metrykalnego, Lwów* 1901, poz. 437, Archiwum Główne Akt Dawnych.

124 I received this information from Barbara Lem in a letter dated July 12, 2012. In Hemar's biography, Anna Mieszkowska published fragments of letters written by Samuel Lehm, which he sent to the artist immediately after the war. However, writing to Hemar in the post-war era was extremely risky and could have endangered the whole family, so the letters were sent by trusted sailors and not by official mail. *Ja, kabareciarz. Marian Hemar – od Lwowa do Londynu*, ed. A. Mieszkowska, Warszawa 2006.

125 Manuscript courtesy of Barbara and Tomasz Lem.

126 *Ja, kabareciarz. Marian Hemar – od Lwowa do Londynu*, p. 105.

127 There are two versions of Sabina Lehm's name in the archives: Wollner (or Wolner) or Gottfried. There is a note added to the marriage certificate: "The name of the fiancée is Wolner and not Gottfried, she is the daughter of Itzig Szyja and Breindla née Gottfried, Mr. and Mrs. Wolner." As inspector Paweł Staniszewski explains, "Such an amendment in the record means that the grandparents of Stanisław Lem on his mother's side had to register their marriage with Izraelicki Urząd Metrykalny (Jewish Vital Records Office). At the same time, the spelling of the writer's grandfather's first name was changed from the Hebrew form *Isaac* to the Yiddish form *Itzig*, and the spelling of his last name was Polonized from *Wollner* to *Wolner*. This means that earlier, Stanisław Lem's grandparents on his mother's side had just been married by a rabbi." Based on a marriage certificate from the former Izraelicki Urząd Metrykalny in Lviv. Urząd Stanu Cywilnego Miasta Stołecznego Warszawy, III Wydział Rejestracji Stanu Cywilnego i Ksiąg Zabużańskich, Sekcja Ksiąg Zabużańskich, rok 1919, nr 111.

128 *Księga urodzeń byłego Izraelickiego Urzędu Metrykalnego we Lwowie za rok 1921*. Urząd Stanu Cywilnego Miasta Stołecznego Warszawy, III Wydział Rejestracji Stanu Cywilnego i Ksiąg Zabużańskich, Sekcja Ksiąg Zabużańskich. Until 1890, Samuel Lehm's parents also had just the rabbinical marriage. Archiwum Główne Akt Dawnych, *Księga metrykalna urodzeń gminy wyznania mojżeszowego Lwów z 1879 r.* (I egzemplarz), ks. nr 533, s. 206, poz. 1048.

129 Birth certificate, issued on October 15, 1939. Document courtesy of Barbara and Tomasz Lem.
130 Archiwum Państwowe Obwodu Lwowskiego we Lwowie, Akta realności domu przy ulicy Brajerowskiej 4 Urzędu Nadzoru Budowlanego Król. Stołecznego Miasta Lwowa, f. 2, on. 2, spr. 562.
131 E. Mendelsohn, "Jewish Assimilation in Lvov: The Case of Wilhelm Feldman," *Slavic Review* 1969, vol. 28, no. 4, p. 577–590.
132 L. Wolff, *Galicyjscy Żydzi*, transl. into Polish M. Duda-Gryc [in:] *Mit Galicji*, ed. J. Purchla, W. Kos, Ż. Komar, M. Rygier, W.M. Schwarz, Kraków 2014, p. 125. Cf. also: J. Shanes, *Tworzenie się narodu. Żydzi galicyjscy w państwie austriackim*, transl. into Polish M. Duda-Gryc [in:] ibid, p. 165–170.
133 Cf. E. Mendelsohn, "Jewish Assimilation in Lvov: The Case of Wilhelm Feldman," p. 577–590.
134 T. Snyder, *Bloodlands. Europe Between Hitler and Stalin*, London 2011, p. 1.
135 Cf. e.g. "Lista płatników składki Gminy wyznaniowej żydowskiej we Lwowie, w powiecie lwowskim, województwie lwowskim na rok 1936," Centralne Państwowe Archiwum we Lwowie, f. 701, on. 3, spr. 2066. I would like to thank Dr. Nadiya Polishchuk from the University of Lviv for finding this document and checking many archival records that did not include the name of the Lehm family.
136 *Sprawozdanie Roczne Wydziału Towarzystwa Rygorozantów (Żydowski Dom Akademicki) we Lwowie za Rok Akademicki 1927/1928*, Lwów 1928, p. 27.
137 Jurasz moved to Poznań in 1920, and Samuel Lehm worked as an assistant at least until 1923. Samuel Lehm's personal file containing documents concerning his appointment as an assistant at the University of Lviv clinic. Archiwum Państwowe Obwodu Lwowskiego we Lwowie, f. 12, op. 93.
138 Ibid.
139 S. Lehm, *Przypadek wrodzonej przegrody błoniastej w krtani*, "Lwowski Tygodnik Lekarski" September 26, 1912, p. 645–646. The journal also regularly published reports on the meetings of the Polish Otolaryngological Society, including Samuel Lehm's papers.
140 S. Lehm, M. Panchyshyn [Polish: Pańczyszyn], *O leczniczym wpływie promieni Roentgena na twardziel głębszych dróg oddechowych*, "Przegląd Lekarski" October 26, 1918, no. 43, p. 289–290. I would like to thank Prof. Alexander Kitsera from the Department of Otorhinolaryngology at the Danylo Halytsky Lviv National Medical University for his conversation about Samuel Lehm and his research, and Dr. Volodymyr Hrynovets from the Chair of Therapeutic Dentistry of the Lviv National Medical University for his discussion on the history of medicine in Lviv.
141 Cf. O. Hnatiuk, *Odwaga i strach*, Wojnowice 2019, p. 80.
142 In the 1930s, Panchyshyn's involvement in the Ukrainian national movement deepened, and his death was linked to the Polish–Ukrainian conflict during the occupation of Lviv. In 1943 *Kedyw* [Directorate of Diversion of the Polish Home Army] ordered the shooting of Andriy Lastovetsky, a Ukrainian physicist who worked at the Medical Department of the Lviv State Medical Institute, on the street, after he was accused – wrongly – of not admitting Poles to the university in Lviv. In retaliation, a Ukrainian activist, most likely Panchyshyn's son, shot Bolesław Jałowy, a histopathologist from the Medical University on October 1. Marian Panchyshyn then went into hiding with Metropolitan Archbishop Sheptytsky, where he died of a heart attack. See *Kronika 2350 dni wojny i okupacji Lwowa 1 IX 1939 – 5 II 1946*, p. 380. Currently, his home in Lviv houses the Marian Panchyshyn Museum of Medicine.
143 Cf. e.g. S. Lem, *List z 2 kwietnia 1978* [in:] idem, *Sława i fortuna. Listy do Michaela Kandla*, p. 634–637.
144 T. Epsztein, *Inwentarz archiwum Towarzystwa Ochrony Zdrowia Ludności Żydowskiej w Polsce przy Centralnym Komitecie Żydów w Polsce (1945) 1946–1949 (1950)*, Archiwum ŻIH 324/1425.

145 Ibid. 324/394.
146 Stanisław Lem to Prof. Władysław Kapuściński, *List z 20 sierpnia 1973*, deposited with the Museum of Literature in Warsaw, (Muzeum Literatury w Warszawie, sygn. 3740).
147 M. Orwid, *Przeżyć … I co dalej?* p. 89.
148 S. Lem, *Highcastle*, p. 7.
149 Idem, *Czas nieutracony*, p. 619.
150 Ibid., p. 24.
151 This is likely an allusion to Copernicus's friend, Tiedemann Giese.
152 S. Lem *Solaris*, transl. from the French J. Kilmartin, S. Cox, San Diego–New York–London 1987, p. 161–162.
153 Idem, *List z 24 stycznia 1974* [in:] idem, *Sława i fortuna. Listy do Michaela Kandla*, p. 184.
154 Idem, *Solaris*, p. 90.
155 Ibid., p. 102.
156 Ibid., p. 142.
157 S. Lem, *Highcastle*, p. 142.
158 Idem, *Hospital of the Transfiguration*, p. 161.
159 Idem, *Czas Nieutracony*, p. 621–622.
160 Idem, *Return from the Stars*, transl. B. Marszal, F. Simpson, New York–London 1980, p. 62.
161 Ibid., p. 69.
162 L. L. Langer, *Holocaust Testimonies: The Ruins of Memory*, New Haven, 1991, p. 198.
163 S. Lem, Return from the Stars, p. 67.
164 Ibid.
165 Ibid., p. 78.
166 Ibid., p. 184.
167 Lem explained his position on emigration to Israel to Kandel in the 1970s, in a letter in which he referred to the opinion of those who decided to emigrate and were disappointed with the home and foreign policy of Israel. See S. Lem, *List 18 stycznia 1974* [in:] idem, *Sława i fortuna. Listy do Michaela Kandla*, p. 179.
168 G. Niziołek, *Polski teatr Zagłady*, p. 235.
169 Dawid Kahane's file, Akta operacyjne "Kahane Dawid," IPN BU 01178/36/D. IPN BU 01178/36/D. On the social and political situation of the Jewish minority in Poland, see A. Rykała, *Przemiany sytuacji społeczno-politycznej mniejszości żydowskiej w Polsce po drugiej wojny światowej*, Łódź 2007.
170 On the subject of problems related to IPN documents, see for example: M. Napiórkowski, *Prawda archiwów*, "Kultura Współczesna" 2011, no. 4, p. 12–26.
171 D. Stola, *Emigracja pomarcowa*, "Prace Migracyjne" 2000, no. 34, p. 4, 6.
172 Ibid, p. 21–22.
173 M. Saryusz-Wolska, "Wprowadzenie" [in:] *Pamięć zbiorowa i kulturowa. Perspektywa niemiecka*, ed. M. Saryusz-Wolska, Kraków 2009, p. 32.
174 S. Lem, *Pod prysznicem* [in:] idem, *Lube czasy*, p. 48.
175 Idem, *His Master's Voice*, p. 163.
176 Ibid., p. 156.
177 Cf. S.M. Ulam, *Adventures of a Mathematician*. New York 1983.
178 E. Wiegandt, *Austria Felix, czyli o micie Galicji w polskiej prozie współczesnej*, Poznań 1988, p. 46.
179 A. Ubertowska, *Świadectwo – trauma – głos. Literackie reprezentacje Holocaustu*, Kraków 2007, p. 71. I was inspired by a chapter on Michał Głowiński, entitled *Między "słownikiem Zagłady" a figurą autobiografii* (ibid., 75–106).
180 S. Lem, *Return from the Stars*, p. 3.
181 Ibid., p. 110.
182 H. Steinhaus, *Wspomnienia i zapiski*, ed. A. Zgorzelska, London 1992, p. 47. It is worth noting that according to Steinhaus, set theory is given too much attention in

Poland; he indicated that Lviv mathematicians were interested in, among others, the theory of operations and probability theory; ibid., p. 115.

183 In his article *Matematyka w twórczości Stanisława Lema*, Mateusz Głowacki overlooked the context of the Lviv-Warsaw school as important for the mathematical themes in *Return from the Stars*. In my opinion, a significant part of Lem's work is rooted in the history of science associated with pre-war discoveries. Cf. M. Głowacki, *Matematyka w twórczości Stanisława Lema*, "MISHELLANEA: pismo studentów MISH UW" 2001, no. 2–3, p. 25–38.

184 H. White, *The Practical Past*, Evanston, 2014, p. 10.

185 S. Lem, *Highcastle*, p. 3. The phrases *pustka pojemna* ("capacious void") and *biurko duszy* ("soul's desk") are missing from the English edition.

186 Ibid., 1–2.

187 The similarities between *Ferdydurke* and *Highcastle* were interpreted in detail by Ewa Szczepkowska. Cf. Por. E. Szczepkowska, "Gra z autobiografią w 'Wysokim Zamku'" [in:] *Stanisław Lem: pisarz, myśliciel, człowiek*, ed. J. Jarzębski, A. Sulikowski, Kraków 2003, p. 371–373.

188 S. Lem, *Highcastle*, p. 1.

189 Ibid., p. 28.

190 S. Sontag, *On Photography*, New York 2001, p. 22.

191 Ibid., p. 21.

192 S. Lem, *Highcastle*, p. 34.

193 Ibid.

194 G. M. Spiegel, "The Task of the Historian," *The American Historical Review*, Vol. 114, no. 1, February 2009, p. 1–15.

195 S. Lem, *Highcastle*, p. 94.

196 Cf. information on censuses in Galicia and the issue of national identity declaration in Galicia: G. Hryciuk, *Przemiany narodowościowe i ludnościowe w Galicji Wschodniej i na Wołyniu w latach 1931–1948*. Hryciuk also emphasizes that "During the interwar era, Eastern Galicia maintained the character of an ethnically heterogeneous area, in which, however, one of the largest, and in some parts clearly dominating group were Ukrainians. Adolf Krysinski, expert in nationality issues, counted *Ziemia Czerwińska* among the regions of Europe with the most complicated ethnic relations, along with Crimea, northern shores of the Sea of Azov and Black Sea, Bessarabia to Dobrudja and the regions of Vojvodina, Bantu and Transylvania." Ibid., p. 77.

197 In an interview with Tomasz Fiałkowski, Lem noticed that when asked what Lviv meant to him, he answered "his Homeland" (spelled with a capital letter), and though he had been living in Krakow for half a century, he felt like an "asylum seeker." Then he added: "I am exiled." *Świat na krawędzi – ze Stanisławem Lemem rozmawia Tomasz Fiałkowski*, Kraków 2000, p. 69.

198 S. Lem, *Highcastle*, p. 22.

199 Ibid., p. 23.

3

HOLOCAUST IN SPACE

Survivor

In the opening scene of the novel *Człowiek z Marsa* (Man from Mars), published in installments, the protagonist and narrator is abducted from the street. Drifting in New York 3 months after the capitulation of Germany, the unemployed journalist gets irritated when a driver asks him rudely what day of the week it is and answers "Friday" instead of "Wednesday." Based on that, he is assumed to be privy to secret scientific research on an extraterrestrial being and is promptly transported to an isolated center. The mistake is quickly discovered, but since McMoor has already found out where the group of insiders are residing, he cannot leave the center. McMoor is actually happy about this abduction because earlier he had no idea what to do. In the opening scenes, it seems that the story is set not so much in New York but in ravaged Europe, where the end of the war marked the beginning of a struggle against poverty and violence.[1] Even the unemployment of the reporter, who once worked for a popular newspaper, does not quite explain why he is now aimlessly wandering around the city, unwashed, in ragged clothes and hungry,[2] even though he has enough money in his pocket to buy the *New York Times*. When his mistaken identity is discovered, McMoor, handcuffed, suspects that he has been kidnapped by fascists and will soon be killed. Then he tries to find a way out of this situation:

> Two days of enforced fasting took its toll, but did not affect my brain any I could tell. If anything, the hunger brought with it certain levity, not to say a heightened sense of indifference, with which I reviewed these extraordinary dealings.[3]

When it begins to dawn on the protagonist that he is about to be killed, he asks the strangers for something to eat before he dies. The memory of hunger and

DOI: 10.4324/9780367855642-4

symptoms associated with starvation disease (the clarity of mind that appears in the initial phase[4]) would later become a recurring theme in Lem's prose, as he was one of those writers who make sure that their characters eat hearty meals (often sandwiches), drink aromatic coffee from a thermos and, in exceptional (usually critical) circumstances, open a bottle of expensive alcohol. This is the case in *Eden*, *Hospital of the Transfiguration*, *The Invincible*, *Memoirs Found in a Bathtub*, *His Master's Voice*, *Tales of Pirx the Pilot* and *The Star Diaries*.[5]

In *Man from Mars*, McMoor has dinner and is subsequently put to the test during a meeting with people he considers to be a fascist gang:

> I have to admit, the whole conversation made me feel odd. Earlier, when these strange people condemned me to disappear, in other words to die, I was acutely aware of the hopelessness of my position, but this novel turn of events filled me with renewed strength. Up against the wall, a man becomes apathetic, listless. But give him the tiniest ray of hope and his strength grows a hundredfold, his senses fire up to peak levels, and he turns into a single coiled muscle ready to explode in an effort to save his life. That's what happened to me.[6]

McMoor's account is unique, as his resistance and fight against his captors will save his health (he was about to undergo a memory reset) and he will join a team of researchers working on a body/machine from Mars. This strange beginning to the novel and the presentation of the characters are evocative of the reality of life under occupation (abduction, hunger, one's survival depending on physical fitness, cunning and bravado) and contain many autobiographical allusions. Just like Lem, the protagonist, McMoor, studied medicine for several years and then became a reporter. Aside from having his serialized novel published in a magazine, Lem, as a member of the Scientific Conservatory of the Jagiellonian University, started writing regular articles for the scientific monthly *Życie Nauki*. At the time, he was particularly interested in the workings of the brain, as well as the importance of plasma in the life creation process.[7]

In Lem's prose, McMoor is the first in a whole parade of Robinson-like characters – not so much heroic as clever, attentive and desperate for a solution in hopeless situations. They are the ones who live – sometimes as sole survivors – through the confrontation with aliens or the hostile world of cosmic space and tell the story of their missing, dead, murdered companions and the discoveries they made together. These Robinsons include the *Eden* crew, Bregg from *Return from the Stars*, Rohan from *The Invincible*, Pirx the Pilot and Tichy, to name but a few. The convention of an adventure novel unexpectedly makes it possible to write about survival and escape from death: "Now," McMoor says at the end of the novel, "I was no longer on the side of the Martian, oh, no! Now it was all about life."[8] In *Eden*, Lem directly refers to the analogy between survivors from the spaceship and the adventures of Daniel Defoe's most famous protagonist. He simply calls them "interplanetary Robinsons," who have to save themselves and at all costs leave the dangerous planet, the very opposite of paradise. Grzegorz Niziołek analyzed the post-war Robinsonade theme on the example of the film *Robinson Warszawski* (lit. "The Warsaw Robinson," distributed as *Unvanquished City*), written by Czesław Miłosz and Jerzy Andrzejewski, as well as in the plays by Józef Szajna (*Replika*) and Tadeusz Kantor *(The Dead Class)*. The researcher pointed out that the idea of referring to this theme in the context of survival "should be considered radical, allowing to focus on the difficult work of survival, deliverance through human effort and not metaphysical forces."[9] In my opinion, this theme has a similar meaning in the prose of Stanisław Lem, who creatively transformed the eighteenth-century novel and used it to demonstrate the difficulty of survival in a hostile space, full of dangers and enemies.[10] In *Eden*, salvation is divided into two levels: the first concerns the ship's crew, who finally leave the scene of the crime, while the other is associated with the weak resistance movement and survival strategies developed by the persecuted doublers themselves, who often choose suicide as the only way out of a dangerous situation. Some of the participants of the expedition repeatedly oppose the risk that the ship's crew constantly takes up. When the ship's doctor decides to return to the dangerous city, his companion shouts:

> If we all survived the crash and emerged from the grave that this ship became – if after taking the incalculable risk of exploring this planet as if it were a place for walking tours – it wasn't so that now, with this damned, stupid drivel![11]

Such unfinished, grammatically precarious and incomplete sentences are hardly ever encountered in Lem's prose. How could this sentence be finished? It wasn't so that now, with this damned, stupid drivel, we would die, lose our lives now, when the prospect of rescue is near? The sentence breaks off and no one heeds the warning, although the crew do try to improve the safety system.

Officer Rohan from *The Invincible* manages to survive the attack of a swarm of machines and the hostile space of Regis III twice. The first time he is saved by coincidence as, at a critical moment of the unexpected attack, he falls into a stupor, and the machines fail to detect his presence. Thus, his survival is not his own doing but rather a result of blind chance. The second time, he deliberately faces a deadly risk to confirm if his missing companions are dead. Unarmed, with only scarce food supply, the protagonist moves around the contaminated area, encountering only eyeless, dismembered corpses. It turns out that to the ship's crew he is just the one who "[would] return and report what he had found out about their companions' deaths."[12] In order to bring news of the death of his colleagues, he must make a heroic attempt to return to the ship. When he manages to confuse the scouting deadly machines, he stands up "on shaky legs. Suddenly he felt ridiculous standing there with the Weyr gun he had taken so hastily from the dead man: he felt so superfluous in this realm of perfected death, where only dead forms could emerge victoriously."[13]

Despite being exhausted, discouraged and psychologically shocked by the mortal danger and discovery of the massacred corpses of his colleagues, Rohan makes somewhat mechanical effort to return to the base, trying at all costs to overcome the temptation to rest and sleep:

> Every muscle fiber had had enough by now; every cell of his body was screaming for him to stop and throw himself down onto the seemingly cool, harmless, cracked glass sheets on the grounds. … Sobbing, he gasped for air. He scrambled to his feet again, staggered on for a few steps, until the rhythm returned and carried him along. … He had forgotten the dead. … Would this ceaseless running, would this night ever take an end?"[14]

The returning images of dead friends Rohan sees in his mind make it impossible to undertake the effort of saving himself; only when he focuses on his breathing and heartbeat, on the strength of his own muscles, is he able to run, which saves his life. These last scenes of *The Invincible* tell a non-heroic version of the adventures of this interplanetary Robinson, equipped with neither a higher level of civilizational development nor cunning. It is the physical fitness and the fear of sharing the fate of his companions that energize his weakened body. In her review of *The Invincible*, Ursula Le Guin stressed that Rohan's courage and the fact that he is not defeated in the end has nothing to do with a mere test of virility *à la* Hemingway, and the final scene does not serve to show dedication to the cause or absolute obedience. According to Le Guin, the situation presented in the novel is tailored to human needs and reveals the difficult moral choices that the protagonist has to make. Thus, the adventure has an ethical dimension and is therefore extremely moving.[15] In the reviewer's opinion, against the background of science fiction, which abounds with easy optimism and equally easily depicted despair, Lem's novel is highly complex. After the utter failure of the *Invincible*, after Rohan's extremely difficult and unsuccessful search mission, readers might find a message hidden between the lines, that, after all, something has been saved.[16]

Peter Haffner, who analyzed the construction of characters in the context of classical novel formulas based on the intellectual and spiritual development of the protagonist (*Bildungsroman*), presented a very helpful interpretation of Pirx's adventures in the context of the Robinson theme. To get to know oneself usually means to get to know and understand the world. In Pirx's case, the transformation of a cadet into a commander follows a different path: the eager, awkward hero turns into a lonely old man over the course of many years of travels. Pirx is special, Haffner stresses, although his intelligence is not outstanding. Yet, he has instinct and a way of looking at things that differs from machines and his technocratic colleagues. The critic stresses that Pirx often finds a way out of a dramatic situation by pure chance, but always achieves the goal because he intuitively recognizes the signs that offer an unconventional solution. Confronted with perfect machines, Pirx manages to show the imperfection of the human condition, which sometimes makes survival possible (e.g. in *Ananke*).[17]

In Lem's later novels, the figure of Robinson fighting for his life appears only sporadically, replaced by either doubting scientists or misanthropic or grotesque machines. Nevertheless, it is noteworthy that just a dozen or so years after the war, the writer created protagonists who owe their deliverance to their own vigilance and a happy coincidence.

Witness

> "You don't know what you're talking about!" uncle started getting excited.
>
> "You are, my dear, witness to a crime, you have seen everything with your own eyes. Germans remember such things for a long time."[18]
>
> Stanisław Lem, *Time Not Lost*

In 1947, the magazine *Co Tydzień Powieść* (Weekly novels) published Stanisław Lem's short story *Plan anti-V*, about a double agent looking for the plans of a new German ballistic technology. The story is set in a historical context (the intelligence discovery of the Peenemünde Experimental Center in February 1943[19]) and refers to popular spy stories. Nevertheless, the narrative has a dreamlike quality. In successive scenes, overwhelming fear accumulates, and subsequent events are loosely connected with the main theme. An English agent is sent to Hamburg as a renowned engineer because he looks just like a German scientist captured by the Allies. The theme of a doppelganger, recurring in Lem's works, multiplies problems of identity and brings an element of horror into the prose. Engineer Seydlitz's double, Hughes, is a Scotsman, a British agent, sent to German armaments factories. During a test launch on the training grounds, the Allied agent witnesses the murder of prisoners in the Auschwitz camp, and immediately afterward he is taken to a masked ball, where he is disguised as a Scottish bagpiper. Afraid that he has been compromised and is going to be exposed, he decides to commit suicide. What follows is a sequence of traumatic images, accumulated and distorted, leading to a tragic finale. The temporal and spatial relationships, as well as historical references, are also disturbed. For example, Hamburg is more than 300 kilometers from Peenemünde, and the main storylines take place within 2 days, which is unlikely due to the distances and the number of events. Also prisoners forced to produce weapons were brought to Peenemünde from the Buchenwald concentration camp rather than from Auschwitz. The figure of the Holocaust witness seems to be particularly important in this anxious narrative structure. On the training grounds, the English spy is forced to watch how a ballistic missile turns oxygen into ozone, which soon leads to the prisoners suffocating in the middle of a meadow and dying after prolonged agony. The very idea of a ballistic missile that would deplete the atmosphere of oxygen seems disconcerting, especially since V-1, V-2 and V-3 missiles were made at Peenemünde, and although the manufacture claimed many lives, the missiles were not directly used in the extermination camps. Prisoners die the way they would have died in a gas chamber, although the setting is significantly different, as instead of brick buildings, behind tightly sealed doors, they are in a green meadow: "all that was visible were twisting bodies and terrible, swollen faces with wide open mouths covered in raspberry-colored froth .... There were more and more tangled, twitching bodies."[20] Ostensibly, the only reactions of the English agent are his hands, painfully clenched on a metal railing, and his professional determination to find out where the victims were brought from, to pass it on. Right afterward, the protagonist unexpectedly finds himself at a masked ball, where it turns out that instead of additional camouflage, the costume prepared by the hostess in fact reveals his identity. Disguised as a Scotsman, "he stood naked in the middle of a large circle of masks, closing in on him. He looked around desperately."[21] Before the agent decides to swallow cyanide, he observes his face in the mirror twice: "From the depths of the black glass, his own face, pale as paper, leaned over the console in the lodge. It lasted just a moment, like a warning";[22] "he saw himself in the depths of a tall mirror, with his face exposed by a vertical light, down to the finest wrinkles."[23] In her analyses of armed conflicts, which prove the fragility of life, Judith Butler pointed out that the subject always remains outside themselves because who they are is determined by their relationships with others. It is impossible to survive beyond relationships with others, which indicates the social nature of the existence of the human animal.[24] Lem's prose, on the other hand, reveals the effort of survival among others, who can unmask the true, carefully hidden identity. The mirror, agents and death by suffocation are obsessively recurring themes in this prose, building an atmosphere of incredibility and improbability. Multiplied images of oneself blur the unwanted identity, but a reflection in the mirror can shake the characters' sense of security, especially if they are agents. Long agony caused by a lack of oxygen is a subject of Lem's both realistic and science fiction works, and while it seems justified in the setting of space, the detailed description of the suffering and the slow agony of the victims, as well as the pain of the witnesses, forms one of the most moving death scenes in this prose.

The witness of the Holocaust in the short story *Plan anti-V* is a double agent and a participant in a masquerade, who tries to recognize his own face in a mirror because he has to put on a costume, dress up and forget about his old life and who he is. Disclosure of identity means death; it destroys the protagonist's psychological immunity, leading to paranoia and self-destruction. Being a witness also means compromising one's own safety. The condition of the witness appears in an even more distorted form in *Memoirs Found in a Bathtub*, when the protagonist – just before making the suicidal decision to surrender to the machine of the Building – finds himself in a museum, where

> On display were hands – hands severed at the wrist. ... Frozen in an incredible number of poses, they seemed caught forever in roles of a vast drama, a theater under glass. ... I passed: the hands of a saint (praying) and the hands of a sinner (dealing cards); fists of anger, fists of despair, and triumphant fists; then challenging hands and hands of denial; senile fingers giving a

> shaky blessing, senile fingers begging for bread; then some indecent gestures; over here, the shy blossoming of sweet innocence in the shadow of doom, and over there, a mother's relentless concern.[25]

The recording of theatrical gestures reflects various attitudes in the last moments of the victims' lives. Watching successive showcases filled with hands, the protagonist is struck by the illusion that the fingers of the exhibits point at him, which terrifies him and forces him to run away. Then he notices a man with an expression of frantic fear on his face, running toward him, and when he tries to stop, he bumps into a mirror. In narratives structured into nightmarish visions, this important theme of a mirror in Lem's writing serves to unmask the apparent power of "double agents" who seem to be able to escape death. In *Memoirs*, looking into a mirror is accompanied by finger-pointing by the remains of the bodies of those who, with their last gesture (reaching out through barred windows?), point to people who escaped their fate, which turns out to put too much pressure on the protagonist and leads him to suicidal thoughts. Such an ambiguous status as a witness features in Lem's prose in various unreal settings of spacecraft and alien planets. A strong sense of identification with the victims will lead the protagonists to madness or attempts to push the recurring images away. From silence about the atrocities in *Man from Mars* to round-ups in the ghetto in *Eden* and the nightmare of discovering mass graves in *The Invincible*, the main ethical challenges of the survivors are identified. The testimony of the dead in Lem's works is presented in an extreme way: encounters with the horror and suffering of others may lead to the loss of integrality, madness and suicide attempts.

In *Man from Mars*, the story of a vivisected alien visitor is set within a clear time limit, between the capitulation of Germany and the bombing of Hiroshima and Nagasaki. Separated from the city, researchers and a random journalist face a nuclear-powered Martian, whose strength and build far exceed human cognitive capacity. The protagonists witness the extraordinary technical capabilities of the creature, which they sometimes consider to be an object, sometimes an animal, and at the same time constantly compare it to a human being. Professor Widdletton, who is in charge of the project, learns the terrible secret of Martian civilization and concludes that it is so cruel that he should keep silent about it. This is why he tells his surviving companions in the laboratory building, "It is impossible to explain to people what you've experienced, how dare I, whom an alien from foreign worlds has put to the most difficult test?"[26] Widdletton comes to the conclusion that what saved him from the Martian's cruel story was the love for his family and the slightest shadow of faith in other people. The team wants to know the secret of the Alien's crime, so they are trying to get their leader to tell them what he has experienced and what he has seen in his vision:

> "Or perhaps you're hiding something terrible from us? Maybe they feed on blood, maybe they kill one another, maybe they eat one another?" I said.

> "Go ahead, Professor, we know this … from Earthly relations, what else could scare us?"[27]

Despite these insistencies and references to universal history, Widdletton remains silent and never divulges the dark secret. The testimony is not revealed but becomes a burden that the professor will have to bear alone.

This novel reflects the mechanism described by Dori Laub, who points out that the Holocaust is virtually devoid of witnesses who understand what they experienced and who are able to convey the horror of their experience:

> The Nazi system turned out therefore to be foolproof, not only in the sense that there were in theory no outside witnesses but also in the sense that it convinced its victims, the potential witnesses from the inside, that what was affirmed about their "otherness" and their inhumanity was correct and that their experiences were no longer communicable even to themselves, and therefore perhaps never took place. This loss of the capacity to be a witness to oneself and thus to witness from the inside is perhaps the true meaning of annihilation, for when one's history is abolished, one's identity ceases to exist as well.[28]

In *Man from Mars*, the secret of the terrible social organization of Martians is buried in the ruins of the laboratory and in the memory of the project leader. All that remains in the narrative version and in the dialogues are presumptions and associations connected with earthly atrocities. It is uncertain whether the professor will be able to cope with the burden of the secret and self-imposed silence on his own. However, he indubitably saved himself from the fate of engineer Fink, whom the Martian defeated using his mind and body:

> Fink's not human anymore. … Well, [the Martian] just beat Fink. It wasn't Fink under hypnosis, Fink in a cataleptic state, Fink mad … It was only externally Fink … our friend, but something that had his body, his legs and hands, that wore his clothes and that wasn't engineer Fink.[29]

Fink succumbs to the strength of the Alien under the influence of the image of Martian atrocities, and this force turns against his two companions and leads to their deaths. In the context of Laub's findings, Fink would be a character whose identity is taken away by a terrifying experience, leading to total destruction. A similar fate awaits a large part of the *Invincible* crew, who are affected by the loss of memory as a result of an attack by the machines operating on planet Regis III. In this fragment, associations with the exhausted victims of a concentration camp seem rather intentional:

> The other thirteen men, whose rigid masklike faces were especially terrifying, were brought to an isolated room where they allowed themselves

> to be put to bed without any resistance. They had to be undressed. They were as helpless as newborn babies. Rohan witnessed the scene silently. He stood in the corridor between the rows of cots. He noticed that most of the men remained passive, although those that had been carried off by force continued to whine eerily.[30]

The loss of identity associated with amnesia makes victims forget how they can satisfy their hunger and thirst, so they starve to death. To prevent this, they need to be cared for, fed, dressed and taught how to speak. They will never remember who they were again; in this case, the loss of identity as a result of a shock is irreversible.

Eden radically illustrates the position of the bystander/witness[31] of the extermination of a large part of the planet's population. As Fredric Jameson put it when interpreting this novel:

> It is as though alien anthropologists, on their first visit to Earth, landed in Auschwitz and attempted to construct a rational model of human society on the basis of what they found there.[32]

The reason why some doublers hunt others is gradually discovered by the protagonists, who finally find out that the source of violence is the theory of stronger doublers, convinced that the weaker group is just a genetic error, meaning that half of the planet's population is considered worthless. The astronauts from the wrecked spacecraft play the role of witnesses, constantly facing the risk of death, although they are not fully familiar with the social relations on the planet. The problem of passive observers of someone else's suffering can be interpreted as an analysis of the process of breaking ties with the persecuted, who are presented precisely as residents of a foreign planet, characters who do not form any community with the observers, who are not similar to the observers, just as their torturers are not similar to the crew of the ship.

In the initial phase of exploring Eden, scientists try to determine their own attitude toward doublers by asking the doctor performing an autopsy whether a doubler is an animal, whether it is intelligent and what its dual form means (skin folds and a hull resembling a child's torso). At the same time, exploration of the planet and encounters with new life forms provoke revulsion and disgust in the six scientists at every step, and everything smells revolting to them. Unable to understand the social relations on the planet, the scientists call it the "civilization of lunatics." After finding successive piles of corpses, when the researchers think that the whole planet consists of nothing but graves, the engineer asks the Doctor: "Maybe they were only animals." To which the Doctor replies, "And what are we?"[33] The settlements where doublers live are reminiscent of ghettos, and the creatures, plunged into poverty and fear, panic at every sign of an invasion (operation?) and desperately rush to escape. Doublers-attackers, on the other hand, wear silvery clothes and helmets. Looking for analogies to situations known from Earth, the participants in the expedition begin to think that doubler settlements are a refuge for mentally ill people. Once again – after *Hospital of the Transfiguration* – Lem reminds us of the story that marked the beginning of Nazi thinking about mass extermination, this time presenting the event in the convention of science fiction.

Although in *Eden* the protagonists do not speak much about world history (references concern religious wars rather than the most recent events, known to the reader from the late 1950s), the system of references they present is quite startling: a concentration camp, hunting, cannibalism, medical experiments, liquidation operations in psychiatric hospitals. One of the last scenes of the novel is devoted to a conversation with a learned doubler from the persecuted caste, who indicates that the socio-political system of Eden is much more complicated than those analogies. In the descriptions of the expeditions further into the planet, the history of World War Two, and especially the Holocaust, is reproduced, hidden under the mask of the constant wonder of scientists that the Edenian social system may exist at all. The protagonists face being in the position of powerless witnesses, observing acts of cruelty, passively watching mass deaths. Every attempt to support the persecuted caste ends in an open conflict and the death of those in whose defense they tried to act.

The adventures in *The Invincible* correspond to the main determinants of the science fiction convention, in its most classic version. The mission of the ship landing on Regis III seems simple: its goal is to determine the cause of death of the *Condor*'s crew. Changing the mode of reading this story – one of the most ephemeral in Lem's oeuvre – reveals issues it addresses concerning the mechanisms of memory operation and gradual adjustment to tragic, cruel events. The story begins with a scene of landing on the planet and the commanding officer's order not to leave the ship, which is met with disapproval: "Almost one hundred men who had not heard the rustling of the wind for many months, who had learned to hate the emptiness of space in the manner of those who have become too familiar with it."[34] The ship's crew is therefore extremely isolated, and the need to climb out seems more important than their own safety, even though they have spent much of their journey in a state of hibernation. The main question asked by the commander and scientists is how to collect information on the cause of the *Condor*'s disappearance, secure evidence and prevent a repeat of the tragedy. Finally, the crew manages to work out safety rules, and scouts headed by Rohan discover what they consider to be the ruins of a city whose buildings are perforated like "multilayered honeycombs or sieves"[35] and "above everything hung the breath of deadly loneliness and isolation."[36] The story of the two spaceships – the *Invincible* and the *Condor* – is a story of two possible scenarios of the crew's fate; the ships are identical, in the story they are described as doppelgangers, and their double nature draws attention to the possible alternative fate and chances of survival with the same security measures. Eighty-three of the *Invincible* men are protected by the power of the ship and the far-reaching caution of the commander, yet they are annoyed by the isolation, the state of "sleep," the stagnation and repetitiveness of the activities performed in the same closed, claustrophobic space. When they finally leave the ship, they soon find out where the *Condor* landed. On arrival, they find human skulls, bones, body remains and mummified corpses strewn around the ship. Rohan, as a commanding officer, checks all the rooms of the ship – they are in disarray, and the corpses of the crew lie about:

> Rohan was one of the last to leave the Condor. He felt dizzy. Nausea overcame him in spurts and it took all his will power to fight off the recurring attacks. He felt as if he had just awakened from some incredibly horrible dream. But one look at the men's faces told him that the whole thing had been real.[37]

At the sight of decaying corpses, bones lying in disarray and dead faces with frozen expressions of fear and panic, Rohan feels sick and wants to forget everything. He realizes that he is not the only witness, so he tries to assimilate those images and assist in arranging the discovered corpses in neat rows, constantly fearing that he will find a familiar face among the dead. When the crew of the *Invincible* finds a body frozen in the hibernator, everyone begins to feel (futile) hope that perhaps one of the crew members survived:

> There was no indication that this man had been intended to survive his stay in the hibernator. He had most likely stumbled inside by accident – another riddle, just as nonsensical as everything else that had happened on board the Condor.[38]

The description of finding dead bodies, bones, remains and the accompanying feelings of terror, fear and disgust could also apply to the discovery of mass graves or the dragging the bodies of those murdered by the NKVD out to the courtyard at Brygidki. Rohan – even after his return from the *Condor* – "No matter which wall or corner he looked at, he could not banish the images of insanity that had been etched in his brain."[39]

Called to determine the causes of death of the crew, Doctor Nygren explains that about 100 people died of hunger and exhaustion – that even though they had access to food, they had lost the knowledge about how to satisfy their hunger. During the debate among scientists trying to explain this horrifying phenomenon, one physicist stresses that he believes that

> we lack the courage to call some of the things we observed on board the Condor by their right name. … Just remember, it is necessary, for our own sake as well as for that of the dead crew of the Candor, to face the facts with an open mind. I'd like to urge you – in fact, I insist – that we all speak out freely: what was it that shocked you most when you were at the Condor? Something that you have not been able to confide to anybody yet, something so horrible you'd rather forget than even mention it.[40]

This is the most poignant fragment of *The Invincible* because it leads to difficult confessions and brings out images that the protagonists could not cope with, tried to push away and forget about, finding comfort in the fact that concealing that information would protect the good memory of the victims. After this appeal, Rohan confesses that he noticed tooth marks in bars of soap, another scientist mentions books and maps smeared with human excrement, someone talks about impressions of teeth on an unopened can of food, and yet another analyzes meaningless scrawls found in the ship's log book. This return of images that the protagonists' psyches tried to push back at all costs to avoid assimilating them, does little to help explain what happened on board the *Condor*, so the scene is meaningless from the point of view of the story's dynamics. However, if we look at Laub's concept of the mechanisms of non-assimilation of images associated with being a witness to the Holocaust, the protagonists' discussion may become more comprehensible:

> The horror of the historical experience continues in the testimony only as an elusive memory that feels as if it no longer resembles any reality. The horror is, indeed, compelling not only in its reality, but even more so, in its flagrant distortion and subversion of reality.[41]

The repetition of the most shocking memories does not explain the causes of the catastrophe, but shows the scale of the shock of the incomprehensible phenomena, and also their abject aspect. The physiology of extermination and the various stages of starvation leave their marks on objects left by the dead, and their discovery causes shock, but also a sense of disgust, against the background of solid machines that were supposed to protect life and formations reminiscent of burnt-out walls of the city.

The Invincible is a story that reveals the mechanisms of distancing oneself from the images one sees, but also indicates the need to extract and work through them in order to make them comprehensible. The process of forgetting and becoming accustomed to the horrors of events is complemented by a reflection on the ethical obligations toward the dead. Once all the bodies have been found and deposited in the special chambers of the operational ship,

> The men whose job it was to continue to search the sand around the Condor, or to rummage through the ship's interior, experienced boredom rather than a sense of relief. They seemed to have grown oblivious to the fate of the former crew. Their efforts now concentrated on collecting bits of memorabilia, meaningless knick-knacks that had survived their anonymous owners – an old, workworn harmonica or a Chinese puzzle. These objects quickly lost all traces of their origin, and were soon circulated and used as communal property among the *Invincible*'s crew.
>
> Rohan would never have believed it possible, but in less than a week he was behaving no differently than the rest of the crew.[42]

Analyzing this mechanism, the officer comes to the conclusion that its only purpose is self-deception while everyone expects some accident to happen and that the crew of the *Invincible* will share the fate of the dead from the *Condor*. The use of the deceased's belongings by those awaiting annihilation is not stigmatized, and the protagonist treats this phenomenon only as a transitional stage between the death of the previous crew and that of the current. Setting aside the genre of this short story, there are allusions to using objects left after the murdered victims of a war. The boredom of people talking about the catastrophe and the appropriation of things that once belonged to the dead show how tragic events are repressed and how quickly the process of forgetting and silencing shocking images progresses. *The Invincible* was written between 1962 and 1963, 20 years after the mass extermination of Jews and only 2 years before *Highcastle*, in which the subject of eradicated material traces of the dead returns repeatedly:

> What is it about the objects and cobblestones surrounding us in childhood that is so magical, so irreplaceable? Whence comes their demand that after the destruction of war and with them piled in rubbish heaps, I testify to their existence? Not many years after the idyllic time presented here, inanimate things were envied their permanence, for day by day people were taken from their midst, and suddenly the things were orphaned, the chairs, canes, and knickknacks abandoned and monstrously useless. As if objects were superior to the living, hardier than they, less vulnerable to the catastrophes of time. As if liberated from their owners, they had gained force and expression – consider the baby carriages and washbasins on the barricades, the eyeglasses there was no one to look through, the piles of letters stepped on. Although in the landscape of war they gained the power of eerie signs, I never held that against them. I believed in their innocence.[43]

It is not objects that are guilty of the war, which deprived them of their owners' care. Things that once belonged to the dead cannot be used as relics; there are too many of them, they were abandoned in bulk, in disarray, haphazardly. Nor did they accompany the loved ones in dying. This is not the first time Lem notices that objects, including machines, can be orphaned and marked by the painful stigma of abandonment.

In *Tales of Pirx the Pilot* there is a cosmic version of Czesław Miłosz's poem *Campo di fiori*. In the first part of the story, *The Albatross*, the pilot describes the luxury of one of the safest spaceships in the world:

> A gay and festive crowd. Live dance music … and live waiters, each decked out like a philharmonic conductor. "The *Transgalactic* offers you nonautomated service, cordial and intimate surroundings, genuinely human hospitality, and a completely live crew, each a master of his trade."[44]

Pirx visits the ship and tries to distance himself from its splendor, when suddenly he feels an unexpected change in the ship's course and decides to find out what caused them to deviate from the route. Soon it turns out that together with other ships, the *Transgalactic* set off to respond to an SOS call from the *Albatross*. Increased speed means inconveniencing passengers, and they are kept informed about the rescue operation. The desperate attempts to come to the aid of the endangered crew are accompanied by horror:

> In that room were veterans of many years' flight experience, but what they heard now was unprecedented. A voice – barely audible, accompanied by a protracted roar, as if trapped behind a wall of flame – was shouting:
>
> "Albatross … every man … coolant in cockpit … temperature unbearable … crew standing by to the end … so long … all lines … out."[45]

Broken words, lack of explanation, and an awareness of the inevitable demise of people dying in the fire fill the cabin of the ship's commanders, leading to a paralyzing fear. Meanwhile, the passengers of the *Transgalactic* are not interested in whether the efforts of several crews resulted in the rescue of people who were in mortal danger, but whether they can go back to dancing already, so they ask when the operation will finally be completed. The ball, which takes place on the deck, enters the space of the cabin where the telegraphs are located – the last witnesses to the crew's death. Pirx is coming up to one of them:

> He was on the verge of asking about the crew of the Albatross, whether anyone had managed to escape, when the operator, sensing that someone was standing behind him, raised his head and looked him straight in the eye. Without saying another word, Pirx took his leave, through the door marked STELLAR PERSONNEL ONLY.[46]

The death and despair of the agony affect the witnesses, and at the end of the operation the captain addresses the passengers, not to inform about the death of the *Albatross* crew – after all, they do not care about them – but to tell them they can continue dancing.

Being both a victim and a witness to the death of one's companions, friends but also strangers, whose suffering seeps into the deepest layers of memory, preserving images of despair and the rhythm of slow dying, features not just in the prose works interpreted above, although they present such themes in a particularly poignant and consistent way. Lem's protagonists usually lose someone and repeatedly reminisce about those fatal accidents and friends lost in space.

Mane Tekel

Lem's correspondence with Michael Kandel is a unique personal document from the writer, testifying to the great trust the author of *His Master's Voice* placed in his American translator. Between giving advice on the principles of neologism building and explaining the literary allusions in his works, in his letters Lem shared information on the origins of some of his texts and reported on his impressions from reading contemporary American novels, drawing attention to the elusive, individual, fascinating relationships between readers and books, comparing them to love and eroticism.[47] In this thoughtful and kind correspondence, particularly interesting is the letter of September 3, 1974, in which Lem passionately discusses Kandel's interpretation of *Memoirs Found in a Bathtub*.

In a letter dated August 26, 1974, the interpreter alluded to the political restrictions associated with living behind the Iron Curtain. In his correspondence 2 years prior, Lem himself had stressed that when writing his *Memoirs*, he did indeed refer to the Stalinist era.[48] Already in his correspondence from 1972, Kandel pointed to the pessimism and lack of hope evident in the novel, seeing the Building as an allegory of the Cosmos, noting Kafka's influence and drawing attention to the determinism of the Universe outlined there. He also wrote that he did not like the novel, precisely because of the strict dependence of events on certain conditions, and he said that the protagonist seemed to him to be "less than human": he is stereotypical, banal and not unlike a puppet, so it is hard to follow his exploits and identify with him.[49] Kandel informed Lem that in his *Memoirs* the writer had managed to maintain a balance between the tragedy of the suffering man and the comical absurdity of the puppet-like character, while it was extremely difficult for him, as a translator, to balance between those two approaches, which is why the English version of the protagonist is somewhat reminiscent of Tichy.[50] In 1974, both artists were aware that their correspondence was censored by the Security Service – Kandel's letter of August 26, 1974 concerning *Memoirs* can be read as an attempt to give encouragement to the person who feels imprisoned in his country. The translator wrote that hope was necessary in life, and its absence may make it impossible to believe in the meaning of creative effort. He emphasized that the most important thing is freedom of mind, intellectual work associated with it and the possibility of meditation and internal development, as well as friendships with fellow prisoners. He believed that the character from *Memoirs* was trapped by his own personality and not by the Building, which, he felt, was extremely weak.[51]

Lem referred all Kandel's remarks not to his present day, but to *Memoirs Found in a Bathtub*, although he set the novel in a different historical context and in his own experience. In response, he noted that his writing was more than just "pure text," without any references to reality, but he also pointed out that:

> The misfortune of a writer like me is that he either speaks to those who know roughly <u>what</u> he is saying anyway, or to those who do not understand him <u>completely</u> – the former share experiences with the writer, while the latter do not – and that's all. The situation described in *Memoirs* is not fiction, not a confabulation, an invention without any material cover, and

> does not refer to any Kafka, but, first and foremost, to my own personal experience.[52]

The author of *His Master's Voice* thus pointed to two cycles of reception of his works – the first circle consisted of people with similar life experiences, understanding his allusions to the past and the present despite the science fiction setting; the other were readers who did not notice the historical context, fascinated by the fantastical convention, focused on intertextual and genre games.

In a letter to the translator, Lem related the fate of the protagonist of *Memoirs* to the situations of occupation and explained that his hero did not seek help and support from other people because in those conditions, every friend could turn out to be a traitor and denounce him. The writer emphasizes:

> Humanity is not only above animalism, but it is also in the opposite direction, lower than the animal condition – and this is the truth, the omission of which I would consider to be a betrayal of literature, identifying it with ordinary fraud, not just literary.[53]

To erase any traces of the rupture caused in literature by the Holocaust would be tantamount to misappropriating the challenge of giving testament to what people are capable of. The writer rejected the translator's interpretation in its entirety and referred the world of the novel directly to the Holocaust. His protagonist, as well as the victims of Nazi policy, were deprived of the ability to make decisions, even if the latter were limited to choosing how they wanted to die. The fate of Father Maksymilian Kolbe was used as a historical example of the situation depicting the cause of the helplessness of the hero of *Memoir.* Lem believed that Kolbe could give his life for another prisoner only because the German supervisor of the camp agreed; both of them could have died in the camp and the memory of them would probably not have lasted long. The writer emphasized:

> But if both were condemned, just like the Jews at the threshold of the gas chamber in that very camp, neither of them would have anything to give for the other, for his life could no longer be a sacrifice to sacrifice. If that is not obvious, then nothing is obvious. Human memory flees from such reminiscences, and culture turns its back on such literature that keeps repeating "mane tekel" too often.[54]

The writer explains to Kandel that the protagonist of *Memoirs* was not spiritually weak, but rather, in the face of the machinery of the Building, he was deprived of any chance to act. Lem agreed with the translator that the only consolation was that the Building would eventually have to fall apart and that no monolithic authority could survive forever. The writer did not ignore this solace, although he emphasized:

> if it crumbles slower than the human body, if it is certain that we will not survive it, but that it will survive us, and that one day it will finally fall down, then, for the only life given to us, it is an insufficient consolation.[55]

Lem noted that literature should not constantly repeat "mane tekel"; it cannot just herald ruin and death. Hence the need for a grotesque distance:

> The scarier the content, the funnier it is served, seasoned with humorous sauce, which is supposed to be something of a counterpoint – so that you can bear the unbearable.[56]

In her article *Humor as a Defense Mechanism during the Holocaust*, Chaya Ostrower analyzed the accounts of survivors who were teenagers during the German occupation. Her findings demonstrate that gallows humor turned out to be one of the most effective tools to reduce the anxiety that accompanied the awareness of death, as well as an efficient mechanism of self-defense and an emotional escape from the brutal reality.[57] Dark humor reflects not only the tragicomic fate of a body exposed to constant danger, but also provides an opportunity to tell a story about an extreme situation, the horror of which provokes a defensive reaction and complete rejection in the readers. Laughter and joy, however, have the power needed to understand the extent of a disaster through acquiring distance.

Thus, Lem indicated the interpretation of *Memoirs Found in a Bathtub*, and the attempt to read this – as Jerzy Jarzębski called it – most mysterious, philosophical and disturbing novel[58] according to the writer's instructions requires more attention to the narrative elements previously considered in the context of the criticism of totalitarian systems. If we treat the labyrinths of the Building as the space of occupied Lviv, where the protagonist wanders helplessly under a false identity, moving between cellars and attics or hiding in the bathroom, the novel becomes less mysterious than when we regard it as a parable. This does not change its emotional dimension, as it remains a haunting study of fear and despair. In a fictional introduction to *Memoir*,[59] explaining the most probable causes of the downfall of the Neogene community associated with paper decay, the anonymous narrator notes: "In place of those great treasuries, those reservoirs of society's memory, lay mounds of gray, powdery ash."[60] Dust, ashes, parts of human skeletons and a unique testimony of that period, that is, the "memoirs," are the elements remaining after the "chaotic" era and the times of the "Great Collapse." One of the fictitious scientists quoted in the introduction hypothesizes that in the period preceding the Neogen in "Ammer-Ka" there were beliefs in "of various Perils – Black, Red, Yellow – evidently cabalistic incantations connected in some way with the mysterious deity Rayss, to whom burnt offerings were apparently made."[61] The mockery concerns both the allusion to apartheid in America and the association of Nazi views with Kabbalistic beliefs among scientists drawing conclusions from archaeological discoveries and after the disintegration of the dictionary of the Chaotic. In addition, views on the human sacrifice made to Rayss have been the subject of dispute between historical schools and remain only one of many hypotheses. As a setting, America, or more precisely the Pentagon and Washington, effectively distract attention from the author's biographical context and placate the censor, while at the same time this allusion (based on the Cold War topography) becomes another of Lem's unintentional prophecies, as in 1993 the United States Holocaust Memorial Museum was established in that city, and testimonies of the survivors are kept there.

In the memoir itself, the map showing the layout of the Building is located inside "St. Juan Mount" (*Góra Świętego Juana*; in Kandel and Rose's English translation it is simply "the mountain"). If we assume that there is no information in the Building that is not encrypted and apply it to the biographical situation indicated in Lem's correspondence, we can assume that the location refers to St. George Hill in Lviv, where the Greek Catholic Cathedral stands. This is important because one of the first scenes of the novel takes place during obsequies in a temple. Funeral rites take place near the hermitage, behind the altar door, leading to a monk's cell, as one of the brothers explains. The protagonist does not heed the ban on entering the hermitage, opens the door and goes to the antechamber, which is blocked with piles of junk, covered with onion skins and coal dust. There he finds another door and decides to enter:

> I reached the other door, stepping gingerly through the debris, and turned a heavy iron handle. Inside, there was shuffling, whispering. By the light of a single candle somewhere on the floor I saw shadowy figures scurry about, crouch in the corners, scuttle under crooked tables or cots. Someone blew out the candle and there were angry whispers and grunts in the darkness. The air was heavy with the stale smell of unwashed bodies. I beat a hasty retreat.[62]

At first, the nameless hero does not return to the scene and does not think about who the figures hiding from him were, although he realizes that only agents and soldiers – uniformed or in plain clothes – are allowed inside the Building. The hermitage as an asylum is evoked once again in the novel as the exhausted, weary and aching hero tries to find a safe way out of the situation:

> I was tired, my bones ached. Once again I decided to leave, go somewhere, perhaps visit that old hermit – no, on second thought, it was too crowded there.[63]

If this set in a historical context, namely the occupation in Lviv, we can assume that the scene alludes to the hiding of Jews by the Metropolitan Archbishop Andriy Sheptytsky in the buildings adjacent to the Greek Catholic Cathedral, but also to the clergy's relations with the Ukrainian Insurgent Army and the Nazis[64] – after all, priests in the novel wear cassocks that hide uniforms underneath. And although, as Dawid Kahane emphasized, many Jews sought shelter with high-ranking church dignitaries, the description of an old man guarding the entrance to the hermitage where refugees are hiding brings to mind the physical condition of the archbishop: "The old man," Kahane writes, "is 86 years old, with a long white beard, half-paralyzed and chairbound for more than ten years, unable to move without someone else's help."[65] Visiting the hermit can also simply mean a decision to live an eremite life, which – ironically in this context, of course – entails ascetism, mortification and meditations in a crowded, suffocating space. This comparison can also be found in Dawid Kahane's account, when he explained that if Jews hiding on the so-called Aryan side did not leave their hometown and stayed with their friends, they were essentially "bricked up alive" in their shelters, unable to leave them until the end of the occupation.[66]

When interpreting *Memoirs*, it is worth asking historical questions, referring to the everyday lives of people living on the so-called Aryan papers during the occupation. The protagonist of the novel has three options: to wander the corridors, pretending to be one of the employees of the Building; to hide at the back of the chapel; or to leave through the door of the Building, which means certain death. These three choices illustrate the experiences of the people in hiding. To live out in the open, in an environment where anyone could be an informer, forced into constant vigilance, the need to pretend to work and participate in occupation-era life.[67] Staying in hiding seemed safer but involved living in darkness and claustrophobic fear, deprived of any chance to move and have any (even illusory) agency regarding one's fate. The only certain way out of this grueling situation could be immediate death, so readily available at every step. In his examination of personal documents of the Holocaust years, Jacek Leociak cites phrases used by Emanuel Ringelblum, who, when writing about Jews that tried to survive outside the ghetto, divided them into "visible" and "invisible." The researcher used comparisons that can be found in Lem's spy fiction, namely the need for camouflage and mimicry and constant performing of someone else's identity. Leociak also offers an interesting take on testimonies concerning an approach to the so-called *gadzinówka* (Polish-language newspapers officially published by and loyal to the German occupation authorities), which consisted in deciphering the news to distinguish actual information about the situation on the front from propaganda.[68] All these actions intended to guarantee survival were only an unheroic attempt to stay alive:

> "Outliving" on its surface level may mean outliving your persecutors but also implies outliving those who did not manage to stay alive. This is one of the most pervasive microbes infecting humiliated memory.[69]

The protagonist of *Memoirs* is no longer a Robinson, but a victim sentenced to death in life.

Dreams

Memoirs Found in a Bathtub has the structure of a dream. The narrative does not follow causal rules; individual events are linked by the associative character of the narrator's actions, his being lost in time and space and incomprehensible language. For this reason, details, keywords and elements around which revolves the imagination of the protagonist receiving instructions, i.e. blank white cards or empty folders, become essential. In *The Theme of the Three Caskets*, Sigmund Freud pointed out that the necessity to make a choice whose consequences one cannot know, and hiding – the inability to find someone – are themes associated with death.[70] In her article *Dreams as a Source for Research on the Holocaust*, Barbara Engelking argues that recorded dreams concerning the occupation may be a valuable source of information for historians because they "show us historical events through the emotions and experiences of their participants. … After all, the Holocaust is not only a historical event – it is a human experience, a boundary existential situation, experiencing one's own death during one's lifetime."[71]

For Langer, a dream is an expression of deep memory, therefore "the nightmare [it] describes is not a metaphor but a reality. Nothing is disguised, and no one is needed to analyze its concealed meanings."[72] Fear, resignation, dullness and constant attempts to get out of the dangerous space dominate the nightmare that makes up the plot of *Memoirs*. There are also references to dreaming when the narrator wonders whether what he is experiencing is a dream from which he can wake up, or whether he is only a character in someone else's dream, so he has no agency and will be annihilated once it ends. As Engelking put it:

> A dreaming person is not free – they have no free will, they cannot do what they want. It is the dream that imposes on them the themes, characters, motifs and the way they are presented. … The dream gives us freedom and at the same time keeps us in its power, enclosing us within its own narrative.[73]

This theme of "imprisonment" in a dream is very significant for *Memoirs*, as the book recreates the reality of the occupation, especially in the emotional aspect, referring to the sense of constant threat and awareness that one's life depends on pure chance. The protagonist who wants to read his destiny knows that death is the only certainty. The narrator meets people who, thinking that they have been exposed, swallow poison or shoot themselves in the head, while spies in grey uniforms holding machine guns patrol the corridors of the building.[74] Upon finding blank documents, the protagonist starts thinking about cutting his wrists with a razor:

> More and more I could see before me the image of my own face, the cringing, sweaty face of a condemned man. I was defeated, destroyed – what

> more was there to lose? … This ugly face, bathed in sweat and twisted in fear, would soon cease to exist. The thought was almost pleasant. Ah, but I had known all along that it would come to this![75]

Fragments concerning resignation reproduce the mood present in the literature of personal document, because there the present time becomes final, and "Tomorrow has the quality of a postponed execution that did not happen today."[76] Analyzing oral testimonies of the Holocaust survivors, Langer emphasized that memory is not only a spring, flowing from the well of the past, but also a tomb, whose contents cling like withered ivy to the mind. For the witnesses, the Holocaust is at once a lived event and a "died" event: the paradox of how one survives a died event is one of the most urgent (if unobtrusive) topics of their testimonies.[77]

In Lem's prose, there are many fragments devoted to the protagonists' reflections on their own death, accepting it and deciding to face it peacefully. They are the culmination of many scenes. Some characters – like the agent in the story *Plan anti-V* – commit suicide, as the hero of *Memoir* also intends to do on a number of occasions, clenching a razor in his hand. Others avoid death at the last moment, usually with little involvement on their part, although that does not break the emotional numbness to which they already succumbed.

The protagonist of *Memoirs* feels insecure because he does not understand the principles and dynamics of the Building's functioning, and there is no place for him to hide. As soon as he receives a record of his mission from one of the commanders, it turns out that it is hidden in a yellow folder:

> "The color signifies something?"
> My innocence amused him.
> "Does it signify something, he asks. That's great."[78]

Just like food coupons, the yellow color that marks the fate of the protagonist is a direct reference to everyday life during the occupation. If we assume that the narrator of the memoirs was a Jew hiding on the so-called Aryan side, certain fragments and vague allusions also become significant: when the General[79] chooses the hero for a dangerous mission, during which he will likely be killed, he utters an odd phrase: "You got a difficult body." [the English translation reads "the Old Boy gave you a tough nut to crack"].[80] This is followed by a scene of burning the original documents, during which the General's associate "marveled at the naturalness of my face, particularly the nose – then I realized he assumed it was false."[81] The protagonist must also answer the question of whether he yawns and snores because, as the lieutenant explains to him, "many of our people have come to a bad end by snoring."[82] In order to illustrate what happened to those who inadvertently yawned or snored, the officer takes him to the Department of Collections, a room without windows, where chests filled with teeth, pearls and hair are kept. In this warehouse of curiosities there are also tapestries made of beards, sideburns and wigs: "After some hesitation, Blanderdash pointed out one dignitary's coat in the panorama: the lapels were neatly trimmed black sideburns; I was given to understand they originally belonged to an enemy agent this dignitary had unmasked."[83] This entire storage of things made from human bodies is a secret that cannot be discussed. To become an object is a fate that awaits those who betray their hiding place by snoring. Such processing of human bodies, their transformation into objects, is preceded by an execution, but with time it becomes more and more mechanized. As the agent in the bathroom puts it:

> And they took care of you without all these rights and grounds today – good old cloak-and-dagger, everything hush-hush, a knock at the door and a visit to the Cellar Section, a little slapping around, a little boot in the kisser, a tooth or two, sign here and you're through. The most they do now is have an occasional shoot-out.[84]

Brutal beatings and torture in the Building were replaced by gunshots in the streets–corridors, which does not change the fact that the presence of double and triple agents causes fear and turns the men hiding in the bathroom, to quote one of them, into "window dressing." They do not trust one another, either. The fact that anyone can become a snitch or inadvertently contribute to the deaths of others frightens the protagonist, who is paralyzed with terror by every person he meets, even if they are not armed. After all, one of the spies gives him the following advice: "Above all, keep up your strength. Regular meals, an occasional snack, cookies and milk, some cake."[85] This simple principle – just like the hero's shaving, washing and frequently sleeping in his clothes – can have a real impact on survival in such a dangerous place as the Building.

Husks

The above interpretation of *Memoirs Found in a Bathtub* indicates that similar themes can be found in others of Lem's works. In *The Eleventh Voyage* from *Star Diaries*, beginning with Tichy's observation that his robot has broken down and is no longer tidying up properly, the pilot is called to a case of "cosmic importance" – he is to be an agent sent in disguise to the Secret Planet, ruled by rebellious robots who escaped from a spaceship that went missing.[86] Subsequent undercover agents sent by the secret organization did not return from the mission on Cercia (called Kareliria in the original version)[87] but it has been established that robots on that planet call people offensive names, such as "mucilids" and "gook," considering them unworthy of life. A representative of mechanical psychiatry acts as a defender of dangerous machines, stressing that they have become aggressive toward people because they have absorbed

> a comprehensive knowledge of such matters as the history of Jack the Ripper, the Boston Strangler, the Strangler of Gloomspick, also the

> biography of Sacher-Masoch, the memoirs of the Marquis de Sade, and the records of the flagellant sect of Pirpinact, and a first edition of Murmuropoulos's *Impalement through the Centuries*, as well as that famous collector's item from the Abercrombie library – *Stabbing*, in manuscript, by one Hapsodor, beheaded in the year 1673 in London and better known under the alias of "the Baby Butcher." [88]

In other words, they learned violence from people. This scientific explanation does not help solve the puzzles of the planet. Regardless of the danger, Tichy undertakes a dangerous mission and sets off in camouflage, disguised as a robot, on a secret space expedition. Just as in *Memoirs*, as he is being trained to be an agent, the issue of loud breathing and eating emerges, two elements that can expose the pilot and contribute to his death. When Tichy prepares for the expedition to Cerulia, he first reads ominous newspaper announcements:

> THE BURDEL OF GOMORRHEUM
> OPNETH TO-DAY ITS YATES!
> OUR RESTAURACION OFFRETH
> TASTEE DISSHE NE BIFOREN
> FETURED!! MUCILYDE BABEE,
> VITAILLE YSERVE ATTE BORDAND CARIE-OOT!!![89]

Translated and deciphered neologisms turn out to be an advertisement composed of expressions such as brothel, Sodom and Gomorrah, selection of human children and modest belongings to take away. Sodom evokes associations with the few survivors from that city and Lot's wife, who turned away in spite of God's prohibition, and who, realizing the enormity of the suffering, turned into a pillar of salt. Tichy's suspicions of the cruelty of the machines are confirmed when he enters the home of one of them:

> Down the steps I went, deafened by the racket, as though someone were hewing an iron stump to slivers. It came from the parlor. My host, stripped down to his iron torso, was with a curiously fashioned cleaver hacking away at a large doll that lay upon the table.
>
> "Entre, goode my gest! Ye moote werken your hertes delyte upon yon carcase," he said, leaving off his chopping when he saw me and pointing to another, somewhat smaller doll lying there on the floor. When I drew near, the thing sat up, opened its eyes, and began in a faint voice to say, over and over:
>
> "Sire – I yam an innocent chylde – spare me – sire – I yam an innocent chylde – spare me."
>
> My host handed me an ax, similar to a halberd, but with a shorter shaft.
>
> "Nowe then, noble gest, awey with care, awey with sorowe – hav to, and smyte smerte!"

"But I – I do no cure for children ..." I feebly protested. He froze.

"No cure?" he repeated. "A pitee. Ye putten me in sore perplexitee, my frend. What shal you doon? I hav but litel oons – tis my wekenesse, ywis. Woldstow then trie a calf?"

And from out of the cupboard he brought a perfectly serviceable plastic calf, which, when squeezed, produced a timorous bleat. What could I do? Not wishing to unmask myself, I slashed away at the unfortunate puppet, tiring myself out completely in the process. Meanwhile my host had drawn and quartered both dolls, put aside his instrument, which he called his bone-buster, and asked if I were content. I assured him that I had not known such pleasure for quite some time."[90]

Readers would be hard-pressed to find a fragment quite like this one in Polish literature, where the archaic stylization and language of Polish classics such as Pasek and Sienkiewicz are used to tell about the Holocaust. Scenes of a selection of children being murdered with axes, their requests and supplications disregarded, are presented in a grotesque and highly stylized fashion, with an ironic distance that undermines the authenticity of associations with historical events. Between the begging child and a plastic puppet, between the murder of infants and a plastic calf, a vague image emerges, followed by a series of understatements intensified by archaization. The terms "dolls" (*lale* in the Polish version) bring to mind the Nazi word *Figuren*, which already appeared in *Time Not Lost* and *Memoirs*. If we read this passage several times and try to understand what kind of situation it replicates, we have to consider its repulsive power. Describing such situations, when testimonies include recollections unbearable to listeners, which we instinctively want to push away, the researcher of tormented memory wrote:

> We validate the significance of these testimonies by listening to their voices until we hear what Nelly Sachs, in a poem about survivors, called "the mutilated music of their lives." To share this dissonance with a perception built from the ruins of mutilation without being crippled by it ourselves is the summons we face when we embrace the legacy of these testimonies, which bear witness to the simultaneous destruction and survival of European Jewry.[91]

The ironic and grotesque tone of Tichy's adventures on the enslaved planet, where he has to hide his identity, also concerns the hunger he feels. After being imprisoned by robots, the pilot is deprived of access to the modest food supplies he had in his rocket:

> Four more days went by. My biggest problem was food. I made do with the belt from my trousers, soaking it in the water they brought me once a day. The guard carried the pot at arm's length, as if it were poison.
>
> After a week the belt ran out, but fortunately I had on high laced boots of goatskin – their tongues were the very best thing I ate during my stay in the cell.[92]

Eating one's own clothes, soaking inedible objects in water, boot tongue consumed with a side of shoelaces are examples of a dark, gallows sense of humor of a person who is sentenced to death and has nothing to lose. The ironic distance helps Tichy see his own tragicomic situation, at the same time evoking the most difficult moments of the occupation-era reality, namely the overwhelming hunger and thirst.

Tichy's *Eleventh Voyage* can be considered as an illustration of one of the most popular quotes from Zofia Nałkowska's *Medallions*, "People dealt this fate to people," although in Lem's story they pretend to one another that they are no longer people at all. Tichy's provocations lead to the discovery that the robots cruelly killing children are in fact corrupt emissaries from the Earth, diligently obeying the Calculator, who turns out to be a grumpy old man following the orders issued by an unspecified superior authority with clerical meticulousness. People report on other people to save their lives or to gain acknowledgement from the Computer, forget words from their own language and speak in phrases from propaganda posters. When Tichy discovers that it was people who destroyed his ship and reported on him to the Computer, he gets angry:

> But the Computer wasn't satisfied merely to neutralize its enemies – it made of each a champion of its cause, and by requiring them to turn in others, the new arrivals, it gave still further proof of its diabolical cunning, for who could best distinguish men from robots if not those very men, who after all were privy to all the secrets of Intelligence!
>
> And so each man, unmasked, included in the register and sworn in, felt himself isolated, and possibly even feared his own kind more than the robots, for the robots were not necessarily agents of the secret police, while the men were – to a man.[93]

The practice of exploiting those over whom one has absolute power, the participation of the "grey market," blackmailers, "navy blue" police and former colleagues in the practice of denouncing others before they denounce you, illustrated in this fragment of the story, points to a poignant sense of alienation and fear of other human beings. We find echoes of these observations in the ironic conclusion:

> Thus concluded one of the most unusual of my adventures and voyages. Notwithstanding all the hardship and pain it had occasioned me, I was glad of the outcome, since it restored my faith, shaken by corrupt cosmic office-holders, in the natural decency of electronic brains. Yes, it's comforting to know, when you think about it, that only man can be a bastard.[94]

Tichy represents historical non-heroic and anti-monumental narration, and in the conclusion, he parodies historians' attempts to write a comforting, compensatory ending to the story of genocide. The way he speaks about the past is nothing like the classic approach, according to which humans are capable of extraordinary acts and unlimited sacrifice in the name of the common good. "Unheroic memory," Langer stresses, "is imbued with a spirit of irony, its defense against a reconciliation that it cannot embrace."[95] It is impossible to build a community with people who report on each other and thus expose others to death, and hence in Tichy this need for loneliness and expeditions to the farthest regions of the universe arises.

What is Hamlet asking?

Intertextual references, pastiche and parodies are the most recognizable features of Stanisław Lem's writing and are often analyzed by Lemologists. As Jerzy Jarzębski put it, "Even a superficial reading of *Solaris*, *The Cyberiad*, *A Perfect Vacuum* or *Fiasco* makes it evident that Lem turned intertextual games into a method,"[96] while Helena Eilstein called this quality of Lem's prose simply "hellish erudition."[97] It would be impossible to compile a comprehensive list of the titles the writer knew, as he was a truly avid reader, following all new releases and, at the same time, returning to eighteenth-century philosophical treatises. Moreover, he read most of the books in their original languages, which makes it very difficult to follow the chronology of his reading interests.[98] The textual games in *Memoirs Found in a Bathtub*, interpreted by researchers, often lead to enumerations, as a result of which the exegetical commentary erodes and shifts toward entropy.[99] Nevertheless, some of the references have obvious literary prototypes, which means that in *Memoirs* we constantly encounter language inspired by Bruno Schulz, Witold Gombrowicz or William Shakespeare. It is difficult to ignore such clear signs, especially when pondering the significance of those games in the context of literature after the Holocaust. What does the allusion to Gombrowicz's *Virginity* mean after the wartime violence, rape and mass murder of women? Is the Schulz-inspired language of descriptions of the appearance of soldiers in grey uniforms and double agents an attempt to transfer that writer's output to the present day, like a posthumous literary revenge? Finally, how to ask the melancholy question "To be or not to be?" during the occupation and persecution?

When, after desperately attacking an agent, the protagonist of *Memoirs Found in a Bathtub* goes to the hospital, he looks at the exhibits in the doctor's office and reaches for the skull:

> *It must have been most carefully macerated – it shone as if coated with a thin layer of fat, but the shine was dry.* – here was a contemporary skull: clean, hygienic, scrubbed.[100]

The hero takes it in his hands, looks at it, compares its surface to a lunar landscape, estimates its weight. The two-page description of the skull is extremely sensual, and the protagonist, touching and looking at the bone, finally decides to smell it:

> Only dust, harmless, … but then a whiff, a trace of something, something … until my nose touched the cold surface and I inhaled – yes – a faint, the faintest stink – another sniff – oh, foul play! Corruption!!
>
> The reek betrayed the crime within. Like a drunkard, I breathed in the bloodiest, the most hideous murders behind that ivory elegance.[101]

Comparing the protagonist of *Memoirs* to Hamlet, who wonders whether to stay alive, seems, in the context of the actions presented in the novel, to be another part of the basic dilemma the lost and vulnerable narrator faces. However, it is evident that the context of this question, including the meaning of the prop, has shifted: the skull in the hospital is contemporary, a medical exhibit obtained as a result of a murder, and the traces of the victim's identity have been erased. A similar association will appear later in the case of a skeleton, as its hands will remind the protagonist of a person who committed suicide in his presence. Medical preparations and models are another effect of the Building's efficient machine, which transforms bodies into useful artifacts and scientific aids and uses the bodies of murder victims for technological progress.

In his autobiographical essay *Chance and Order*, Lem undermined the links between his childhood fascination with bones, resulting from his upbringing in a family of doctors, the time of the Holocaust and the philosophy of chance. In the same fragment, he added that the skull depicted in *Memoirs Found in a Bathtub* evoked the memory of his uncle (Gecel [Marek] Wolner), murdered by the Wehrmacht in the first days after the Germans entered Lviv:

> That bone – or, rather, its fictional counterpart – is to be found in another novel of mine, "Memoirs Found in a Bathtub." In this book, the bone became a whole skull cleanly dissected from a corpse, that was kept by a doctor in a ward – one of the many stations in the hero's odyssey through a labyrinthine building. A complete skull like this was owned by my uncle, my mother's brother, who was also a physician. He was murdered two days after the Wehrmacht marched into Lviv. At that time, several non-Jewish Poles were also killed – mostly university professors – and Tadeusz Boy-Żelenski, one of the best-known Polish writers. They were taken from their apartments during the night and shot.[102]

Short declarative sentences, devoid of emotional burden, are woven into an ironic childhood story; they appear in passing, on the margin or in interjections. Following this succinct information, in which the time difference between childhood and the occupation is blurred, is a paragraph filled with contradictions:

> Now, then, what objective, extrinsic connection – i.e., not one imagined by me and consisting solely of associations – could there be between a little boy's fascination with the parts of a human skeleton and the era of the Holocaust? Was this apparently significant and fitting omen a matter of

chains of chance, purely of coincidence? In my opinion, it was. I do not believe in manifest destiny or predetermination.[103]

The logical chaos and the questions the author asks himself generate uncertainty and make the proposed hypotheses unstable. If we compare this fragment with reflections in *Highcastle* (which *Chance and Order* follows in terms of the story), it is evident that it concerns not only the link between the skull and the death of Gecel Wolner, but also an issue that was troubling the writer, namely the awareness that the Jewish community in the inter-war era did not foresee the mortal danger the symptoms of which had appeared already in the 1930s. Today, the skull in *Memoirs* evokes associations with murder, but before the war, who could have expected that Jewish bodies would be used as medical preparations on a mass scale? In the inter-war era, there were debates at medical universities, inspired by an anti-Semitic atmosphere, during which nationalists demanded that Jewish students perform autopsies exclusively on Jewish cadavers. Such a postulate was virtually impossible to carry out, as the Jewish community provided burial for even the poorest Jewish residents, so their bodies were not taken to the dissecting rooms.[104] Meanwhile, during the occupation, body parts and entire skeletons were sent to many research institutes in the areas occupied by the German army.

Selection of robots

Although *Return from the Stars* is not one of Stanisław Lem's most frequently discussed novels, it is nevertheless an important point on the map of reflections on carnality, mechanization and violence in his prose. It is also one of the few books that deal with the emotional relations between the characters and contain erotic scenes. There are disturbing fragments in this novel: the main protagonist makes a number of unsuccessful suicide attempts, and many political and historical allusions indicate that it is a palimpsest, although subsequent layers are formed not so much by hints and quotes as by the simultaneous occurrence of several temporal planes, as if Einstein's time paradox affected not just the main theme but always appeared at key moments of the story. Significantly, in a letter to Sławomir Mrożek from 1960, when he was working on the novel, Lem added, "Krakow, as if on January 23, 1960 (but who is to know that, anyway?)"[105] In previous sections, I have already stated that in my opinion the novel can also be read in the context of the so-called "little realism," and I have pointed out the themes of the wartime temporal fracture related to Hal Bregg's return to the Earth after more than a hundred years. However, one of the most poignant scenes in the novel is when Bregg visits the city selex-station as an inspector, guided by his housemate, the engineer Marger. There, the time turbulence seems to be particularly important, as the burnt-out and smashed husks are reminiscent of twentieth-century history.

The selex-station is a cybernetic scrap yard, as the frugality and prudence of the future civilization requires that all raw materials be recycled. The place makes Bregg realize that the society he is trying to understand has isolated its own life from machines and automata, although its prosperity is based on their work. Defective, damaged or inefficient robots and equipment are disassembled and placed under a press. By chance, the protagonist passes by a tin barrack and, although the heat discourages him from entering the dark, he decides to explore the area because he hears "human voices – distorted, merging in a hoarse chorus, blurred, babbling, as though in the gloom a pile of defective telephones were talking";[106] later, significantly, he calls them "voices in the dark."[107] From under his feet there are pleas, requests, assurances about being fault-free and fit for work, and one of the voices says a rhyme, reminiscent of a prayer. The cacophony of sounds is arranged into a haunting complaint, evoking fear and compassion.

> "Please, me … only me … it is a mistake …"
>
> "Pleash … shir … haff …"
>
> "I will save you …"
>
> "Who is that …"
>
> "What …"
>
> "Who saves?"
>
> "Repeat after me: the fire will not consume me utterly, and the water will not turn me all to rust, both elements will be a gate unto me, and I shall enter …"
>
> "Hush-sh-sh!"
>
> "The contemplation of the cathode –"
>
> "Cathodoplation –"
>
> "I am here by mistake … I think… I think, after all …"
>
> "I am the mirror of betrayal …"
>
> "Pleash … shir … yer shervet … haff a look ar-round …"
>
> "O flight of the transfinite, O flight of the nebulae … O flight of the stars …"
>
> "He is here!!!" something cried; and a sudden silence fell, a silence almost as penetrating in its terrible tension as the many-voiced chorus that had preceded it.
>
> "Sir!!!" said something; I do not know why I was so sure, but I felt that these words were directed to me, I did not respond.
>
> "Sir, please … a moment of your time. Sir, I – am different. I am here by mistake."
>
> There was a stir.
>
> "Silence! I am living!" This outshouted the rest. "Yes, I was thrown in here, they dressed me in metal on purpose, so no one would know, but please, only put your ear to me and you will hear a pulse!"
>
> "I also!" came a second voice over the first. "I also! Sir! I was ill; during my illness I imagined that I was a machine, that was my madness, but now I am well!"[108]

When Bregg tries to find out what those voices mean, the engineer patiently explains to him that it is scrap metal to be melted, after selection. The word "selection" provokes an emotional response in the hero, so he asks who does the selection. It turns out that the process has been completely mechanized; robots are not repaired because it is unprofitable, and humans only watch over the full synchronization of the melt, not interfering in the selection itself. Bregg unsuccessfully attempts to erase the memory of the barrack, explains to himself that these were just mechanisms, wires and glass, and is constantly accompanied by the feeling that he witnessed the distressing "agony of mechanical death." A visit to the selection leads the protagonist to a nervous breakdown, as he realizes that he is unable to look at the beautiful landscape in front of him: "as if I did not have the right to look, as if there lay a horrible deception in this, squeezing at my throat. I sat down among the trees, buried my face in my hands; I regretted having returned."[109] The grief associated with the return is synonymous with death, because not to return from the stars means to die during the space mission. It is not until the arrival of his friend Olaf, who has shared the same fate, that Gregg overcomes his despair.

The episode concerning the slow death of robots, which otherwise constantly surround the protagonist, is not mentioned later, nor does it significantly affect the way Bregg perceives the earthly civilization. In his correspondence with his translator, Lem reported that Rafail Nudelman, who discussed the micromodels in his novels on specific subjects, independent of the plot, found the scene of scrapping robots in *Return from the Stars* reminiscent of a selection in a concentration camp.[110] Such associations can be expanded further, because the scene with the machine swearing that it is human is rather similar to the tragicomic episode that Rappaport narrates to Hogarth, in which a Jew tries to convince a German soldier in Yiddish that he is not Jewish. Moreover, the way used robot bodies are destroyed, disposed of and depersonified connotes the mass extermination of slave workers from ghettos and camps, while prayers and supplications bring to mind the final moments of people waiting for mass executions. Above all that, there is a plethora of characters from Leśmian's poetry, mutilated, incomplete entities, phantoms and specters, as well as heroes who do not realize that they have died.

Phantoms and ghosts

> How Jewish ghosts will reinhabit the New Europe, of which Poland is now a part, will certainly affect the place of the Holocaust in the public memory.[111]
>
> (David G. Roskies, *What is Holocaust Literature?*)

Lem's 1957 essay *Zagęszczanie duchów* (Concentration of ghosts) begins with an ironic allusion to the present day:

> In our country influenza germs are the only beings untroubled by housing concerns. Recently they chose me as their place of residence and moved

> in (so to speak) with me by force, so this violation of biological lawfulness bound me to the bed for some time.[112]

Further, the writer reports on what he decided to read during his convalescence, namely contemporary literature (Hłasko), war documents and diaries, descriptions of life in the camps, testimonies of criminals, a book on atomic and hydrogen strategy. Finally, he comes across an English book about ghosts and vampires, which provides him with some entertainment and provokes a hollow laugh:

> how are we to be afraid of a horrible dead man, supporting himself with his own pelvis, rattling his teeth like a tractor, today, in the era of memorable ovens, H-bombs and experiences brought upon us by these novelties of the twentieth century?[113]

Ghostly visitations must therefore take on new forms in new times, or disappear completely. After the age of ovens, are there not specters of those who were not buried with proper rites? Do the suffering and screams of the victims not return persistently in the literary texts of survivors?

Despite his declarations, echoes of the despair of dying and shadows of the dead are present in Lem's science fiction prose, because astronauts typically have no graves – their unburied bodies float in space or accompany the protagonists on ships throughout the voyage, building emotional tension and provoking thoughts of death. This is particularly evident in *Tales of Pirx the Pilot*, in which ghostly visitation and faith in the spectral existence after death are often discussed. In *On Patrol*, young Pirx spots a mysterious light unnoticed by radars and concludes that it cannot be a shining halo of a spirit, because "he didn't believe in spirits, although occasionally, especially in the company of women, he might shoot the breeze about them, but even then it was not born of any spiritualistic convictions."[114] The joke concerning the idea of "the communion of saints" in the era of space flight, as well as spiritualists' belief that foreign planets are inhabited by spiritual beings, is that the pilot probably told that story to women he tried to seduce, even though the art of flirtation and romance are hardly – to put it euphemistically – his strongest suit. The spiritualism, however, is more than just part of a punchline, since the specters of the deceased in his stories communicate with sound signs (Morse code), thus using typology.

Untangling the mystery of the death of his two colleagues, Pirx notes that "On the whole, people tend to trust too much in the evidence of their senses; if they should happen to see a deceased acquaintance in public, they would sooner believe in a resurrection than admit to their own insanity."[115] Pirx's rationality helps him discover the cause of death of his companions, and the illusion of light reflection perceived by the senses is exposed, though only until the pilot boards a haunted ship. Named after the tragic Roman commander, the *Coriolanus* from the story *Terminus* (likely a nod to Shakespeare), brings to mind medieval torture and triggers biblical-apocalyptic visions. Its outer shell is in shreds, which is why the shuttle looks like it has been skinned, the gantry stretches like Jacob's ladder and the ship is compared to Noah's Ark, but it makes so many sounds that Pirx is sure he would not hear the call to the Last Judgement. The text explicitly draws on the gothic tradition: a weary traveler arrives at a new place, notes the gloomy and rusty structure of the ship and climbs the gantry, when he hears the cry "Over here!" but cannot locate the source. He reaches the central area, where he finds the pilot's seat – "its shadowy projection looming like the last navigator's ghost"[116] – the tools and handles are "polished smooth from handling"[117] and on the walls there are hastily patched holes and handprints in cement. Low, dark corridors remind the pilot of the underground, and he compares the interior to a fortress wall. Finally, he spots an image of a skull and crossbones, and it is only after a while that he realizes that it is a warning against radioactive radiation. At the atomic pyre he finds the eponymous Terminus, that is, a crumbling robot: "The robot rocked back and forth, more like a knight in armor than an automaton."[118] Pirx soon discovers the grim past of the ship, which had collided with the Leonids several years prior and was accidentally found much later by a patrol ship on a routine flight. The investigating committee concluded that the accident had been caused by force majeure, through no fault of anyone's. As for the crew,

> [t]he evidence indicated that not all of them had been killed instantly … that among the survivors was the skipper, and that, thanks to him, the crew – though cut off from one another by the collapsing bulkheads and with no hope of being rescued – had held out to the end, down to the last oxygen bottle.[119]

This heroic version of the story is soon confronted with the log of the crew's final moments, encrypted as a Morse code message inside Terminus, a witness to their deaths. The machine unknowingly works to the rhythm of the remembered sounds transmitted by the dying members of the crew, who communicated by tapping on the pipes connecting individual levels of the ship. The dying crew lives in the robot like a dybbuk and speaks with their own voices in its every activity. When Pirx discovers this recording, he wonders if he should be listening to it:

> There was something obscene about it, about being a spectator to someone else's death throes, witnessing it in all its gruesome detail and later analyzing every signal, every plea for oxygen, every shriek … It was immoral – if you could do nothing to help.[120]

The most shocking discovery is that the dying spirits can be asked questions through Terminus by tapping them in Morse code. "One thing was clear: his recorder was far from dead. Whoever those people were – those voices, those signals – you could talk to them, converse with them. You just had to have the guts, that was all."[121] The fear of talking to the ghosts is the fear of helplessness in the face of dying beings that cannot be helped or told that they have already died. The only solution seems to be to annihilate the machine along with their recorded agony. Wondering about how it is possible to communicate with the spirits of the deceased crew, Pirx comes to the conclusion that this situation resembles a dream and a dialogue taking place within a particular person, but also points to the fact that every night the self splits up,

> divides, and begets pseudopersonalities. These dream personalities can be invented, or taken from real life. Don't we sometimes dream of the dead? Carry on conversations with them?[122]

This rational explanation is at odds with the pilot's growing fear of the returning wave of cries for help, complaints about the lack of oxygen and the horror of dying that still fill the ship.

It is not just in *Terminus* that Lem draws on Jewish legends and creatures that populate them, such as dybbuks, demons and golems, and his spectral characters are related to the beings inhabiting the poetry of Bolesław Leśmian, who do not know that they have died, like Don Juan, terrified by the sight of their own funeral, lasting in a residual form despite the disintegration of their body, capable of only the slightest impact on the abandoned world. In Lem's prose, the deceased appear in spectral, dreamlike afterimages usually when they become aware that they have died, and their presence is signaled by screaming, noise, begging for help. This is what happens during the robot agony in *Return from the Stars*: moaning and mysterious voices come from behind the walls of the Building in *Memoirs Found in a Bathtub*, and the final words of the crew dying in the fire will also be heard by the commanders of the luxury intergalactic ship in *Albatross*. Most of the specters are the shadows of people who died from asphyxiation, which Pirx calls by the medical term "anoxia." The pilot becomes a witness to death or hears a story about those who died of lack of oxygen, and their dying and suffering fills the space for a long time, even when their bodies are found and buried. In *The Conditioned Reflex*, the protagonists report on the death of members of the lunar expedition, during which part of the crew dies immediately under an avalanche of stones, and only the transport driver manages to escape:

> He became the lone survivor of the disaster, outliving his companions by only a few hours. For the witnesses those few hours became a living hell. The driver, a French-Canadian named Roget, who either remained conscious or regained consciousness later on, started radioing for help from somewhere inside the white cloud – his receiver had been damaged, but not his transmitter. There was no locating the injured man.[123]

The visibility is very poor, so Roget's rescue is impossible, and his slow dying, his weakening breath and pulse, are followed by all surviving crew members.

Listening to the sounds of dying overwhelms the protagonists psychologically, leaving a mark on their personalities. Pirx will not be freed from the ghosts of the dead even by the decision to use Terminus for scrap metal, destroying the dead crew's dybbuk-like existence imprinted on the machine. After all, he did not allow the dybbuk to speak, he did not ask what it needed, and for fear of his own integrality, he annihilated the traces of the dying. In retrospect, the pilot feels that scrapping Terminus was wrong, and the punishment the machine received for someone else's crime – too cruel.

Notes

1 Jerzy Jarzębski points out that reflected all too clearly in *Man from Mars* is the post-war fear of entirely earthly totalitarianism. J. Jarzębski, "Chaos jako wyzwanie: późna eseistyka Lema" [in:] idem, *Wszechświat Lema*, Kraków 2003, p. 235.

2 Professor "looked critically at my clothes, which, apart from the traces of the recent battle in the library, bore prominent signs of wear and tear" (S. Lem, "Człowiek z Marsa" [in:] idem, *Człowiek z Marsa. Opowiadania młodzieńcze. Wiersze*, Warszawa 2009, p. 20); "The next moment I was standing under the tempting, hot shower and enjoyed the foam of expensive, fragrant soap, which I had to do without for so long" (ibid., p. 25).

3 S. Lem, *Man From Mars*, transl. P. Swirski, <https://www.wordswithoutborders.org/article/from-man-from-mars?src=wwbweekend> [accessed online March 18, 2019]. So far, only fragments of the novel have been translated into English. Unless otherwise indicated, the cited fragments have been translated for the purpose of this volume from the Polish edition, *Człowiek z Marsa. Opowiadania młodzieńcze. Wiersze*, Warszawa 2009.

4 On the subject of starvation, see *Choroba głodowa. Badania kliniczne nad głodem wykonane w Getcie Warszawskim w roku 1942*, ed. E. Apfelbaum, intr. I. Milejkowski, Warszawa 1946.

5 In *The Invincible*: "After the two probes had safely returned … Rohan, Jarg and the five other men ate their first hot meal of that day"; "Once they had blown oxygen into the tiny space, they set about eating sandwiches, washing them down with coffee from thermos flasks"; "After he had finished eating his meager provisions, he felt much better"; *Memoirs Found in a Bathtub*: "Lunch wasn't very good: a limp salad, leathery roast beef, the usual mashed potatoes, vile coffee as black as tar"; "Today it was macaroni and cheese – terrible, but it put off the moment when I would have to set forth again"; *Star Diaries*: "According to my calculations I would be making contact with the edge of the first vortex at around eleven, and therefore hurriedly prepared lunch, not wanting to face the danger on an empty stomach"; *More Tales of Pirx the Pilot*: "It was 0620 hours – breakfast time for any sensible person. He was tempted by the thought of coffee."

6 S. Lem, *Man From Mars*, transl. P. Swirski <https://www.wordswithoutborders.org/article/from-man-from-mars?src=wwbweekend> [access online March 18, 2019].

7 "Perhaps it will be possible to discover the systemic laws that govern plasma, which is a carrier of heredity." S. Lem, *Omówienie książek Jeana Rostanda*, "Życie Nauki" 1948, no. 33–34, p. 299.

8 S. Lem, *Człowiek z Marsa*, p. 84.

9 G. Niziołek, *Polski teatr Zagłady*, Warszawa 2013, p. 148. Another example of the Robinsonade theme is the account from *Farby wodne* by Lidia Ostałowska: "In the children's block there was a small stage and shows twice a week. Jiří Fränkl wrote a play about Robinson Crusoe for six-year-old boys, with the following song: 'Apart from us, no human has ever set foot on the island, but I believe in God and

that I will return home healthy, into my daddy's and mommy's arms.'" Metaphysical themes in this story are linked to the tale of Robinson's survival. L. Ostałowska, *Farby wodne*, Wołowiec 2011, p. 23–24.

10 American post-war science fiction (both film and novel) uses Robinson's character differently. In the Cold War reality, the annihilation of humanity is often presented in positive terms, and the plot focuses on protagonists who, despite adversity (extinction of other species, nuclear contamination, hostile environment) manage to survive. The catastrophe is an opportunity to repeat the pioneer myth and stir up fear of communists, and is sometimes seen as a quasi-Darwinian development. Critics saw such transformations as a typical example of capitalist individualism. In her 1950 novel *Shadow on the Hearth*, Judith Merril casts a woman as Robinson – a housewife who, in the absence of her husband, saves her family from nuclear annihilation. See M. K. Booker, *The Beginning or the End? Post-Holocaust Novels and Films. 1946–1964* [in:] idem, *Monsters, Mushroom Clouds, and the Cold War: American Science Fiction and the Roots of Postmodernism, 1946–1964*, Greenwood Press 2001, p. 65–72.

11 S. Lem, *Eden*, transl. M. E. Heine, San Diego–New York–London, 1989, p. 93.

12 Idem, *The Invincible*, transl. (from the 1967 German edition) W. Ackerman, New York, 1973, p. 179.

13 Ibid.

14 Ibid, s. 180.

15 U.K. Le Guin, "European SF: Rottensteiner's Anthology, the Strugatskys, and Lem," *Science Fiction Studies* 1975, vol. 1, no. 3, p. 184.

16 Ibid, p. 185.

17 P. Haffner, "Stanislaw Lem: A Moralist Who Doesn't Moralize," *Science Fiction Studies* 2001, vol. 28, no. 1, p. 149–150.

18 S. Lem, *Czas Nieutracony*, p. 255.

19 Cf. V. Vitaliev, "The Wall of Terror and Deception," *Engineering & Technology*, Jun 2015, vol. 10, no. 5, p. 60–64.

20 S. Lem, *Plan anti-V* [in:] idem, *Człowiek z Marsa. Opowiadania młodzieńcze. Wiersze*, p. 178.

21 Ibid., p. 184.

22 Ibid., pp. 183–184.

23 Ibid., p. 184.

24 J. Butler, *Frames of War: When is Life Grievable?* p. 49.

25 S. Lem, *Memoirs Found in a Bathtub*, p. 176.

26 S. Jerzy Jarzębski considered this ending to be at odds with the science fiction convention at the time, as it overstepped the frame of the genre and was an unusual solution for the whole writer's output. Cf. J. Jarzębski, "Przygody Rycerzy świętego Kontaktu" [in:] idem, *Wszechświat Lema*, p. 215–216.

27 S. Lem, *Człowiek z Marsa*, p. 96.

28 D. Laub, "An Event without a Witness. Truth, Testimony, and Survival," [in:] D. Laub, S. Felman *Testimony: Crises of Witnessing in Literature, Psychoanalysis, and History*, New York 1992, p. 81–82.

29 S. Lem, *Człowiek z Marsa*, p. 99, 101.

30 Idem, *The Invincible*, p. 92.

31 Cf. G. Niziołek, *Polski teatr Zagłady*.

32 F. Jameson, *Archaeologies of the Future: The Desire Called Utopia and Other Science Fictions*, London–New York 2005, p. 123.

33 S. Lem, *Eden*, p. 80.

34 S. Lem, *The Invincible*, p. 6.

35 Ibid., p. 31.

36 Ibid., p. 33.

37 Ibid., p. 44.

38 Ibid., p. 45.

39 Ibid., p. 52.

40 Ibid., p. 55.
41 Laub, p. 62.
42 S. Lem, *The Invincible*, p. 75.
43 Idem., *Highcastle*, p. 131.
44 Idem., "Albatross" [in:] idem, *Tales of Pirx the Pilot*, transl. L. Iribarne, San Diego–New York–London 1979, p. 140.
45 Ibid., p. 150.
46 Ibid., p. 156.
47 "I'm beginning to think that a particular attraction, a preference results from a resonance in the soul of the reader with the text, a resonance in which an important role is played by certain elements ('structures'), unconscious, unaware, of exactly the same type (but not of the same origin!), which make a particular man generally like a particular type of woman, though he cannot justify it (justifications are always a secondary rationalization of the original attraction)." S. Lem, *List z 15 czerwca 1975* [in:] *Sława i fortuna. Listy do Michaela Kandla 1972–1987*, Krakow 2013, p. 383.
48 Michael Kandel reviewed his correspondence and kindly shared all the letters he wrote about *Memoirs Found in a Bathtub*. The quoted letter was written on May 25, 1972. Letter in English, courtesy of the author.
49 Ibid.
50 Michael Kandel, letter in English dated September 19, 1972. Courtesy of the author.
51 Idem, letter in English dated August 26, 1974. Courtesy of the author.
52 S. Lem, *List z 3 września 1975* [in:] *Sława i fortuna. Listy do Michaela Kandla 1972–1987*, p. 261–262. In 1972, Lem presented a different interpretation of *Memoirs Found in a Bathtub*, indicating that it is a novel about Stalinism (Jerzy Jarzębski used this letter in his analyses). In my opinion, this discrepancy can be explained in two ways: firstly, *Memoirs* has a great metaphorical potential, which makes it possible to embed its realities in any system that opposes its citizens. Secondly, with each subsequent year of correspondence, Lem trusted Kandel more and, when asked about his biography, he began to share more details of his life before the war and during the occupation. Cf. S. Lem, *List z 9 czerwca 1972* [in:] ibid., p. 53–57. Cf. J. Jarzębski, "Lektura świata. Stanisław Lem jako czytelnik" [in:] idem, *Wszechświat Lema*, p. 269–270.
53 S. Lem, *List z 3 września 1974* [in:] *Sława i fortuna. Listy do Michaela Kandla 1972–1987*, p. 262.
54 Ibid., p. 263.
55 Ibid., p. 265.
56 Ibid.
57 Ch. Ostrower, "Humor as a Defense Mechanism during the Holocaust," *Interpretation: A Journal of Bible and Theology* 2015, vol. 69, no. 2, p. 191.
58 J. Jarzębski, "Podróż do kresu znaczenia," Afterword in: *S. Lem, Pamiętnik znaleziony w wannie*, p. 226.
59 In a letter to his Russian translator, Konstantin Duszenko, Lem admitted that at the beginning of the 1960s he had been pressured by the publishing house to write an introduction to *Memoirs*. Because of the censors, the novel had to be set in the United Statesd in order to be approved for publication. However, the author decided to keep the introduction in the Russian translation released in the 1990s. He emphasized that it was a document of the era. As a result, in the Russian edition, the introduction was moved to the Appendix. M. Krajewska, "'Cieplica to wystygła zimnica.' Wizerunek tłumacza na tle korespondencji z pisarzem," [in:] *Lem i tłumacze*, eds. E. Skibińska, J. Rzeszotnik, Kraków 2010, p. 127–128.
60 S. Lem, *Memoirs Found in a Bathtub*, p. 2.
61 Ibid., p. 6.
62 Ibid., p. 45.
63 Ibid., p. 115.

64 For information on the principles of the network to help Jews organized by the Metropolitan Archbishop, as well as on the most important problems related to the evaluation of his conduct during the German occupation, see S. Redlich, *Moralność i rzeczywistość: metropolita Andriej Szeptycki i Żydzi w czasach Holocaustu i II wojny światowej*, "Zagłada Żydów. Studia i Materiały" 2008, no. 4, p. 241–259.
65 Dawid Kahane, account from Lviv [in:] *Życie i zagłada Żydów polskich 1939–1945. Relacje świadków*, eds. M. Grynberg, M. Kotowska, Warszawa 2003, p. 267.
66 Ibid., p. 266. Cf. K.I. Lewin, *Przeżyłem. Saga Świętego Jura spisana w roku 1946 przez syna rabina Lwowa*, Warszawa 2006.
67 "We hear all the time about Jews discovered in hiding places, new victims. I firmly believe that without the help of the local population, Germans would absolutely not have been able to find so many Jews. Many Jews could have been saved if it had not been for these additional denunciations of the Polish and Ukrainian population." Dawid Kahane, *Przeżyłem. Saga Świętego Jura spisana w roku 1946 przez syna rabina Lwowa*, Warszawa 2006.
68 J. Leociak, "Literatura dokumentu osobistego" [in:] *Literatura polska wobec Zagłady*, eds. S. Buryła, D. Krawczyńska, J. Leociak, Warszawa 2012, p. 42, 62–67.
69 L.L. Langer, *Holocaust Testimonies: The Ruins of Memory*, New Haven, 1991, p. 107.
70 S. Freud, "The Theme of the Three Caskets" [in:] idem, *Writings on Art and Literature*, Stanford 1997, p. 109.
71 B. Engelking, *Sny jako źródło do badań nad Zagładą*, "Zagłada Żydów. Studia i Materiały" 2013, no. 9, p. 45.
72 L.L. Langer, *Holocaust Testimonies: The Ruins of Memory*, p. 8.
73 Ibid.
74 In a letter dated November 4, 1972, Lem praises Kandel's translation of *Memoirs Found in a Bathtub* and explains that he modelled his spy songs in this novel on Horst-Wessel-Lied, which is particularly evident in the German translation. S. Lem, *List z 4 listopada 1972* [in:] *Sława i fortuna. Listy do Michaela Kandla 1972–1987*, p. 98. Władysław Bartoszewski also told an anecdote about the Horst-Wessel-Lied anthem and Stanisław Lem: "Another time my wife and I are leaving Vienna for Bavaria, a taxi driver is supposed to take us to the station. An elderly Austrian arrives and Staszek [Lem] goes out in front of the house in his shirt, because it was the end of the summer, suddenly raises his hand in a Nazi salute and starts singing the Nazi anthem off tune: 'Die Fahne hoch! Die Reihen fest geschlossen!' (Banners up! Our ranks are closed!). It was the beginning of Horst-Wessel-Lied, the anthem of the Nazi SA militia! The taxi driver is speechless. He looks at Staszek, at me, says – in German – 'Gentlemen, no one is allowed to sing this song.' And Staszek – also in German – replies, 'I am allowed.' Then the driver, when he drove us to the station, didn't say a word." W. Bartoszewski, *Mój przyjaciel pesymista* [Stanisław Lem], [in:] idem, *Pisma wybrane 2002–2012*, selection, ed. and footnotes by A.K. Kunert, vol. 6, Kraków 2012, p. 364.
75 S. Lem, *Memoirs Found in a Bathtub*, p. 70.
76 SJ. Leociak, "Literatura dokumentu osobistego," p. 33.
77 L. L. Langer, *Holocaust Testimonies: The Ruins of Memory*, p. 69.
78 S. Lem, *Memoirs Found in a Bathtub*, p. 55.
79 *Komenderał* in the Polish edition, most likely coined by combining *komendant* ("commander") and *generał*. The original is peppered with such neologisms, some of which have been retained in translation, such as Infernalist, Counterinformant First Class, Macerator, Master Cremator or Osteophage Provocateur.
80 S. Lem, *Memoirs Found in a Bathtub*, p. 51.
81 Ibid., p. 20.
82 Ibid.
83 Ibid., p. 22.
84 Ibid., p. 119.
85 Ibid., p. 123.

86 The censor saw in these games allusions to the political system of socialist Poland and pointed to the possibility of interpreting *The Eleventh Voyage* as a condemnation of the terrorist system. Cited in: K. Mojsak, "Cenzura wobec prozy groteskowej w latach 1956–1965" [in:] *'Lancetem, a nie maczugą.' Cenzura wobec literatury i jej twórców w latach 1945–1965*, eds. K. Budrowska, M. Woźniak-Łabieniec, Warszawa 2012, p. 241.
87 The name of the planet in the Polish version, Kareliria, evokes associations with Kakania, which is a term used in literature to describe the Austro-Hungarian empire.
88 S. Lem, "The Eleventh Voyage" [in:] *The Star Diaries, Further Reminiscences of Ijon Tichy*, transl. M. Kandel, New York 1976, p. 47.
89 Ibid., p. 52.
90 Ibid., p. 59.
91 L.L. Langer, *Holocaust Testimonies: The Ruins of Memory*, p. 38.
92 S. Lem, "The Eleventh Voyage" [in:] *The Star Diaries, Further Reminiscences of Ijon Tichy*, p. 63.
93 Ibid., p. 68.
94 Ibid., p. 71.
95 L.L. Langer, *Holocaust Testimonies: The Ruins of Memory*, p. 170.
96 J. Jarzębski, "Intertekstualność a poznanie u Lema" [in:] idem, *Wszechświat Lema*, p. 103–104.
97 N. Pospieszalska [H. Eilstein], *"Głos Pana," czyli zwierciadło z nieba*, part I, "Nurt" 1969, no. 8, p. 38.
98 On the subject of Lem's reading inspirations, see I. Csicsery-Ronay, Jr., "Twenty-Two Answers and Two Postscripts: An Interview with Stanislaw Lem," transl. M. Lugowski, *Science Fiction Studies* 1986, vol. 13, p. 242–260. In this interview, Lem also explains that *Memoirs Found in a Bathtub* was not inspired by Kafka's work.
99 Marcin Wołk presented these problems convincingly. See M. Wolk, "Interteksty 'Pamiętnika znalezionego w wannie'" [in:] *Stanisław Lem: pisarz, myśliciel, człowiek*, ed. J. Jarzębski, A. Sulikowski, Kraków 2003, p. 376–399.
100 S. Lem, *Memoirs Found in a Bathtub*, p. 135. The portion of the quote in italics is missing in the English translation.
101 Ibid.
102 S. Lem, *Chance and Order*, transl. F. Rottensteiner, *The New Yorker* 59, January 30 1984, p. 88–98.
103 Ibid.
104 Cf. T. Kielanowski, "Wspomnienie o lekarzach lwowskich," Archiwum ŻIH, ref. 302/279; *Kronika Uniwersytetu Jana Kazimierza we Lwowie za rok szkolny 1929/1930, stanowiąca sprawozdanie rektora i dziekanów*, compiled by prof. dr. hab. H. Schramm, Rector in the school year 1929/1930, Lwów 1931, p. 72.
105 S. Lem, *List z 23 stycznia 1960* [in:] idem, S. Mrożek, *Listy 1956–1978*, Kraków 2011, p. 26.
106 S. Lem, *Return from the Stars*, p. 134.
107 *Głosy w ciemności* [Voices in the dark] was the title of Julian Stryjkowski's novel, written shortly after the war and published only after 1956, the first volume of his Galician tetralogy on shtetls.
108 S. Lem, *Return from the Stars*, p. 134–135.
109 Ibid., p. 140.
110 Idem, *List 18 października 1974*, [in:] *Sława i fortuna. Listy do Michaela Kandla 197–1987*, p. 278.
111 D.G. Roskies, "What is Holocaust literature?" [in:] *Jews, Catholics and the Burden of History*, ed. E. Lederhendler, Oxford 2006, p. 202.
112 S. Lem, "Zagęszczanie duchów" [in:] idem, *Wejście na orbitę*, Kraków 1962, p. 75.
113 Ibid., p. 76.
114 S. Lem, "On Patrol" [in:] idem, *Tales of Pirx the Pilot*, p. 126.
115 Ibid.

116 Idem, "Terminus," p. 161.
117 Ibid.
118 Ibid., p. 165.
119 Ibid. p. 170.
120 Ibid. p. 189.
121 Ibid. p. 204.
122 Ibid.
123 S. Lem. "The Conditioned Reflex" [in:] idem *Tales of Pirx the Pilot*, p. 93.

CONCLUSION

While confronting realistic novels with historical or political contexts does not usually provoke much opposition among literary scholars, references to the Holocaust in science fiction prose are not that obvious, especially when it comes to grotesque, ironic works, full of stylization and intertextual games. Dominick LaCapra points out, however, that in their works, many historical traumatists usually refer to conventional narratives instead of outstanding modern literature, even though its untypical and original character might contribute much to the reflection on absence and loss.[1] As the researcher notes,

> It is curious that theoreticians who know much better nonetheless seem to assume the most conventional form of narrative (particularly nineteenth-century realism read in a rather limited manner) when they generalize about the nature of narrative, often to criticize its conventionalizing or ideological nature.[2]

LaCapra stresses that it is precisely such distorted narratives that are critical of mythical images and other ways of representation.[3] The science fiction setting and ambiguous allusions to historical events in Lem's genre prose can be read as a residue of personal, generational and family traumas, stored in unusual spaces reminiscent of crusted lava, alienated and lonely, hidden on foreign planets and in windowless rooms. Alternative history, written alongside community clichés and political simplifications, makes it possible to tell unpopular versions, reveal anxiety structures and break the melancholic and pathos-filled tone of the Holocaust narrative. The bitter taste of cruelty and wartime violence is overcome by grotesque distortions, jokes, the self-ironic distance of the protagonists and narrators, and this distanced approach to narrating makes it difficult to decipher historical and traumatic burden – a multi-level game addressed to those who understand allusions to traumatic events, complicated by chronological disturbances and events located in timeless zones.

The themes of the Holocaust and Jewish protagonists feature surprisingly often in Stanisław Lem's prose, especially for works regarded as science fiction or philosophical treatises on the past. In the volume *Sezam* [Sesame], the short story "*Kryształowa kula*" [Crystal ball] describes, for example, the figure of an outstandingly talented Jewish boy who lost his life because his executioner saw a golden tooth in his open mouth. This episode is not repeated in *Fiasko* [Fiasco], which quotes that 1954 short story, but the spirits of the dead are present in this novel, which begins with an ethical discussion about whom the protagonists will save by wakening them from a coma. The writer's literary strategy enabled him to express the fear of the survivors, and the seemingly non-functional anecdotes, interrupted storylines and episodes unrelated to the main plot lead the readers toward the past and help them understand alternative history, for which there is no place in collective memory. Focusing on particular themes and stories of protagonists – masks needed to mediate the narration multiple times – I see in them the posthumous existence of victims. Traces of the despair of the dying are accompanied by astonishment at the silence about genocide after the war; all the while, propaganda exploited the suffering of the victims. Between silence and an attempt to save the memory of the victims, there is the life of the survivor, constantly moving in his literary work between the ditches full of bodies and offices of scholars debating ethical obligations toward humanity; between the Holocaust and the stars.

* * *

In one of his letters, Michael Kandel asked me why Stanisław Lem's Jewish roots were such an important topic in contemporary Polish reflections on the writer. While I was writing my book, a documentary film about the author was also made, directed by Borys Lankosz and written by Wojciech Orliński, and Kandel was asked to address that issue. At the same time, Kandel explained that the question of Jewish identity was highly complex and delicate because there was no single answer to the question of what it means to be Jewish. He pointed out that a person with no connection to the religion, history or Yiddish culture could be a Jew for reasons more important and deeper than genetics.[4] It was not the first time Kandel touched upon the issues that are of key importance for my research, making me face again, after completing the book, the challenge of explaining my own intentions and intuitions and the significance of my investigations.

In his autobiography titled *Ex-prodigy: My Childhood and Youth*, which Lem mentions in *Highcastle*, Norbert Wiener wonders what his own Jewish background means to him. Analyzing the life of his family in Krotoszyn, Poznań and Białystok at the turn of the nineteenth and twentieth centuries, the author of *The Human Use of Human Beings* stressed that in his case, Jewishness was not related to any religious, linguistic or "racial" affiliation, or to Zionism or morality.

The emphasis, however, was on the impact of the family, where the awareness of Jewish roots was preserved; this was important for the understanding of who one was, and this was conducive to the right orientation in the surrounding world. Wiener studied the history of his family and reconstructed how his ancestors' choices enabled him to become one of the most famous cyberneticians. For example, he stressed the importance of his grandfather's decision to stop speaking the Yiddish language and to send his son to a Lutheran school.[5] He also ironically summarized the educational path of his father, who first went to a medical school:

> I dare say that at least in part his motive was one so common in Jewish families, which generally desire to have at least one son a professional man, if possible a doctor. The motive is strong and easily understandable in a group long underestimated in society. God knows how many shy rabbis, shy lawyers, and unskilled doctors this motivation has produced.[6]

The description of the emphasis on education in Jewish families is parallel to the life choices of the Lems and the Wolners, among whom we find both a lawyer and doctors, including the writer himself, as he studied medicine after the war.

Stanisław Lem is emblematic of the history of the twentieth century in this part of Europe. His fate is the fate of a victim of Nazism, Stalinism, the People's Republic of Poland, a victim who was constantly tracked, hunted down and observed, permanently and throughout his life. At the same time, the writer wanted to grow in Poland as an artist, which sometimes brought him awards granted by the state. Hiding one's own identity under such circumstances must have been agonizing; he had to keep silent on extremely important issues, unable to go through mourning, feeling the sense of the futility of explaining his own existential choices. This life experience left its mark on the writer's oeuvre, and he made the game of unveiling and covering up the historical context his own literary strategy, engaging in discussions about the crisis of humanism and speaking out against racism, xenophobia and hate speech. The multiple readings of his novels and confronting them with historical data and the layout of Lviv helped me, I believe, to unearth one of the countless layers of interpretation. Lem divided his readers into those who understood his writings because they shared similar life experience, and those who did not, thus challenging the researchers of his works. My book is an attempt to understand, despite the lack of common experience.

Discovering the untold story of a Nazi victim expelled from Lviv, I had to reconstruct the way the writer operated in the meanders of the cultural policy of communist Poland, as well as in the post-war anti-Semitism, with dates that mark subsequent milestones in the dark history of Poland: August 11, 1945; July 4, 1946; 1956; March 1968. Both the death of a close relative in the Kielce pogrom and the closely supervised Polish Writers' Union confirmed Lem's fears that talking about his own past could be used against him and his family. It also meant that after the war, Stanisław Lem could not stop hiding. If he had revealed his background, he would most likely have been forced to emigrate or handed a one-way ticket to Israel. Traces of that exhausting situation, combined with grief and depression, can be found in Jan Józef Szczepański's diary, published on October 18, 1976:

> Lem came by this morning. He keeps talking about possible emigration. Today, for the first time, he said that he was close to informing the authorities that, as a "dirty Jew," he wanted to go to Israel. He's aged a lot and got very bitter.[7]

However, at the end of his life, even though still in Poland, Lem started to talk more and more openly about his roots, which is why I decided to reveal the story of his life during the occupation, the life that shines through the storylines in the novels that the whole world knows.

Notes

1 D. LaCapra, "Trauma, Absence, Loss," [in:] *Writing History, Writing Trauma*, Baltimore 2014, p. 63.
2 Ibid.
3 Ibid.
4 Two letters from Michael Kandel dated September 29, 2015.
5 N. Wiener, *Ex-prodigy. My Childhood and Youth*, Cambridge 1953, p. 9–12.
6 Ibid., p. 14.
7 J.J. Szczepański, *Dziennik 1973–1980*, vol. 4, Kraków 2015, p. 320.

INDEX

Adorno, T.W. 102
Agamben, G. 50
Aldrovandi, U. 28
Andrzejewski, J. 8, 120
Arendt, H. 11–12
Assmann, J. 101

Baronowa, E. 93
Bartoszewski, W. 46, 79
Bellow, S. 54
Berenstein, T. 49
Bereś, S. 46
Bessie, K. 26
Błoński, J. 45–46
Blumenfeld, R. 77
Borges, J.L. 28
Borowski, T. 89
Bosch, H. 28, 54
Breughel, P. 28
Buryła, S. 7
Butler, J. 21–22, 29, 84–86, 123
Buxdorf, P. 92

Camus, A. 47
Cantor, G. 103
Čapek, K. 14–15
Carnap, R. 16
Carroll, L. 28
Caruth, C. 23–24
Cervantes, M. 7
Chamayou, G. 21–22, 51
Chandler, R. 90
Coché, S. 51
Csicsery-Ronay, I. 82
Czermińska, M. 9

Dajnowski, M. 27
Darwin, Ch. 4, 18, 20
Defoe, D. 119
Derrida, J. 18
Diderot, D. 7
Dmowski, R. 3
Dürer, A. 28
Dushenko, K. 5
Dybowski, B. 40
Dzieduszycki, W. 40

Edith, P. 26
Eilstein, H. 81, 143
Einstein, A. 98, 103, 145
Engelking, B. 137
Enser, I. 92

Federman, R. 6, 13
Fiałkowski, T. 46
Flaubert, G. 7
Foucault, M. 22
Freud, S. 23, 137

Głowiński, M. 24, 43, 59
Gombrowicz, W. 105, 143
Gomel, E. 52
Gottliebova, D. 26
Grabowicz, G.G. 37
Grosz, E. 18
Gutman, I. 26

Haffner, P. 6, 121
Hayles, K.N. 2, 81
Hemar, M. (Hescheles J.M.) 92
Hemingway, E. 121
Hersey, J. 15–16
Hirszman, Ch. 72
Hitler, A. 26
Hłasko, M. 148
Hogarth, W. 28
Hryciuk, G. 40, 44
Huxley, A. 5

Iwasiów, I. 74

Jakubowska, W. 89
Jałowiecki, B. 3
Jameson, F. 80, 126
Janicki, J. 37, 44
Jarzębski, J. 2, 7, 47, 81, 134, 143
Jones, E. 77–78
Jurasz, A. 94

Kafka, F. 132–133
Kahane, D. 26, 46, 77, 100, 136
Kahane, S. 76
Kandel, M. 12, 22, 50, 80, 90, 92, 96, 101, 131–133, 135, 158
Kantor, T. 120
Kapuściński, W. 12, 95
Katzmann, F. 87
Kolbe, M. 133
Koselleck, R. 104
Kotyńska, K. 38, 42
Krall, H. 57, 74
Kremin, W. 76–78
Kuryluk, E. 28, 49

LaCapra, D. 56, 157
Langer, L L. 7, 24, 26, 41, 58, 75, 83, 137–138, 143
Lankosz, B. 158
Lanzmann, C. 50
Laub, D. 125, 129
Le Guin, U. 6, 121
Lehm (Bick) S.L. 91
Lehm, A. 92
Lehm, B. 92, 93
Lehm, Ch. 92
Lehm, E. 92
Lehm, F. 76, 88, 92–93, 107
Lehm, H.N. 91
Lehm, J. 92
Lehm, M. 92
Lehm, S. 91–98, 100
Lem, B. 76
Leociak, J. 136
Leśmian, B. 150
Lesser, G. 86
Lewin, K.I. 77
Lipski, L. 7
Lubash, M. 79

Madejski, J. 42
Makuszyński, K. 42
Malewska, H. 27
Mann, T. 101
Masłowska, J. 48
McCagg, W.O. 50
Miłosz, Cz. 120, 130
Mokłowski, K. 49
Mróz, D. 28
Mrożek, S. 145
Muzyczuk, D. 16

Nałkowska, Z. 142
Niziołek, G. 23–25, 59, 75, 90, 100, 120
Nudelman, R. 147

Oramus, D. 5
Ordonówna, H. 92
Orliński, W. 158
Orwell, G. 5, 17
Orwid, M. 95
Ostrower, Ch. 27, 134

Panchyshyn, M. 94
Para, A. 28
Parandowski, J. 42, 44
Pasek, J.H. 141
Piskorski, J M. 3
Podłuski 77
Pospíšil, T. 15

Rauch, J. 51
Reder, R. 72
Ringelblum, E. 136
Roskies, D. 12, 24, 39, 147
Rzeszotnik, J. 5

Sacher-Masoch, L. von 140
Sachs, N. 141
Sade, D.A.F. de 140
Sandauer, A. 74
Schindler, O. 56
Schulz, B. 98, 106, 143
Semczyszyn, M. 38
Sennett, R. 43
Shakespeare, W. 143, 148

Shallcross, B. 47
Sheptytsky, A. 135
Sienkiewicz, H. 141
Sitkiewicz, P. 28
Snyder, T. 49, 93
Sontag, S. 105
Sowa, J. 43
Spielberg, S. 56
Steinhaus, H. 103
Stryjkowski, J. 14, 45
Swift, J. 8
Szajna, J. 120
Szczepański, J.J. 7, 27, 160
Szczypiorski, A. 8

Tomasik, K. 79

Ubertowska, A. 102
Ulam, S. 102

Vávra, O. 15
Vorobyov, A.M. 78

Wagner, H. 11
Ważyk, A. 45
Welbel, S. 17
Weliczker, L. 51
Wells, H.G. 8, 14, 52
Wessel, H.L. 11
White, H. 8, 104
White, T.H. 28
Wiegandt, E. 102
Wiener, N. 20, 158
Wittlin, J. 15, 42
Wolff, L. 93
Wolner, G. (M.) 76, 144–145
Wolner, S. (Lem S.) 92
Wóycicka, Z. 4, 73
Wróblewski, J. 17
Wylegała, A. 45

Zajdel, E. 37
Zamorski, K. 37
Zamyatin, Y. 5
Zaremba, M. 49
Zarycki, T. 3
Zawieyski, J. 7, 8
Zieniewicz, A. 4, 84
Żuławski, M. 14
Żywulska, K. 26

CPSIA information can be obtained
at www.ICGtesting.com
Printed in the USA
LVHW081921030222
710079LV00007B/251